THE SECRET AGENT:

CENTENNIAL ESSAYS

Edited by

Allan H. Simmons

and

J. H. Stape

Cover design: Pier Post

Maps by Donald J. Shewan © The Joseph Conrad Society (UK)

The paper on which this book is printed meets the requirements of "ISO 9706: 1994, Information and documentation – Paper for documents – Requirements for permanence."

ISBN-13: 978-90-420-2176-1

Printed in The Netherlands

CONTENTS

Foreword

IN RESPONSE TO reviews of *The Secret Agent* in 1907, Conrad fulminated: "I've been so cried up of late as a sort of freak, an amazing bloody foreigner writing in English" (*CL3* 488). Foreignness is a hallmark of this novel, from its factual source in the "Greenwich Outrage" of 1894 to Conrad's explanation for its "honourable failure": "I suppose there is something in me that is unsympathetic to the general public. ... Foreignness, I suppose" (*CL4* 9-10).

When early reviewers referred to the author as a "Slav," they touched a raw nerve: Conrad, who had adopted British nationality, countered to his friend Edward Garnett, "you seem to forget that I am a Pole" (*CL3* 492), at the time a linguistic and cultural rather than a national identity. Foreignness had topical currency, as the Alien Act of 1905 demonstrated. Begun in Montpellier in February 1906, *The Secret Agent* is the first of Conrad's novels with an English setting. It centres on a potential act of anarchism perpetrated by a foreign power on British soil, and is likewise a departure in being "a spy novel" whose narrative methods and pervasive, but not corrosive, irony make heavy demands on the reader.

The Secret Agent is the central novel in the political trilogy, comprising *Nostromo* and *Under Western Eyes* as well, that crowns Conrad's greatness as a writer. It is also his great metropolitan novel, aware in a special way of the Condition of England fiction then popular. But the novel makes the familiar life of London strange and anatomizes its society and institutions. As Garnett noted in the same offending review: "It is good for us to have Mr Conrad in our midst visualising for us aspects of life we are constitutionally unable to perceive" (in Sherry, ed., 1973: 191).

It has long been realized that Conrad brought a Continental influence to bear upon the English novel, but the vision here is also fundamentally English. London life is dissected with the scalpel last used (though for the making of wider cuts) by Dickens. In his 1933 essay on *The Secret Agent*, the German novelist Thomas Mann described the "spirit of the narration" as "impressively English, and at the same time ... ultra-modern, post-middle-class," concluding that modern art "sees life as tragic-comedy, with the result that the grotesque is its most genuine style" (240-41).

When Conrad became interested in the theatre he chose this novel to dramatize. Its production on the London stage in November 1922 was a resounding failure, the mounting perhaps too experimental, the actors under-rehearsed, and Conrad's adaptation hostile or insouciant to contemporary stage conventions. But, lacking its narrative layering, the story's bleakness surely had much to do with discouraging potential audiences. And it has taken some time for the novel to achieve the centrality it now enjoys in Conrad's canon.

Whilst it has grown in critical estimation over the past few decades, contemporary events have also brought it once again to the attention of a wider public curious about the nature and psychology of political terrorism. Anchored firmly in its time, with its references to Lombroso, capital punishment, anarchism, and the Greenwich Outrage, *The Secret Agent* none the less manages to speak loudly and with uncanny prescience to our own. The domestic tragedy of the Verloc marriage continues to fascinate, however much the status of women has altered, and the hapless Stevie remains one of the most touching characters in Modernist fiction. The essays collected here testify to the novel's capacity to excite highly diverse interests and judgments a century after its first publication.

Allan H. Simmons
J. H. Stape

Works cited

Garnett, Edward. Review of *The Secret Agent* in the *Nation*, 28 September 1907. Rpt. in *Conrad: The Critical Heritage*, edited by Norman Sherry. 191-93. London: Routledge & Kegan Paul, 1973.

Mann, Thomas. *Past Masters and Other Papers*, translated by H. T. Lowe-Porter. London: Martin Secker, 1933.

Note

All references to the text of *The Secret Agent* are to the critical edition produced by Bruce Harkness and S. W. Reid for The Cambridge Edition of the Works of Joseph Conrad (Cambridge University Press, 1990). References to other works by Conrad are to Dent's Collected Edition, except for *Notes on Life and Letters* also in the Cambridge Edition. References to Conrad's letters, abbreviated *CL*, are to *The Collected Letters of Joseph Conrad*, edited by Laurence Davies *et al.* (Cambridge University Press, 1983–).

Contributors

DAVID MULRY has taught in England, France, and Greece, and currently teaches English at Longview Community College in Missouri. He has published on Conrad and on folklore, and is the author of websites and CD-Roms of composition readers and writing handbooks. He is working on a monograph on *The Secret Agent.*

PAUL WAKE, Lecturer in English at Manchester Metropolitan University, co-edited *The Routledge Companion to Critical Theory* (2006) with Simon Malpas. He is currently completing *Conrad's Marlow: Narrative and Death in "Youth," "Heart of Darkness," Lord Jim, and Chance*, to be published by Manchester University Press in 2007.

PAT PYE, a research student at Royal Holloway College in the University of London, is working on a thesis about the aurality of Conrad's London fiction. She also teaches English at colleges of Further Education.

YUET MAY CHING, Associate Professor of English in the Chinese University of Hong Kong, has published essays on Pound, Joyce, and Yeats. She is particularly interested in the motif of sacrifice in literature.

DAVID PRICKETT works for a foreign aid charity. His doctoral thesis explored the themes of subjectivity and self-governance in some of Conrad's major novels. His current research concerns the tensions between practical action and thought in Conrad's fiction, particularly in the Marlow narratives.

ELLEN BURTON HARRINGTON, Assistant Professor of English at South Alabama University, has written on Conrad, Wilkie Collins, Arthur Conan Doyle, and Dickens. She is currently editing *Scribbling Women and the Form of the Short Story* for the Society for the Study of the Short Story, and is continuing to work on gender and criminality in Conrad.

CEDRIC WATTS is Research Professor of English in the University of Sussex. His many books on Conrad include *The Deceptive Text* (1984), *Joseph Conrad: A Literary Life* (1989), *Joseph Conrad: "Nostromo"* (1990), *A Preface to Conrad* (2nd edn., 1993), and *Joseph Conrad* (1994). He has written widely on other writers, including Shakespeare.

LUDMILLA VOITKOVSKA, Assistant Professor of Slavic Studies at the University of Saskatchewan, has published articles on Conrad and is working on a book titled *Living in Translation: Exile as a Continuum in Conrad's Fiction*. **ZOFIA VORONTSOVA,** a doctoral student in Behavioural Neuropsychology at the University of Waterloo, has done research in identity construction in seniors and police officers. Her present research is on physical mobility and working memory in ageing. She has also published as a creative writer.

LUDWIG SCHNAUDER, who has just completed his doctoral dissertation on *Free Will and Determinism in Joseph Conrad's Major Fiction*, is a Junior Lecturer in the English Department at Vienna University.

J. H. STAPE, Research Fellow in St Mary's College, Strawberry Hill, is the author of *The Several Lives of Joseph Conrad* (forthcoming August 2007) and General Editor of the seven Conrad texts appearing in Penguin Classics in 2007, for which he has edited *Typhoon and Other Stories*. His edition of Conrad's *A Personal Record*, co-edited with Zdzisław Najder, is to appear in the Cambridge Edition in 2007. **ALLAN H. SIMMONS**, Lecturer in English in St Mary's College, Strawberry Hill, has recently published *Joseph Conrad* in Palgrave's Critical Issues series and a monograph on "Heart of Darkness" for Continuum. For Penguin Classics he has co-edited *Lord Jim* with J. H. Stape and *The Nigger of the "Narcissus" and Other Stories* with Gail Fraser and J. H. Stape (both forthcoming 2007).

HUGH EPSTEIN, Honorary Secretary of the Joseph Conrad Society (UK), works in Further Education in London. He has published on Conrad's fiction in *The Conradian* and *Conradiana* and has given papers at conferences of the Joseph Conrad Society (UK) and in Vancouver in 2002.

MICHAEL NEWTON, Universitair Docent, Universiteit Leiden, is the author of *Savage Girls and Wild Boys: A History of Feral Children* (2002) and a book on *Kind Hearts and Coronets* in BFI's Film Classics series (2003). He has edited Edmund Gosse's *Father and Son* for Oxford World's Classics. His Penguin Classics edition of *The Secret Agent* appears in 2007. He is currently completing a book on the cultural history of assassination and political violence.

MARY BURGOYNE is reading English at St Mary's College, Strawberry Hill.

The Anarchist in the House: The Politics of Conrad's *The Secret Agent*

David Mulry
Longview Community College, Lee's Summit, Missouri

ANARCHISM, along with several major political ideologies -- "conservatism, liberalism and socialism … in recognizably their modern form" – can, according to David Miller, be traced to the aftermath of the French Revolution, although he also acknowledges that its philosophical roots, perhaps like those of any radical rebellion, lie much deeper (1984: 3-4). With the French Revolution, the Myth of Revolution was born; it showed that a government, a social order, and even a belief system could fall and rise up fundamentally altered. This underlying idea inspires the anarchists of Conrad's mid-period fiction in general and his London novel in particular. Miller in his history and analysis is quick to point out that anarchism itself is hard to pin down and broaches the possibility that it is, perhaps, not an ideology *per se* but "rather the point of intersection of several ideologies" that coincide in their opposition to authority and capitalism (1984: 3). The sense of anarchism as a sub-set of other more dominant ideologies, like socialism or communism, is a fairly common conflation in commentary about the political left (not always as neutrally as Miller presents the idea, and sometimes disingenuously). It is even there in Vladimir's estimation of Verloc's pose "You – a member of a starving proletariat – never! You – a desperate socialist or anarchist – which is it?" (22). Vladimir's question is posed without any real investment in the response, since any reply Verloc might proffer would be roundly ridiculed, and there is some echo of it in the critical discussions that range over Conrad's minor characters in *The Secret Agent.*

Many commentators on the novel tend to disregard or belittle its revolutionaries, prompted, it must be said, by Conrad's own ostensible estimation. Richard Curle dismissed them cursorily: "of the four anarchists each indelibly individualized, only one, the man called The Professor, is worth much attention psychologically" (1957: 133). Conrad's depiction of the others, especially, is a deal-breaker for Irving Howe who notes that Conrad "repeatedly abandoned his established subjects and turned, with a visible shudder of distaste, to the world of London anarchists, Russian émigrés, [and] Latin revolutionaries" (1992: 76). Howe goes on to describe their treatment as a "coarse spirited burlesque" and especially critiques Conrad's disclaimers about the seriousness of his subject (or lack thereof), suggesting that not to treat the subject of anarchism and anarchists seriously does a disservice to the "complexities of the radical mind" and ultimately undermines the novel's grasp and scope, "our sense of what 'really happens'" (1992: 97, 98, 100). Eloise Knapp Hay responds to Howe's criticism by sidestepping it shifting the subject – in her words, "Martial Bourdin's fiasco" (1981: 250) – and essentially refusing to see the drama's central "terrorist" act as a legitimate political gesture, but instead, as Conrad dismisses it in his preface, as a "blood-stained inanity" (5). Hay turns, as have others, to the subsequent "domestic drama" that the Assistant Commissioner identifies in Chapter X in part to reflect the weight of the plot's domestic element but in part to deflect Howe's criticism of Conrad's political acuity or honesty.

Recent commentary, like that by Anthony Fothergill (2005), also discusses *The Secret Agent* at length, pointing to the enduring political relevance of Conrad's depiction of anarchism, although, of course, current interest in the text pivots around its treatment of terror and terrorism (see Mallios 2005). Fothergill remarks that Conrad "does look into anarchy and the culture within which, for a while, it flourished. He has a much better informed insiderly knowledge of the cultural and political complexities of the anarchist movement than his evasive prefatory comments on *The Secret Agent* and *A Set of Six* would imply" (2005: 140).

Even a cursory analysis of Conrad's novel reveals as much, and perhaps one can press further by saying that not only does Conrad exhibit a keen awareness of the subtleties of the anarchist movement but also that that awareness is essential to his creative endeavour and the fundamental mechanisms of plot and character. In fact, the framework of anarchist ideas as expressed in the pantheon of revolutionaries is key to understanding the novel, both in terms of its major themes and in the hinging of the plot. Still the weight of commentary on the anarchists tends to disregard them as individuals, to shy away from labelling them as anarchists, or to suggest that their treatment reveals Conrad's contempt for anarchist ideology. The consensus seems to be that Michaelis, Yundt, and Ossipon, and to a degree even The Professor serve little purpose except as fearful grotesques – broad evidence of conservative reaction perhaps but hardly legitimate insights into the world of revolt and terror. Thus many observers regard their presence in the scheme of the novel as merely enforcing a condemnation of anarchist ideology through the gross caricatural representation and conflation of anarchist types – even though such a perspective might be characterized as journalistic or "newspaperly" (in a pejorative sense) rather than Conradian.[1] From a certain point of view, such a response is perfectly understandable.

Admittedly, as a tableau, the anarchists grouped together in Verloc's kitchen are deliciously funny, but unremittingly grim. And it is delightful that Conrad chooses to stage his scene in an eminently domestic space, rather than in a secret backroom, a Continental café, or a filthy tavern. They are by turns, cadaverous, corpulent, and prurient, and universally self-serving (who in the novel is not?); they prey on women in every way imaginable; and, perhaps worst of all, are complete humbugs – they utter imprecations and vociferations upon which they will never act, driving Verloc himself to fulfil Vladimir's command to shift from seeming to being. So much for the revolutionaries, runs the typical analysis. But that is precisely Conrad's point. Where such a dismissal of the anarchists fails is in not understanding that Conrad does not make them impotent mouthers of mere cant to dismiss them, but because their inaction is an historical inevitability, a philosophical necessity, and a vital aspect of his manipulation of both his narrative and audience.

After all, one way of looking at the sequencing of the plot is as a kind of loose, but none the less compelling, corollary of anarchist ideology. When we first see the *agent provocateur*, Verloc, he is comfortably, like the anarchists with whom he associates and observes, ensconced in the anarchist milieu of propaganda by word – the attempt to subvert the state and educate the masses via oratory, print, and illustration.[2] But after his interview with Vladimir he is jolted out of this position and forced to embrace the inevitable philosophical extension of it, the "Propaganda by

---

[1] Page after page of newspaper coverage of anarchist activity points to international conspiracy. In the *Pall Mall Gazette*'s treatment of the Greenwich bombing in its issue of 16 February 1894, there is simultaneously a report on the London outrage, the Café de Terminus bombing by Henry, and two bombings in Spain. Subsequent coverage juxtaposes Fenian acts with anarchist ones and notes the anarchist conspiracy in America, Spain, and France, and as close to home as Dover and Glasgow in an attempt to show readers associations and connections where there were, in reality, none.

[2] Of course Verloc's true agenda could not be more different – he mouths the anarchist position without believing in it, or even caring for it – but he, like the group he moves, in represents Propaganda by Word (hence the pervasiveness of print-culture propaganda and pamphlets in the novel).

Deed" advocated by Bakunin in the early 1870s when he said "this is no longer the time for ideas; but for deeds" (cited in Oliver 1983: 12). The philosophical shift marked a distinct evolution of perspective, so that the Italian anarchist Carlo Cafiero when he advocated, in 1880, the urgent need to generate and propagate ideas "by permanent revolt, by spoken and written words, by the dagger, the gun, dynamite," was catching and conveying the mood of the time (*Ibid.*, 13).[3] That broader movement in anarchist ideas is manifested by the task set for Verloc who may no longer remain "*Vox et [præterea nihil]*," a voice and nothing else.[4] Attempts to assert his voice during his interview with Vladimir come to nothing. Though his "lips quivered before they came widely open … [and] he boomed out in his great, clear, oratorical bass," Vladimir curtly silences him: "Don't roar like this" (23). Subsequently Verloc narrates the value of his own disembodied voice:

> His voice, famous for years at open air meetings and at workmen's assemblies in large halls, had contributed, he said, to his reputation of a good and trustworthy comrade. It was, therefore, a part of his usefulness. It had inspired confidence in his principles. "I was always put up to speak by the leaders at a critical moment," Mr Verloc declared, with obvious satisfaction. There was no uproar above which he could not make himself heard, he added; and suddenly he made a demonstration. (23-24)

---

[3] That was reflected at the London Congress in 1881 (Conrad was apparently in the city) where there was a resolution to arouse the working and peasant classes by examples of insurrectionary deeds and the prosecution of violent means. Ironically, the resolution passed unnoticed by the press and public, which goes some way to explaining the kind of frustration that Vladimir expresses about Britain as a safe haven for terrorists. In fact, little attention was paid to the Congress, although its policy decision was to herald the "era of outrages" and touch off a new Terror in Europe.

[4] The phrase comes from Plutarch, a high-culture allusion made by Vladimir and mocked by Verloc, in the form of a coded and clipped "*Vox et* …" (24). It originally referred to a nightingale, dismissed as a mere nothing despite all its singing, and one can see how the allusion fits Vladimir's perspective of Verloc. Curiously this is also perhaps an example of Conrad's "multiple thought" or at least a satirically allusive style, given that a "nightingale" was also late-Victorian and early modern slang alternately for an informer and, depending upon the context, a prostitute (as in T. S. Eliot's "Sweeney among the Nightingales"), which is, of course, a fairly pithy summation of the Verlocs.

The "demonstration" is telling, not least for the damningly complacent description of the policeman in the square, which represents Verloc's (and perhaps the contemporary reader's) actual perspective, "watching idly the gorgeous perambulator of a wealthy baby being wheeled in state" (24). As for the startling effect of Verloc's effortless voice on the constable who spun round "as if prodded by a sharp instrument" (24), one might draw all sorts of conclusions about Verloc's effectiveness as a police agent and *provocateur*, or indeed of the police as responsive agents of Verloc's insinuations and intelligence. Indeed, Verloc's contention, which Vladimir, who wants deeds, mocks, is that his voice is a valuable instrument – perhaps sharp – but certainly of use for whichever cause controls it.

From a certain point of view, rather than being merely "a domestic tragedy," the whole story expressly revolves around this shift from propaganda by word to propaganda by deed because the consuming question for Verloc in the tale's early development becomes: Who will not merely speak, but act?

Any discussion of the political dimension of Conrad's *The Secret Agent* runs up against a range of what have become fairly iconic statements made in the letters and essays, the so-called "left-handed writing" that sometimes illuminates the novels, but as often obscures them. Early on Conrad remarks, for example, that "England was the only barrier to the pressure of infernal doctrines born in continental back-slums" (*CL*1 16). Yet in the "Author's Note" to *The Secret Agent* he confesses, perhaps with an eye to the æsthetic/economic impact of such radical *frisson* on his reading public and his peers: "I have no doubt … that there had been moments during the writing of the book when I was an extreme revolutionist" (8). To Edward Garnett he plays up the incendiary angle of his writing, identifying, Hamlet-like, "words, words, words" exploding "like stored powder barrels" where "An explosion is the most lasting thing in the universe. It leaves disorder, remembrance, room to move, a clear space" (*CL*1 344). But of his own anarchist characters he is less expansive. In response to criticism by Cunninghame Graham he wrote dismissively: "All these people are not revolutionaries – they are shams" (*CL*2 491). Conrad's letter to Cunninghame Graham seems to enforce a conservative reading of the novel, but still there is a need to redress the perception of their contribution to the novel since they are types or expressions of the anarchist movement and as such represent an important nexus of ideas.

The ideas canvassed by Michaelis, Karl Yundt, and Ossipon, are clearly derived from the concerns of anarchist theorists; these three types (suggesting Conrad's intention perhaps) also encompass in their ideologies, different stages in the progression or development of anarchist positions. Hay moves some way towards this when she argues that the revolutionaries are pathetic "in the way each contradicts himself while promoting the theories of the 'supermen' – Nietzsche, Nechaev, and Marx," and she equally distinguishes between them comfortably observing Conrad's "communist, anarchist, nihilist, and police spy" (1981: 250, 242). Those distinctions are perhaps a little arbitrary and artificial – the kind of conflation of approaches mentioned earlier. Moreover, while this is not meant to be a discussion of sources, Conrad's figures often echo figures from key stages in anarchist thought.

Michaelis offers an insightful rebuff to his colleagues as we join Chapter III in the middle of an on-going (and presumably long-standing) verbal conflict between various anarchist ideologies (a reflection of the kinds of philosophical and political schisms that divided anarchist "communities" as well as demarcating anarchist from communist and socialist groups throughout the late nineteenth century): "No one can tell what will be the form the social organisation may take in the future. Then why indulge in prophetic phantasies? At best they can only interpret the mind of the prophet, and can have no objective value. Leave that pastime to the moralists, my boy" (37). Possibly an oblique reference to Utopians such as Wells, to whom the novel is dedicated, it is a remote and Olympian kind of discourse. The effects are, first, that Michaelis's utterance is rather pompous and, as such, easily disregarded by his immediate audience or the reader; secondly, his remarks seem neutral or abstract (part of his dream-like musing) because they do not seem to pertain to his surroundings or his company, for after all, there are few "prophets" among the motley gang of anarchists. (It does, however, reinforce the mystico-religious aspect of Michaelis's Utopianism.)

In an ironic sense, however, these anarchists are indeed prophets, conduits of ideas, albeit self-styled, egocentric prophets of destruction and change. In the first passage, Michaelis's observation is in response to his colleagues' visions of the future. A sharp rebuke based on an economic understanding of historical change, it is strongly reminiscent of the phrase coined by the early anarchist ideologue Pierre-Joseph Proudhon, "property is theft," which appeared in a pamphlet in 1840 (Joll 1979: 45). Like Proudhon, Michaelis "saw already the end of all private property coming along logically, unavoidably, by the mere development of its inherent viciousness" (38). And like Proudhon, Michaelis, originally from the labouring class, turned to an economic reading of history and revolt arguing that "we must destroy the royal rule of gold," a vision that may have appealed to Conrad who had completed his account of the royal rule of silver in *Nostromo*.

In fact, the different "temperaments" on display in Chapter III are indicative of standards of anarchist thought that are eerily prescient when compared to the language of early anarchist ideologues. Here, for example, is Bakunin (the Master, Bakunin the Destroyer, in Zola's *Germinal*)[5] who instituted the shift towards propaganda by deed, speaking of the revolutionary potential of the right kind of men: "Three men alone if they stand united already form an important beginning of strength … Now what will happen when you organize your country to the extent of some hundreds?" (cited in Joll 1979: 90). He found one such man in the Russian anarchist, Sergei Nechaev, described by James Joll in *The Anarchists* as "a self-made revolutionary, a dark, lonely tortuous man, part poseur, part fanatic, part idealist, part criminal" (1979: 76). Bakunin writes of Nechaev:

> I have with me … one of those fanatical young men who know no doubts, who fear nothing and who have decided in an absolute way that many, very many of them must perish at the hands of the government, but who will not stop because of that until the Russian people rise. They are magnificent, these young fanatics, believers without gods, heroes without phrases. (Cited in Joll 1979: 76)

Nechaev himself remarks:

> The revolutionary despises and hates present-day social morality in all its forms … he regards everything as moral which helps the triumph of revolution. … All soft and enervating feelings of friendship, relationship, love, gratitude, even honour, must be stifled in him by a cold passion for the revolutionary cause. … Day and night he must have one thought, one aim – merciless destruction. (*Ibid.*, 78)

---

[5] Souvarine, the Russian terrorist in Zola's novel, embraces Bakunin's philosophy and goes on to endorse the prosecution of terror, of changing things: "by fire, poison, and the dagger. The real hero is the murderer," he asserts, "for he is the avenger of the people, the revolutionary is action, not someone just trotting out phrases out of books. We must have a series of appalling cataclysms to horrify the rulers and awaken the people" (cited in Joll 1979: 236).

Consider these sentiments against the expression of Karl Yundt in *The Secret Agent*, who is seen spouting much the same sentiments in the gathering at Verloc's home:

> "I have always dreamed," he mouthed fiercely, "of a band of men absolute in their resolve to discard all scruples in the choice of means, strong enough to give themselves frankly the name of destroyers, and free from the taint of that resigned pessimism which rots the world. No pity for anything on earth, including themselves – and death – enlisted for good and all in the service of humanity – that's what I would have liked to see. …
>
> And I could never get as many as three such men together." (38)

Note again Bakunin's earlier comment: "Three men alone if they stand united already form an important beginning of strength."

Ossipon, on the other hand, represents a different stage of anarchism, the new generation wedded to science (or pseudo-science) and reason. The Italian anarchist Malatesta was a student doctor and might be a potential model since Ossipon is "nicknamed the Doctor, ex-medical student without a degree" (40). Equally, Kropotkin, who assumed leadership of the anarchist movement after Bakunin's death, might be a possible influence on the robust Ossipon with his fascination for science and his belief "that it was by means of the printed word that the cause of the revolution could best be served and that a clandestine pamphlet was worth more than the terrorist's bomb or the assassin's dagger" (Joll 1979: 131).[6]

In The Professor, too, there are a range of interesting elements. Worthy, as Conrad notes, of serious examination, the foundation of The Professor's extremism is religious zeal. Described as the son of a "dark enthusiast," Conrad explains how The Professor had nursed his

---

[6] Kropotkin was a keen advocate of scientific progress for the freedoms it could confer upon humanity. He was excited, for example, by the invention of the washing machine as a labour-saving device. Ironically, in the pages of the serialization of *The Secret Agent* in *Ridgway's Militant Weekly*, there is an advertisement for a washing machine which stresses the troublesome nature of servants: "Cook going on 'short notice' – housemaid refusing to stay 'another minute,' or perhaps it's the 'wash-lady' getting out in a hurry and leaving part of the clothes in the tub and the rest on the floor. Do you find it hard to keep good servants because of the troubles of wash-day?" Far from freeing individuals from menial labour, as Kropotkin optimistically envisaged, technological advancement threatened to free them into unemployment ("save time and trouble and servant worries," the advertisement promises) and a major new phase of social unrest (61).

"frenzied puritanism of ambition … into something secularly holy" (66). There has been a good deal of previous work linking this character to possible anarchist antecedents (such as Dr MacDonald, who was allegedly implicated in the Greenwich bombing), but perhaps The Professor, linked though he is, like Ossipon, to science, belongs more to the terroristic bogey men of the 1880s and 1890s, the even more liminal zealots of the anarchist movement like Ravachol, Vaillant, and Henry – notorious propagandists by deed. Joll describes Ravachol, for example, as a figure that even the anarchists found hard to embrace comfortably because he oscillated between acts of sordid criminality (such as the murder and robbery of a hermit) and apparently authentic acts of revolt (explosions aimed against judges who had taken part in the sentencing of workers involved in 1891 May Day demonstrations). It is not difficult to see in a figure like Ravachol the echoes of The Professor in the Silenus Restaurant scene, immediately after the bomb outrage is made public where Ossipon expresses his horror at The Professor's dangerous and ill-conceived policies about distributing his explosives.

For all the various possible influences, and for all the possible antecedents, the anarchists are clearly just that – anarchists. They represent a range of responses, whether chronological or philosophical (or both) that are legitimate expressions of type. But they also represent a problem for the reader since they are not merely conservative reactions to type.

At this point we might cue another iconic statement instead of wrestling with the problem – the stop-gap Conrad letter that allows us comfortably to incorporate his "multiple thought" in his writing, and embrace instead his "irreconcilable antagonisms." After all, Conrad describes how "The only legitimate basis of creative work lies in the courageous recognition of all the irreconcilable antagonisms that make our life so enigmatic, so burdensome, so fascinating – so full of hope" (*CL2* 348-49). But to flee too quickly into the embrace of those "irreconcilable antagonisms" is perhaps an intellectual evasion. The anarchist credo is important to the novel after all, and it is not clear that Conrad is rejecting it in the way that some commentators suggest.

It may be fair to argue that the novel's anarchist figures are compromised by their own weaknesses and failings. But they are merely part of the social critique that Conrad engineers, and the essential truthfulness of their concerns is often supported by other characters. Hay refers to "Conrad's Dickensian tenderness for lower-class nobility" in the Cockney cabman scene (1981: 252), but the sufferings of the poor, poignantly depicted there, are reiterated in Verloc's walk to the Embassy where he observes the policeman "watching idly the gorgeous perambulator of a wealthy baby being wheeled in state across the Square" (24). That complacent and disturbing image is reinforced subsequently when Winnie distractedly responds to Stevie's questions about whether the police might intervene in the "bad world for poor people" epiphany he experiences after the cabbie experience in Chapter VIII:

> "Don't you know what the police are for, Stevie? They are there so that them as have nothing shouldn't take anything away from them who have." …
>
> "What?" he asked at once anxiously. 'Not even if they were hungry? Mustn't they?"
>
> The two had paused in their walk. (133)

Winnie's response is interesting because the question fails to engage her, although Conrad notes her link to the world of anarchists as a preface to her words. She has other more practical things to concern herself with here, however, and no good reason to disillusion Stevie, except that perhaps the claim feels true. It is apparently true at least as far as she perceives it. And the narrator's voice chimes in complacent and remote with its lofty language, after the remark's immediacy: 'Not if they were ever so," said Mrs Verloc, with the equanimity of a person untroubled by the problem of the distribution of wealth, and exploring the roadway for an omnibus of the right colour" (133).

The "bad world for poor people" of Stevie's world view is strikingly juxtaposed against Toodles's moment of epiphany when he discovers that the "extreme selectness" of the Explorers' Club might be compromised. Conrad's irony drips from the observation that "Toodles was revolutionary only in politics; his social beliefs and personal feelings he wished to preserve unchanged through all the years allotted to him on this earth which, upon the whole, he believed to be a nice place to live on" (164). These secret sharers of a sort offer polarized views of their worlds – one, stutteringly drawn to the knowledge that the world is "bad" for the poor (a conclusion that is only too readily endorsed by the tragic closure of the novel and the relentless machine of the plot), the other mincingly affirming the delusion that the world is a "nice place," when it is perfectly evident in Conrad's text that if it is, it is only "nice" for a select few. What is curious here is that when Dickens explores this theme again and again the reader feels for the suffering multitudes, what Proudhon described as "*la classe la plus nombreuse et la plus pauvre*."

Dickens documents social inequities, but at the same time sentimentalizes them, so that at their heart it is no longer a complex issue, just a clear cut case of right or wrong. When Conrad does it we are simultaneously moved by the misery of the many, and revolted by their unredeemed squalor and incipient menace. We feel for the unwashed multitudes, but also fear them, or merely despise them. Yet the social mechanisms of protection and peaceful change are equally conflicted. The police are not to be trusted in *The Secret Agent*, and government is little more than an exclusive gentlemen's club. Howe is correct when he notes that "Few things in the novel, or in all of Conrad, are more gloomily impressive than the care with which he demonstrates that every part of society is implicated in Mr Verloc's fate and responsible for Stevie's death" (1992: 94). Conrad, then, moves the reader from propaganda by word to propaganda by deed, from the words of the anarchist to the actions of Stevie and Winnie, but at no point does he undermine the underlying complaints from the "discredited" anarchists of social inequity, complacence, cruelty, and despair. Conrad's London is more unsettling than Dickens's and more apt, perhaps to shock the reader with its brutality. In fact, the ruthlessness of the politicians, the complacency of the upper classes, the complicity of the police, the very unfolding of the plot itself reinforces the anarchist vision of the world rather than attempting to debunk or discredit it.

In and through Stevie and Winnie, propaganda becomes deed, and the deed in turn becomes a kind of propaganda, not a random act of terror (as it was to become, and as perhaps we witness now), but a concerted effort to arouse the observers to revolution by example. Thus the novel becomes that most sophisticated of detonators, which eludes The Professor but not Conrad, when the act of revolt is modelled for us (again the original sense of propaganda by deed) by Winnie. Conrad's great achievement is that in *The Secret Agent*, while there are the worst excesses of nineteenth-century dynamiters in fiction – the traditional dark, cloaked figure, menacing an innocent populace with arbitrary violence – the novel's true anarchist is Winnie, since one might describe the classical anarchist as a person who discovers himself or herself free to act.

Acknowledgement

A version of this essay was presented at the 32nd Annual International Conference of the Joseph Conrad Society (UK), London, July 2006.

Works cited

Conrad, Joseph. "The Secret Agent." *Ridgway's Militant Weekly*. New York: The Ridgway Co., 6 October 1906 to 15 December 1906.

Curle, Richard. *Joseph Conrad and his Characters*. London: Heinemann, 1957.

Fothergill, Anthony. "Connoisseurs of Terror and the Political Æsthetics of Anarchism: *Nostromo* and *A Set of Six*." In *Conrad in the Twenty-First Century*, edited by Carola M. Kaplan, Peter Mallios, and Andrea White. 137-54. New York: Routledge, 2005.

Howe, Irving. *Politics and the Novel*. New York: Columbia University Press, 1992.

Joll, James. *The Anarchists*. London: Methuen, 1979.

Hay, Eloise Knapp. *The Political Novels of Joseph Conrad: A Critical Study*. Chicago: University of Chicago Press, 1981.

Mallios, Peter. "Reading *The Secret Agent* Now." *Conrad in the Twenty-First Century*, edited by Carola M. Kaplan, Peter Mallios, and Andrea White. 155-72. New York: Routledge, 2005.

Miller, David. *Anarchism*. London: J.M. Dent & Sons, 1984.

Oliver, Hermia. *The International Anarchist Movement in Late Victorian London*. London: Croom Helm, 1983.

Zola, Émile. *Germinal* (1885), translated by Leonard Tancock. Harmondsworth: Penguin, 1983.

The Time of Death: "Passing Away" in *The Secret Agent*

Paul Wake
Manchester Metropolitan University

IN COMMON WITH the work of many of the writers associated with literary Modernism, Conrad's fiction demonstrates a real concern with time. In his essay "Conrad's Clocks" David Leon Higdon goes so far as to describe Conrad as "one of our century's great time novelists" (1991: 8-9). His essay begins: "Conrad's fiction contains a rogue's gallery of malfunctioning, maimed, abused and abusive timepieces which serve their owners perversely… Their presence … unlocks the secret of several paradoxical structural problems in his novels" (1991: 1). Taking Higdon's cue, the present essay considers the "structural problems" that arise in *The Secret Agent*, arguing that they are inherent in the nature of narrative time and derived from the non-narratable nature of the instant.

The "abuse" of these "abusive timepieces" appears in *The Secret Agent* in the form of three distinct attacks on time. The most obvious is the attempted terrorist attack on the Royal Observatory in Greenwich. The second attack can be located in the novel's complex narrative structure and the final and, I will argue, most successful attack comes in the novel's consideration of the instant of death and of the impossibility of that instant's appearing in narrative. As R. W. Stallman (1960) effectively deals with the first two in his "Time and *The Secret Agent*," and the third is the focus here, with the first two discussed only briefly.

Attack One

As Sherry (1966) and others have noted, Conrad based *The Secret Agent* on a real-life attempt to blow up the Royal Observatory in 1894, by which time Greenwich had been recognized as the zero meridian, the point from which all time zones are measured, and therefore as a symbol of universal time it provided the perfect anarchist target. The real-life attempt failed when Martial Bourdin, a French anarchist, was fatally injured in an accidental explosion before reaching his target.[1] Similarly, Verloc's attempt fails when Stevie trips on his way to the Observatory, accidentally detonating the bomb he is carrying. Consequently, the plot of *The Secret Agent* literally charts the failure of this attempt to destroy clock time.

The second, more effective, challenge to clock time occurs not at the plot level but in the novel's narrative structure. Characteristically, in *The Secret Agent* Conrad rarely presents events chronologically, instead circling around key moments, elongating stretches of time, and repeating certain events while compressing and omitting others. The novel thus cries out to be read in a way that registers the distinction between story (what happens) and narrative (the way it is organized), what Gérard Genette describes as narrative's "doubly temporal sequence" (1980: 33).

The novel's structural anachrony has been well documented. Stallman suggests that in terms of story time chronology the chapters would run 1, 2, 3, 8, 9, 4, 5, 6, 7, 10 concurrent with 11, 12, 13. His conclusion is to link the novel's structure with its subject: "The theme of *The Secret Agent* has to do with time, the destruction and confusion of time itself, and the confused chronology of narrated events by their disarrangement from time effects a structure which is at one with the theme" (1960: 246). This double temporality acknowledges the fact that narratives are freed from the constraints of linear time by what Aristotle terms emplotment, the arrangement (or rearrangement) of events. The flipside of this is that, providing the novel adheres to another of Aristotle's tenets, "wholeness," the sequence can be reconstructed by the reader. That is, put back into a linear order – as Stallman so effectively does. Thus, despite its complex narrative structure, *The Secret Agent* does not so much challenge temporal consonance as foreground the human role in shaping time.

Ricoeur and Time

The connection between narrative time and human time is discussed in detail by Paul Ricoeur in his three-volume *Time and Narrative*. In Ricoeur's analysis narrative is a time-bound form, organizing and interpreting events within a temporal framework in order to make them intelligible on what he describes as a "human level." Pursuing the hypothesis that

---

[1] On Bourdin and the historical event, see the collection of documents edited by Burgoyne in the present edition.

narrative is not only *always* temporal but also that it allows the *only* access to temporality Ricoeur argues that "Time becomes human time to the extent that it is organized after the manner of a narrative; narrative, in turn, is meaningful to the extent that it portrays the features of temporal experience" (1984: I:3).

This argument follows from Ricoeur's reading of Augustine and Aristotle. From the former he takes the idea of the "three-fold present." This formulation, which is taken from the *Confessions*, emerges from Augustine's attempt to account for the notion that the present has no duration. Augustine writes:

> the only time that can be called present is an instant …that cannot be divided even into the most minute fractions, and a point of time as small as this passes so rapidly from the future to the past that its duration is without length. For if its duration were prolonged, it could be divided into past and future. When it is present it has no duration. (1984: I:266)

In order to solve this problem Augustine develops the idea of a three-fold present in which time is conceived as having being only inasmuch as the past and future exist in the present of the mind as memory and expectation.

The usefulness of Augustine's formulation for the study of narrative, where past, present, and future can be equated with beginning, middle and end, becomes evident when Ricoeur introduces Aristotle's *Poetics*. Ricoeur builds on the Aristotelian notion of "emplotment," which he describes as "an eminently verbal experience where concordance mends discordance," or, more plainly, as "the organizing of events" (1984: I:31, 34). This organization, which is the narrating activity that allows "human time" to emerge, is readily apparent in *The Secret Agent*'s convoluted narrative structure.

In common with Aristotle's *Poetics*, Ricoeur's analysis pivots on the notion of wholeness, and he quotes Aristotle's claim that "a thing is a whole if it has a beginning, a middle, and an end" going on to state that "it is only in virtue of poetic composition that something counts as a beginning, middle, or end … the ideas of beginning, middle, and end are not taken from experience. They are not features of some real action but the effects of the ordering of the poem" (cited in Ricoeur 1984: I:38-39).

Thus, the human intervention required by Augustine's three-fold present is comparable to the Aristotelian notion of emplotment. Both are activities by which experience is ordered and through which time is understood. Accordingly, Ricoeur's use of Augustine's philosophical analysis of time and Aristotle's discussion of poetics allows him to conclude that: "time becomes human to the extent that it is articulated through a narrative mode, and narrative attains full meaning when it becomes a condition of temporal existence" (1984: I:52). The three-fold present of human time comes into being with narrating activity.

Time and Death

If the narrative structure of *The Secret Agent* succeeds in depicting time as human time, as organized and narratized, it would appear that in doing so it makes it clear that human time is a narrating act for which time is characterized as sequential. In this way time asks a question of narrative: If the three-fold model of time is an act of narrating necessary to allow human time to emerge from a sequence of instants, how is narrative sustained when it encounters the problem of narrating the instant *as* an instant, as the non-passage of time? The attempt to narrate the instant is the third challenge to time in *The Secret Agent* and appears in what will prove to be the limit case for narrative: the instant of death.

Death, as limit, is figured here as a form of border across which it is impossible to step, a figuration that emerges when Augustine's claim that time "cannot be measured after it has passed, because nothing then exists to be measured" (1961: 269) is read alongside Derrida's description of death as an aporia, "as what cannot pass [*passer*] or come to pass" (1993: 23). Thus, according to this reading, in *The Secret Agent*, the instant of death (and death itself) must necessarily be refused narrative.

With this in mind, it is notable that the narrator of *The Secret Agent* makes a point of recording the times of the story's three deaths. Stevie, who stumbles on his way to plant the bomb at the Royal Observatory dies at half past eleven, Ossipon reading the details of his death in a newspaper: "Bomb in Greenwich Park. There isn't much so far. Half past eleven" (59). Adolf Verloc, the next to die, is murdered by his wife at "ten minutes to nine" (198). Finally, Winnie Verloc takes her own life at "five o'clock in the morning" (230). Despite the importance apparently allocated to the times at which the three members of the Verloc household die there is a certain imprecision in the relation. Each of these times is mediated without the impersonal narrator's authority – by a ten-day old newspaper, by a ticking clock noticed by Winnie moments *after* she murders her husband, and by the crew of the trans-Channel ferry who arrive *too late* to witness the instant of death. This tendency is typified by Stevie's death which, in terms of Verloc's plans, comes at the wrong time. Consequently, when Chief Inspector Heat questions Verloc about Stevie's death, asking, "The bang startled you, eh?", Verloc replies: "Yes; it came too soon" (158). As the deaths in *The Secret Agent* demonstrate, the instant of death presents a problem to narrative for which it can only come either too soon or too late, a conflict encapsulated by the disavowal of Winnie's idea that "clocks and watches always stopped at the moment of murder for the undoing of the murderer" (202). This failed attempt at precision, the continued ticking of the clock, suggests a refusal, or inability, to include the instant of death in the narrative.

Given that these three deaths *are* marked, however inaccurately, the obscure manner of their presentation in the narrative is also striking. Stallman notes that, "of the three main events – the explosion, the murder, and the suicide – only the murder scene is presented as point-present action, whereas the first and final events are reported piecemeal through multiple points of view" (1960: 245). Terry Eagleton describes this aspect of the narrative:

> The killing of Stevie is unpresented – happens, so to speak, in the reader's absence; and the murder of Verloc is presented with extreme obliquity, squinted at sideways rather than frontally encountered. Both events reveal sinister forces capable of destroying the quotidian forces which must be "shown" at the same time as the novel proclaims the impossibility of attesting textually to their authentic existence. (cited in Jordan, ed., 160)

Eagleton's use of the word "authentic" indicates what might be described as a doubling of death within narrative. The first death in the narrative is the death of the Other that circulates at the level of language. The second death, the authentic death, which might be called the philosopher's death, is that linked to the aporetic instant and refuses itself to narrative.

This doubling is evident in the depiction of Verloc's murder, which unlike the deaths of Stevie and Winnie, is presented: Verloc, lying on the couch, "saw partly on the ceiling a clenched hand holding a carving knife. It flickered up and down. Its movements were leisurely. They were leisurely enough for Mr Verloc to recognise the limb and the weapon" (197). The "leisurely" nature of the instant in which Winnie Verloc plunges the knife into her husband continues into the next paragraph as Conrad presents Verloc's last thoughts, emphasizing this expanse of time, a "flicker" in which Verloc can do no more than utter the word "Don't." The next three sentences begin "They were leisurely enough" until the sequence (itself a retardation of time) concludes, "But they were not leisurely enough to allow Mr Verloc the time to move either hand or foot" (197). In this final sentence there is a kind of temporal anachrony that distinguishes between the instant of death and the time of death as it appears in the narrative.

Following on from this notion of doubled death/time, reading the passage in which Chief Inspector Heat examines Stevie's remains makes clear the kind of temporal duality that emerges when death appears in *The Secret Agent*:

> The man, whoever he was, had died instantaneously; and yet it seemed impossible to believe that a human body could have reached that state of disintegration without passing through the pangs of inconceivable agony. No physiologist, and still less of a metaphysician, Chief Inspector Heat rose by the force of sympathy, which is a form of fear, above the vulgar conception of time. Instantaneous! He remembered all he had ever read in popular publications of long and terrifying dreams dreamed in the instant of waking; of the whole past life lived with frightful intensity by a drowning man as his doomed head bobs up, screaming, for the last time. The inexplicable mysteries of conscious existence beset Chief Inspector Heat till he evolved a horrible notion that ages of atrocious pain and mental torture could be contained between two successive winks of an eye. And meantime the Chief Inspector went on peering at the table with a calm face and the slightly anxious attention of an indigent customer bending over what may be called the by-products of a butcher's shop with a view to an inexpensive Sunday dinner. (71)

This passage is selected because of its interrelation of the instant with the "meantime," a relation enacted both at the level of story (what the extract says) and at the level of narrative (how it is said). The passage is interesting because of the way it illustrates the narrative's incapacity to render the instant. The word "passage" is used deliberately here: narrative as passage, as movement between beginning and ending, is what this reading focuses on, picking out for attention, at this preliminary stage, "instantaneous," "passing through," "till he evolved," and "meantime."

The instant, the theme of Heat's thoughts, is introduced in the first sentence, "The man, whoever he was, had died instantaneously." As Heat evolves "the horrible notion that ages of atrocious pain and mental torture could be contained within two successive winks of an eye," the narrative enacts its own elongation of the instant by moving back and forth between Chief Inspector's mind and the narrator's voice.

A summary of the narrative structure makes clear the way that the doubly temporal nature of the passage refuses to relate the time of death as an instant. The section begins with a sentence that reveals the process of Heat's thoughts. It then shifts to the voice of the narrator to comment on Heat and his credentials as a theorist of time: he is "No physiologist, and still less of a metaphysician." The third sentence signals a return to Heat's mind, returning both the Chief Inspector and the reader to the opening of the passage, with the repetition of "Instantaneous!", the multiple syllables of this single word refusing the possibility of containing what it speaks of. The next two sentences reveal Heat's thoughts as organized by the narrator, gradually increasing the presence of the narrator, who returns in full in the final sentence. This last sentence shifts the mood, removing the scene from Heat's mind with the grim humour characteristic of the novel. The way in which this passage links Heat's meditation on the instant with the notion of a non-instantaneous "meantime" demonstrates the contradictions inherent in the attempt to "think through" the instant. In the enactment of the "meantime," the extract's narrative structure reveals its nature as passage. Narrative, revealing its three-fold nature must, like the Chief Inspector's thoughts, "evolve" in a "passing through" that characterizes narrative as a "meantime" that assumes the possibility of its ending.

As Conrad's text problematizes the instant, the Chief Inspector cannot help but elongate the instant of Stevie's death. He does this by imagining Stevie at the very moment of it, "passing through the pangs of inconceivable agony." This passing through is exactly what death and the instant refuse to time and, simultaneously, what characterizes narrative. Death admits no "meantime," and the problem of fixing the instant of death, which allows no further passage of time, comes sharply into focus. Recalling Augustine, the three-fold notion of time was introduced to allow the thinking of the present to appear. If the narrative process "humanizes" time, to use Ricoeur's phrase, then the instant of death would appear to institute an *aporia* into this notion of time. How, if the present is understood in relation to the past and the future, can the instant of death, which is that for which there is no passage, appear in narrative?

By way of conclusion, but leaving this question open, I should like to equate the state of Stevie's body with the state of narrative. In a "state of disintegration," it resembles "the by-products of a butcher's shop" (71). There is a degree of irony in the local constable's words when he tells Heat, "He's all there. Every bit of him" (70). As Stallman wryly notes, "Poor Stevie never was all there" (1960: 238). The boy has been scraped up with a shovel and yet the text insists on his completeness: the constable continues, "Well, here he is – all of him I could see" (72), and again, "here he is all complete, velvet collar and all. I don't think I missed a single piece of him as big as a postage stamp" (73). This insistence on Stevie's wholeness suggests that his death has lent him a completeness not possessed during his life. It is this completeness towards which narrative moves, and yet it would seem that there is a certain stumbling in the attempt to pronounce the end that leaves the meantime in a state of disintegration.

Acknowledgement

A version of this essay was presented at the 31st Annual International Conference of the Joseph Conrad Society (UK), Amsterdam, July 2005.

Works cited

Augustine. *Confessions*, translated by R. S. Pine-Coffin. Harmondsworth: Penguin, 1961.

Derrida, Jacques. *Aporias*, translated by Thomas Dutoit. Stanford: Stanford University Press, 1993.

Eagleton, Terry. "Form, Ideology, and *The Secret Agent*." In *Joseph Conrad: Contemporary Critical Essays*, edited by Elaine Jordan. 158-67. Houndmill: Macmillan, 1996.

Genette, Gérard. *Narrative Discourse: An Essay in Method*, translated by Jane E. Lewin. Oxford: Blackwell, 1980.

Higdon, David Leon. "Conrad's Clocks." *The Conradian* 16.1 (1991): 1-18.

Ricoeur, Paul. *Time and Narrative*, translated by Kathleen McLaughlin and David Pallauer. 3 vols. Chicago: Chicago University Press, 1984, 1985, 1988.

Sherry, Norman. *Conrad's Western World.* Cambridge: Cambridge University Press, 1966.

Stallman, R. W. "Time and *The Secret Agent*" (1959). In *Joseph Conrad: A Critical Symposium*, edited by R. W. Stallman. 234-54. East Lansing: Michigan State University Press, 1960.

A City that "disliked to be disturbed": London's Soundscape in *The Secret Agent*

Patricia Pye
Royal Holloway College, University of London

"WHERE IS IT?" asks Aaron Fogel of Conrad's London in *The Secret Agent*, questioning whether this can be called "the great novel of London" (1985: 155). Martin Ray similarly finds an inexact geography that "does not betray any profound intimacy with the capital" (1992: 197). Fogel's question derives from a comparison with Dickens's city; other critics have made this comparison in different terms. Wendy Lesser, for example, traces a shift from Dickens's "bustling central city" to Conrad's "hollowed-out core" (1985: 202). Hugh Epstein identifies a Dickensian city as a result of Conrad's literary "borrowings" but one that nevertheless lacks that novelist's "solidity of specification": London is an "empty and depressing city" and Brett Street "a muffled and finally an abandoned vacuity" (1992: 178). Lesser's and Epstein's descriptions recall the novel's major themes of nihilism, isolation, and despair but also point to the strange auditory quality of Conrad's London. Having chosen the setting of a famously noisy city, Conrad presents streets memorable for their silence.

In this context, it might be argued that the aurality of Conrad's London is significant only for its symbolic value, the novel's auditory impressionism supporting its narrative themes but disassociating it from the actuality of the late-nineteenth-century capital. This essay will argue for a different reading, one that considers the social and cultural factors that might have informed Conrad's subdued city. Despite critical acknowledgement that *The Secret Agent*, to use Mark Eyeington's terms, is "rich in 'period' observations and textures" (2004: 119), this is a neglected area of study.

Before considering the sound of Conrad's London in detail, it is worth recalling what is well-known. First, that his presentation is informed by first-hand experience; secondly, and perhaps paradoxically, that this is an *émigré*'s experience. Conrad's familiarity with London's streets is made clear in the "Author's Note" (1920), wherein he describes his "solitary and nocturnal walks" (7). On first arriving in 1878, he had experienced the city's bewildering combination of "hidden" courts and alleys and "charted and navigable streets" ("Poland Revisited," 122).

Nearly twenty years later, in the autumn of 1897, Conrad walked the streets with Stephen Crane, from lunchtime until the early morning hours. Crane's response to the city is described in his essay "London Impressions," published the same year. He evokes a nocturnal city moving "with the decorum and caution of an undertaker" and compares London's "easy silence" with New York's "loud, fierce, aspiring noise" (1973: 8: 683). Crane's opposition reminds us that his impressions of London are also an outsider's and that a city's aurality may be experienced in comparative terms. Crane describes London at night, but it seems that the relative quietness of the daytime city also struck visitors. An article in the *Pall Mall Gazette* of 1902 refers to the "silence of London" and wonders why this "never fails to impress itself on the foreign visitor," while its residents "are never weary of declaiming against the ceaseless clatter of 'buses, jingling of cabs, and the hum and roar of crowded traffic" (3). The article cites Crane's reactions and Alphonse Daudet's, the latter reportedly commenting to *Le Figaro* that he found London's lack of noise "uncanny" and "disquieting," "conveying the idea of moving amid a swarm of taciturn automata, rushing about in dreamland on a pavement of india-rubber." Daudet's description recalls the Verlocs and the city we "hear" in *The Secret Agent.* Like Winnie, Conrad's London seems best characterized by a "diversity of dreadful silences" (118).

But these silences need locating. This is, after all, a city whose size and social diversity also impacted on visitors. A mid-century German traveller, Max Schlesinger, observed: "No other town presents so strong a contrast between its quarters." He notes, for example that, in the wealthy roads near the parks, "comfort reigns supreme" and the flagstones are "carefully watered" to "deaden the rumbling of the carriages and the step of the horses" (1853: 13). In any city, wealth and comfort might equate with peace and quiet, but class-conscious Victorian London does appear to have been especially diligent in ensuring that aural inequality was maintained in selected districts.[1] If by the turn of the twentieth century, London really was the "quietest of the world's

---

[1] It is possible to produce an aural map of late-Victorian London. *Bartholomew's Road Surface Map* (1908) indicate the persistence of audible inequalities into the Edwardian era, such as the continued use of granite setts, the noisiest of road surfacings, in the city's poorest districts to the east and south.

capitals" (*Pall Mall Gazette* 1902: 3), this was as a result of efforts on the behalf of the city's wealthier classes.

It seems that London was sometimes perceived as audibly "different" from other major cities and that its sounds and silences could be related to specific districts. Noise control was certainly an on-going concern. This is suggested by the existence of organizations such as the "Association for Suppression of Street Noises," whose campaigns were reported in *The Times* in 1897, when Conrad and Crane took their walk "east and north and south again" (*Last Essays*, 153). By the time of *The Secret Agent*'s publication in 1907, controlling noise in wealthy areas was part of a well-established process for the "betterment of London" that had been on the civic agenda for some years. It seems unlikely that Conrad would have been unaware of this, or that its results would have failed to impact on his auditory imagination, as it had done on Crane's and the city's other visitors. But Conrad was also especially well placed to understand this aurality in the context of London's social topographics: he had lived in different parts of the city, and his explorations on foot had taken him "from West to East and back again" (*A Personal Record*, 7). There is much evidence to suggest that *The Secret Agent* was informed by Conrad's awareness of the social significance of London's sounds, and that these might be mapped in a work in that as Robert Hampson has argued – *contra* Fogel, Ray, and Epstein – "topographical exactitudes" are inherent (1992: 174).

Bystreets and Thoroughfares

In *The Strange Case of Dr Jekyll and Mr Hyde* (1886), Robert Louis Stevenson offers the following description of Mr Hyde's locality: "By ten o'clock, when the shops were closed, the bystreet was very solitary and, in spite of the low growl of London, from all round, very silent" (2002: 14). The implied location is Soho, where Conrad placed Brett Street. Stevenson's novella also depicts London "before the era of reconstruction" (9), a process during which many of London's narrow streets either disappeared altogether or were widened into "thoroughfares."[2] Such narrow streets offered a sanctuary from the "stream" of life that passed by. Referring to Holywell Street and Wych Street, for example, demolished

[2] The 1890s saw extensive demolition and re-building across the capital, in a process of improvement that may be traced back to the 1860s and a "fascination with wide, impressive thoroughfares on the Parisian model" (Olsen 1976: 54).

when the Strand was rebuilt, *The London Topographical Record* of 1901 noted that "In their origin and purpose they are linked with the courts and alleys – the pleasant backwater whence the stream could be heard rushing by" (1:20).

Although it is more "sordid lane" (76) than "pleasant backwater," parallels can nevertheless be drawn with the alley off the Tottenham Court Road where Inspector Heat encounters The Professor, "a side corridor of a mansion full of life" (68). This is a street topographically quite separate from the "broad thoroughfare" (77) The Professor emerges into and from which Heat hears the "murmur of town life" (76). Brett Street can also be identified as such a street, acoustically cut off from the sounds emanating from the city's "populous thoroughfares" (155). Although the bystreet is not identified by this term, this movement between sound and silence, between noisy main road and quiet "back-water," is mappable throughout. Conrad establishes this feature of London topography early, through Verloc's progress from busy Piccadilly to a street that "could with every propriety be described as private" (17). Before meeting Heat, The Professor turns from "a long, straight street" into a "narrow and dusky alley" (67). The Assistant Commissioner's perambulatory experience of the city is similar as he walks to and from Whitehall from a "short and narrow street like a wet, muddy trench" into a "broad thoroughfare" (105). Later, he emerges "into the Strand out of a narrow street by Charing Cross Station" (114). London, then, is repeatedly presented in terms of this comparison between noisy thoroughfare and quiet backstreet.

Although focussed on London's sixteenth-century "soundscape,"[3] Bruce R. Smith's work makes acoustic comparisons that can be usefully applied here. In particular, he draws attention to the contrast between the city's aural "surface," as heard in its broad, heavily populated thoroughfares, and its "depth," the auditory experience of its "narrow corridors," its back lanes and alleys (1999: 60). Further sound absorption was provided by the layers of mud on the streets, still a problem in the late nineteenth century, as Conrad evokes in his description of the "enormous town slumbering monstrously on a carpet of mud" (224). Mud piled up especially in neglected bystreets, as Conrad reveals through that reference to the "trench" that the Assistant Commissioner walks

[3] The Canadian composer R. Murray Schafer and communications theorist and composer Barry Truax use this term to refer to sounds that make up the "aural identity of geographical places" (Smith 1999: 44).

through. The trench effect was created because mud and manure were not removed; in the 1880s, road-sweepers dealt with this problem by pushing it to the sides of the street, clearing a path through the middle (Turvey 1996: 134).

Once in the bystreet, back lane, or alley, individual noises from outside the street were hard to differentiate. Smith describes noises that typify a locality as "keynote sounds" (1999: 44). These "keynotes" were overwhelmed by vast numbers of people and excessive traffic, combining them together to create the impression of the "blended noises" that Conrad describes (68). The sound of the resultant effect recurs throughout late-nineteenth century fiction. Conrad's "inarticulate low murmur" (68) recalls Gissing's description from *In the Year of Jubilee*, "Noises far and near blend into a muffled murmur" (1895: 325-26), while Wilde's *A Picture of Dorian Gray* (1891) describes the "dim roar ... like the bourdon note of a distant organ" (1974: 1).

Non-fictional accounts support such impressions. In *English Hours*, Henry James recounts how "The uproar of Piccadilly hummed away at the end of the street" (1905; 1981: 4). This is the sound of London as a "background" that may be understood as the commonest aural experience of the city. It is certainly the auditory impression that Ford presents in *The Soul of London* (1905): "London, in fact, is so essentially a background, a matter so much more of masses than of individuals ... that its essential harmony is not to be caught by any human ear. It can only be treated as a ground bass, a drone" (1995: 11). Ford's impression alludes to an effect that may have led to the contemporary perception of the city as a comparatively noiseless place. The all-encompassing "hum" produced by the enormous "world city" appears to have operated like twentieth-first century "white noise," the process through which individual sounds are masked, thereby replacing them with a single note. Crane's "London Impressions" (1897) also seems to suggest that the origin of the London "silence" might be attributable to this: "There was a low drone, perhaps, a humming contributed inevitably by closely gathered thousands , and yet on second thoughts it was to me a silence" (1973: 8: 683).

On crowded thoroughfares like the Strand, keynotes like footsteps merged together, providing a sound Conrad used in "Karain" (1898) to evoke the "full … and ceaseless stir," the "headlong shuffle and beat" of the massive London crowd (54). In contrast, in bystreets, footsteps were heard as individual sounds, producing a "quaint effect," especially at night, as Stevenson captures in *Dr Jekyll and Mr Hyde*: "the footfalls of a single person, while he is still a long way off, suddenly spring out distinct from the vast hum and clatter of the city" (2002: 14). In *The Secret Agent*, Conrad uses this sound to signify the solitary individual. In the Strand, the footsteps are numerous and swift; in Brett Street, they are distinct, slow, and deliberate: "Down below in the quiet, narrow street measured footsteps approached the house" (48).

These auditory impressions of footsteps alert us to the way in which a bystreet might provide its own acoustic world. Such streets allowed for detachment from the events and affairs of the city at large. "No event in the outer world makes any impression in this street" is how Arthur Morrison in *Tales of Mean Streets* (1894) describes a street in the East End (rpt. 1903: 16), but the same might be said of the Verlocs' street in Soho, where the sound of newsboys outside the street is inaudible: "the echo of their cries drifting along the populous thoroughfares, expired between the dirty brick walls without reaching the threshold of the shop" (155).

With the noisy city in the background, some streets were comparatively quiet. However, as George Sims describes in *How the Poor Live and Horrible London* (1889), the meanest of London's streets generated enough noise of their own, especially at night. In Southwark and in the Mint district, he hears the "shrieking aloud ... of popular songs," the exchange of "ribald jests and foul oaths," and the occasional "cry of murder" (137). Such sounds were also characteristic of London's "unsavoury courts" (13), as Conrad terms them, the enclosed spaces formed between the city's bystreets and accessed by the "narrow alleys" that led off. In a description that suggests the Seven Dials area, *Dorian Gray* evokes these "gloomy courts," with their sounds of "hoarse voices and harsh laughter," "cursing, and chattering," and "shrieks and oaths" (1994: 88).

In contrast, Brett Street recalls where Stevenson's Mr Hyde lives, a street "called quiet" (2002: 6) that, unsurprisingly, was synonymous with "respectable" in the 1880s and 1890s. Number 32 is characteristically free of "unseemly shrieks" (198), until Winnie finally gives way to a "shrill and terrible" one after murdering Verloc (217). Ossipon's fear that she might "pursue him shrieking" into the street (218) indicates the social embarrassment that such a noise would cause. Any inclination to "shriek piercingly," like Stevie, had to be suppressed: the respectable city, characterized by the subdued crowd of wealthy Belgravia, "disliked to be disturbed" (13). The quiet city that made an impression on Crane and Daudet might be best experienced in the wealthiest districts to the west, such as Belgravia, Chelsea, and Mayfair. In "Chesham Square," Conrad depicts the city at its most impressively silent and orderly; there an unaccustomed call from a window, which Verloc provides, is enough to startle a policeman (24). Chesham Square recalls the "artificial abyss" of Hervey's West End square in Conrad's earlier work *The Return* (1898) whose residents experience the "correct silence of walls, of closed doors and curtained windows" (25, 22). But in their considerably poorer home to the east, the Verlocs have also achieved some measure of comfort. The presence of a venetian-blind on their bedroom window confers a measure of respectability; this is a domestic detail noted by Sims, who observes that the desperately poor conduct their lives on the streets, while closed doors and window blinds feature in the homes where the rents are regularly paid (1889: 10).

According to the social mapping of Charles Booth's *Life and Labour* survey (1886-1903), the Verlocs and their bystreet might therefore be located as the "poor quiet," as opposed to the "poor, rough, noisy."[4] That such a distinction might be made draws attention to the precise social topographics of Brett Street and is indicative of Conrad's "insistence on territorial and cultural specificity" (Najder 2003: 1). The aurality of Conrad's London appears to have been informed by such specificity, as a consideration of the location that inspired Brett Street reveals.

Green Street

Hugh Walpole's recollection of a conversation in 1919 provides the only evidence for a possible source for the site of Verloc's shop (Ray, ed., 1990: 136). As Hans van Marle noted (1977: 7; 1987: 138), Conrad's comments at that time placed it in Green, now Irving, Street, which connects Leicester Square and Charing Cross Road (see Fig. 1).[5] Since the novel so clearly places the shop in Soho, the comment to Walpole has been viewed as an inconsistency on Conrad's part (Harkness and

[4] Working Papers (1898): Notebooks B354 and B355.

[5] Conrad referred to the Leicester Galleries, the building still extant today at 20 Irving Street. According to Pevsner, it was constructed in 1875, so predates Conrad's first visit to London by three years and must therefore have been the building he saw, rather than a later one on the same site. The Leicester Galleries moved from its Irving Street site in 1962. Correspondence in *The Times* that year (30 October: 13; 2 November: 13), including a letter from Oliver F. Brown of the Galleries, corroborates the connection and supports the suggestion that Brett Street recalls the Green Street/Irving Street area.

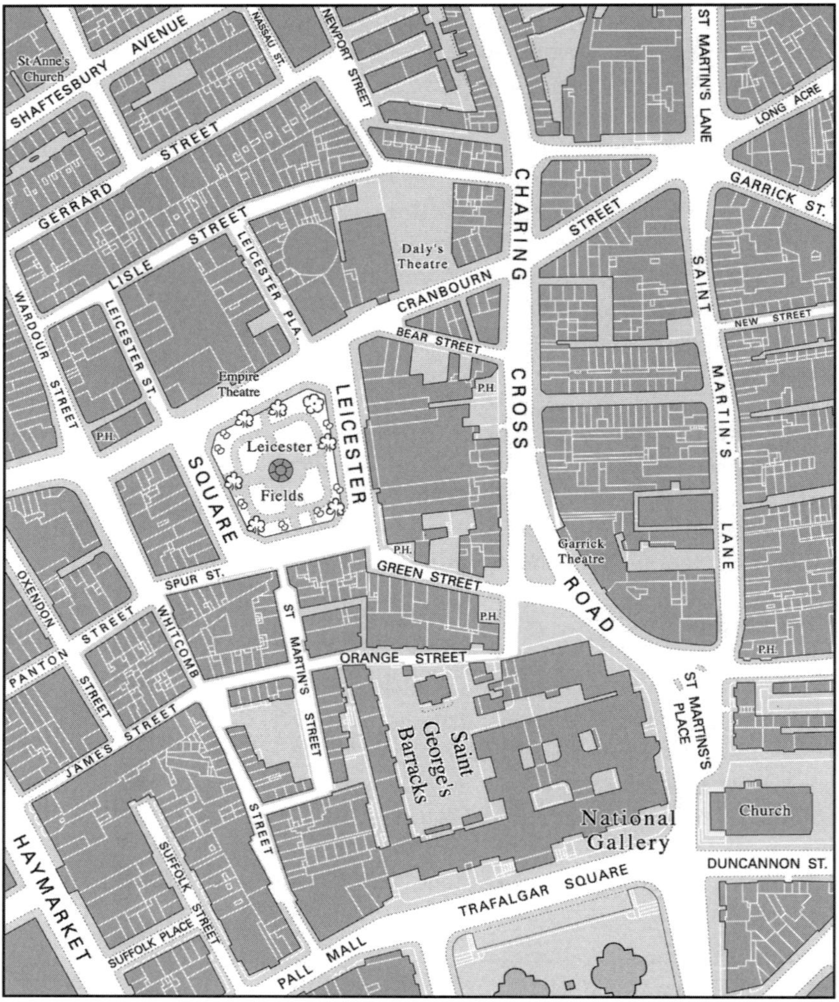

Fig. 1 Green Street and the Leicester Square area: Ordnance Survey, 1894-96 (Alan Godfrey edition, 1996)

Reid 1990: 426). Perhaps because of this, the site has not received much critical attention.[6] Although we may not think of Green Street as part of Soho, technically it was, being in the Parish of St Anne. Leicester Square also had a well-established French community.

If Green Street provided the model for Brett Street, this would also explain some other supposed geographic inconsistencies. For example, Harkness and Reid note that it is "difficult to imagine the constitutionally lethargic Verloc" walking all the way from Soho to Belgravia (1990: 416), while Van Marle suggests that the Blackfriars and Waterloo Bridges would have provided shorter routes for the cab ride to Peckham's almshouses than Westminster Bridge (1987: 140). But a walk from Green Street to Belgravia would have been shorter than one from the environs of Soho Square, and Westminster Bridge provides the quickest route southwards across the river. But, perhaps most significantly, Green Street, which might be termed a bystreet until the late 1890s, was fairly near the Strand, the capital's most important and reputedly noisiest thoroughfare, the sounds of which Conrad depicted in "Karain." As Lynda Nead has noted, the Strand had a symbolic significance for Victorian Londoners: the major linking route between East and West, it connected the centres of finance (The City), commerce (the West End), and government (Whitehall) (2000: 161). In Green Street, Conrad would have found a similarly central and interconnecting location for his novel. A walk westwards led to wealthy Piccadilly, St James's, and Belgravia, while the notoriously deprived Seven Dials area lay in similar proximity to the east. A walk southwards led to the centre of government at Whitehall or to the river and South London beyond.

Conrad knew Green Street well in later life, visiting the Leicester Galleries in it to model for Jacob Epstein's sculpture (Brown 1962: 13). But the street may have become familiar to him during *The Secret Agent*'s composition, as a shortcut through from Charing Cross Station, the terminus for trains from Kent, to the Mont Blanc Restaurant in Gerrard Street, where Edward Garnett hosted weekly lunches during 1904-06 (Najder 1983: 318). A walk through Green Street would not have required a detour or special visit: its sights and sounds would be effortlessly absorbed while traversing the city on day-to-day business.

---

[6] Sherry acknowledges Walpole's reference but draws parallels between Verloc's shop and a jeweller's in Deptford (1971: 317-18). Bagnall argues for Brett Street as a "composite" space; "nominally rooted in Soho," it could "allude to some other district – to Spitalfields, for example, or to Whitechapel" (1999: 222).

The street also has an interesting literary pedigree: Dickens cited it as the location of the "old curiosity shop" (Brennan, ed. 1998: xiii), as Conrad may have known. It is interesting to note that this area's auditory quality inspired Dickens in the 1840s, when narrow alleys and enclosed courts characterized its topography. One such was St Martin's Court, just north of Green Street.[7] Here Dickens's impression of the sound replicates that of Conrad and his contemporaries: "Think of a sick man in such a place as St Martin's court, listening to the footsteps … think of the hum and noise being always present to his senses, and of the stream of life that will not stop" (*The Old Curiosity Shop*, [1841] 1998:8).

Another such enclosed space was provided by the triangular area into which Green Street opened at its eastern end. This was formed by its intersection with Castle Street, a narrow street replaced by Charing Cross Road and completed in 1886. This formation, particularly evident on maps that predate the road widening, is still visible on later maps (see

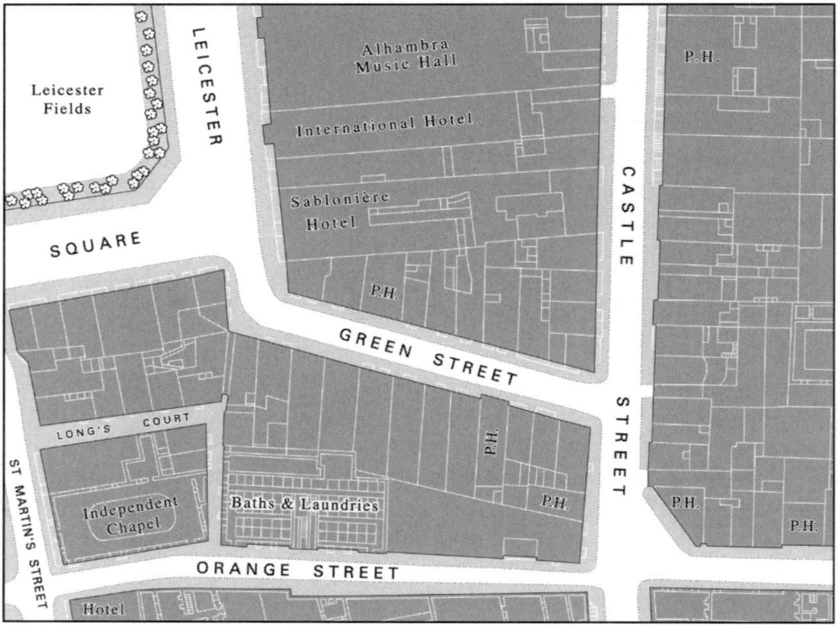

Fig. 2 Green Street and Castle Street (Ordnance Survey, 1871; "P.H." = Public House)

---

[7] See Fig. 1. St Martin's Court, unmarked, is just above Cecil Court, opposite Bear Street.

Figs. 2-3). This area reproduces the shape of *The Secret Agent*'s Brett Place, the "triangular well of asphalt and bricks" into which Winnie runs after murdering Verloc. Recalling that the novel is set in 1887,[8] it may be suggested that Conrad sought to capture the acoustic qualities of a disappearing topographical feature. London's "triangles," like its bystreets, once provided for an impression of material and psychological separation from the city's background, and an aurality where "All sounds of life seemed lost" (207).

During 1890-97, Green Street was widened from a bystreet to a thoroughfare, to accommodate the increase in traffic between Charing Cross Road and Leicester Square (*Survey of London* 34: 503). *Kelly's Directories* for the 1880s and 1890s indicate a street of small businesses, including some fine art dealers on the premises later occupied by the Leicester Galleries. "Not a very likely location for a somewhat shady Soho shop," Van Marle comments, but "the remark does suggest that Conrad had a

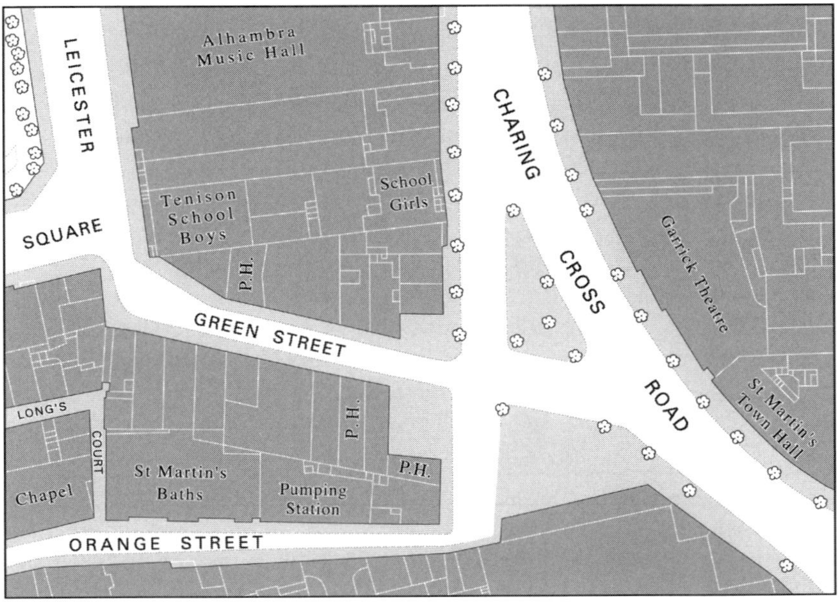

Fig. 3 Green Street and Charing Cross Road (Ordnance Survey, 1894)

[8] See Watts' discussion of the temporal setting in the present collection.

rather precise and real typography in mind when writing *The Secret Agent*, a topography perhaps connected with the Charing Cross Road" (1977: 7). The premises themselves appear to have borne little resemblance to Verloc's shop; however, as Conrad's description of Brett Place suggests, Green Street's topographics and aurality offered some important characteristics on which he could draw.

A street of small businesses, none selling essentials such as food,[9] suggests a quiet place going about its business without "the old needless uproar" of the past that had included, for example, the "disagreeable peculiarity" of street-hawkers' cries (*The Times*, 19 May 1864: 8).[10] However respectable and insular by day, Green Street appears to have taken on some of Brett Street's sinister and sordid qualities at night. This can be ascribed to its location in the very heart of London's entertainment district, with two music-halls, the Alhambra and the Empire, just round the corner in Leicester Square. In 1898, the investigators for Booth's *Life and Labour Survey* noted the large numbers of "pleasure-seekers and prostitutes" frequenting the district at night, and how this aspect made it "peculiar" in terms of classification (*Notebook* B354: 187). While this suggests a noisier, busier place than nocturnal Brett Street, it is nevertheless easy to imagine that the solitary footsteps of the last of the "pleasure-seekers" or of a passing policeman would have had just the eerie and illicit quality ascribed to the sound in *The Secret Agent*.

Green Street also presents a possible source for the impression of desolation that pervades Conrad's London. During the late 1880s, the shops on its northern side were "empty shells awaiting demolition" (67), a sight that may have had a special impact when experienced at the city's heart. The street's north side was demolished between 1890 and 1897; by 1898, new buildings were *in situ*, with some shops untenanted, and many of buildings in the surrounding streets were "down" or "about to come down" (*Notebook* B354: 182-83). The demolition process also caused a

---

[9] *Kelly's Directory 1887* lists businesses that include picture-dealing, ivory-turning, and engraving.

[10] The reports and correspondence in Bass (1864) indicate that by the mid-1860s London had become a quieter place, the famous cries of its street-sellers already controlled by law. Bass also reveals the extent to which noise was a class issue. Disputes over organ-grinders' disturbing the peace of wealthy districts continued into the next century. In 1907, the Betterment of London Association (established in 1902) called for banning them in some residential districts including Kensington, Mayfair, Belgravia, Chelsea, and South Kensington (*The Times*, 6 June 1907: 10).

social transformation; Booth's observers noted the "displacement" of the very poor in St Martin's Street, Orange Street, and Long's Court, which lay immediately behind the site that had inspired Verloc's shop (*Notebook* B354: 183, 187; see Fig. 3). Green Street's social topographics therefore exemplified the way in which, in 1880s London, the desperately poor might live in close proximity to those who were living in relative comfort: a turn out of a quietly respectable bystreet might quickly lead into "narrow alleys" and "unsavoury courts" (13), and entrapment in the "black abyss" (203). Itself mapped "pink," meaning working-class comfort (Booth 1899), pre-reconstruction Green Street was surrounded by pockets of "dark blue," identifying the very poor.

In this way, Green Street's topography might be appreciated not only as a source for the aurality of Conrad's London but also for the way in which it might inspire a fictional narrative of changing social fortune, actual examples of which typified the period (Sims 1889: 138). The slide from relative wealth to desperate poverty could be rapid, and involved journeys across the city's social borders, using means of transport that might also be socially defined by their audibility. While the wealthy of Belgravia could benefit from the "almost silent. swift flow" of the new victoria hansom (17), fitted with noise muffling rubber tyres and window fittings, the poor suffered the discomfort of a four-wheeler, whose "oscillation, noise and rattle"[11] epitomised all that was outmoded and undesirable in the modern city. Such is the lot of Winnie, her mother, and Stevie as they travel to Peckham in a cab that "rattled, jingled, jolted" (128). Conrad's repetition of this sound throughout the journey evokes just how unpleasant an experience could be in an episode that owes much of its poignancy to the preciseness with which he has located the family amongst the "poor quiet." The journey might be traced from pre-reconstruction Green Street, into narrow Castle Street, down Whitehall, and then across Westminster Bridge into South London. The four-wheeler's noisy progress would have been audible in the houses facing onto the narrow streets preceding "the wider space of Whitehall" (121).[12] The house fronts were in close proximity to the "rattling and jingling cab window" (121). Once they have crossed the bridge, and the cab's iron wheels strike the granite road surfacing prevalent in the city's poorer districts, the resultant din becomes painfully apparent, and

[11] Description from an advertisement in *The Illustrated London News* of 30 July 1887 for the "New Victoria Hansom."

[12] Turvey discusses the effects of road noise (1996: 135).

Winnie's mother "screamed … above the noise" (123). The implicit social mapping of London's aurality is most evident in this episode, as she is "overtaken," even symbolically devoured, by the "sinister, noisy, hopeless and rowdy night of South London" (123).

Acknowledgement

I am grateful to Robert Hampson for reading and commenting on drafts of this article and for making many helpful suggestions.

Works cited

Anon. "The 'Cries of London.'" *The Times*, 19 May 1864: 8.
———. "London through Foreign Lens." *Pall Mall Gazette*, 19 June 1902: 3.
———. "New Victoria Hansom" (advertisement). *Illustrated London News*, 30 July 1887: 130.
Bagnall, Peter. "Joseph Conrad and Jack the Ripper, or The Unfortunate Alias of Martin Ricardo." D. Phil thesis, Oxford University, 1999.
Bartholomew's. *Road Surface Map of London*. London: John Bartholomew, 1908.
Bass, Michael T. *Street Music in the Metropolis*. London: Murray, 1864.
Booth, Charles. *Police Notebooks from the Collection of Working Papers for The Survey of Life and Labour of the People in London, 1886-1903*.
———. *Charles Booth Online Archive: Inquiry into the Life and Labour of the People in London, 1886-1903*. London School of Economics and Political Science. <www.booth.lse.ac.uk>.
Brennan, Elizabeth M. Introduction. Charles Dickens, *The Old Curiosity Shop*. vii-xxxii. Oxford World's Classics. Oxford: Oxford University Press, 1998.
Brown, Oliver F. Letter to the Editor. *The Times*, 2 November 1962: 13.
Crane, Stephen. "London Impressions" (1897). In *The Works of Stephen Crane, Vol. 8: Tales, Sketches, and Reports*. 681-89. Charlottesville: University Press of Virginia, 1973.
Epstein, Hugh. "A Pier-Glass in the Cavern: London and *The Secret Agent*." In *Conrad's Cities: Essays for Hans van Marle*, edited by Gene M. Moore. 175-96. Amsterdam: Rodopi, 1992.
Eyeington, Mark. "'Going for the First Meridian': *The Secret Agent*'s Subversiveness." *The Conradian* 29.1 (2004): 119-26.
Fitzgerald, Murroe. Letter to the Editor. *The Times*, 30 October 1962: 13.
Fogel, Aaron. *Coercion to Speak: Conrad's Poetics of Dialogue*. Cambridge, Massachusetts: Harvard University Press, 1985.
Ford, Ford Madox. *The Soul of London: A Survey of A Modern City* (1905). London: Everyman, 1995.
Gissing, George. *In the Year of Jubilee*. London: Lawrence & Bullen, 1895.
Hampson, Robert. "'Topographical mysteries': Conrad and London." In *Conrad's Cities*. 159-74.

Harkness, Bruce, and S. W. Reid. "Notes." *The Secret Agent*, edited by Bruce Harkness and S. W. Reid. 413-27. The Cambridge Edition of Joseph Conrad. Cambridge: Cambridge University Press, 1990.

James, Henry. "London." In *English Hours* (1905), introduced by Leon Edel. Oxford's World Classics. Oxford: Oxford University Press, 1981.

Kelly's Directory of London, 1887. London: Kelly's Directories, 1887.

Lesser, Wendy. "From Dickens to Conrad: A Sentimental Journey." *English Literary History* 52 (1985): 185-208.

London Topographical Society. *London Topographical Record, Vol. 1: Annual Record of the London Topographical Society, 1900*. London: Topographical Society, 1901.

Marle, Hans van. "Shades of Reality: A Little of Conrad in *The Secret Agent*." *The Conradian* 3.1 (1977): 6-8.

———. "Of Lodging, Landladies, and *The Secret Agent*." *The Conradian* 12.2 (1987): 138-49.

Morrison, Arthur. *Tales of Mean Streets*. London: Methuen, 1903.

Najder, Zdzisław. *Joseph Conrad: A Chronicle*, translated by Halina Carroll-Najder. Cambridge: Cambridge University Press, 1983.

———. "Meditations on Conrad's Territoriality: An Essay in Four Tacks." *The Conradian* 28.1 (2003): 1-16.

Nead, Lynda. *Victorian Babylon: People, Streets, and Images in Nineteenth-Century London*. New Haven, Connecticut: Yale University Press, 2000.

Olsen, Donald J. *The Growth of Victorian London*. London: Batsford, 1976.

Pevsner, Nickolaus, and Simon Bradley. *The Buildings of England. London 6: Westminster*. New Haven,Connecticut: Yale University Press, 2003.

Ray, Martin. "The Landscape of *The Secret Agent*." In *Conrad's Cities*. 197-206.

———, ed. *Joseph Conrad: Interviews and Recollections*. Basingstoke: Macmillan, 1990.

Schlesinger, Max. *Saunterings in and about London* (1852), translated by Otto Wenckstern. London: Nathaniel Cook, 1853.

Sherry, Norman. *Conrad's Western World*. Cambridge: Cambridge University Press. 1971.

Sims, George R. *How the Poor Live and Horrible London*. London: Chatto & Windus, 1889.

Smith, Bruce R. *The Acoustic World of Early Modern England: Attending to the 0-Factor*. Chicago: University of Chicago Press, 1999.

Stevenson, Robert Louis. *The Strange Case of Dr Jekyll and Mr Hyde and Other Tales of Terror*, edited by Robert Mighall. London: Penguin, 2002.

Survey of London. *Vol. 34: The Parish of St Anne, Soho*. General editor: F. H. W. Sheppard. London: Athlone Press, 1966.

Turvey, Ralph. "Street Mud, Dust, and Noise." *London Journal* 21.2 (1996): 131-48.

Wilde, Oscar. *The Picture of Dorian Gray*, edited by Isobel Murray. Oxford: Oxford University Press, 1974.

"A heap of nameless fragments": Sacrifice, Cannibalism, and Fragmentation in *The Secret Agent*

Yuet May Ching
Chinese University of Hong Kong

"The doctrine (or the theory) of atonement through suffering . . . is quite simply a sordid abomination."
– Conrad to Marguerite Poradowska (*CL*1 95)

THE ANCIENT RITE of sacrifice, like Proteus, manifests itself in many forms in Modernist literature, revealing the apocalyptic fears and hopes for regeneration in the modern world. Pound's *Cantos* begin with a descent to the Underworld, where Odysseus performs a rite of sacrifice. The severed head of John the Baptist haunts Flaubert's *Hérodias* and Mallarmé's poem *Hérodiade*, and reappears in Yeats's play *A Full Moon in March* and Eliot's "The Love Song of J. Alfred Prufrock." In Joyce's *A Portrait of the Artist as a Young Man*, Stephen's name reminds one of the first Christian martyr, as does Stevie's in Conrad's *The Secret Agent.* The fear of civilization's decline and the sense of alienation unsurprisingly give rise to a desire to build upon the rubble of this world, to bring regeneration in spite of and through death. Sacrifice seems to promise transcendence and rebirth. This function, however, is queried and even challenged in certain Modernist texts,[1] in particular *The Secret Agent,* where Conrad exposes the sham of sacrifice, emphasizing its violence and revealing its close connections with cannibalism. He shows that sacrifice is a ruthless and arbitrary means to achieve social order and spiritual salvation. It gives no solace, and the novel ends bleakly, with every member of the Verloc family dead. The reader, however, has a chance to contemplate the human condition glimpsed through the fragmented narrative, resisting the sacrificial mode of thinking and behaviour.

---

[1] An example would be Pound's *Cantos*; see Ching (1995).

Sacrificial rites figure prominently in both Judæo-Christian and Græco-Roman tradition. In the second half of the nineteenth century, discussions of sacrifice gained momentum as anthropologists from the West re-encountered the rite in the colonial Other. Sir Edward Tylor (1871), William Robertson Smith (1889), Sir James Frazer (1890), and Henri Hubert and Marcel Mauss (1898), among others, put forward hypotheses. The word sacrifice, derived from the Latin *sacrificium*, means to make sacred (Bourdillon, 1980: 10), and hence suggests a relationship between the human and divine mediated through sacrificial ritual. To Tylor, the communication takes the form of a gift to the gods to secure their blessings. To Smith, sacrifice is sacramental: a community partakes in the consumption of the body of god immanent in food. To Frazer, it is the magical means to resurrect divine strength through killing the old and weak. Hubert and Mauss explore the rite's bearing on a society's communal and moral values.

Conrad, at the end of the nineteenth century, was writing in the context of these debates over sacrifice. Andrew Mozina (2001) shows the evolution of the theme of sacrifice in four of Conrad's novels, *The Nigger of the "Narcissus,"* *Lord Jim*, *Under Western Eyes*, and *Chance*. Garry Watson (1998) compares the treatment of the theme of sacrifice in *The Secret Agent* to that in Melville's *Billy Budd*. Both studies make use of the hypotheses advanced by René Girard (1961) who first gives the study of sacrifice a literary turn before gathering it back to the bosom of Christianity. Deriving his inspiration from examples in fiction, he sees desire as mimetic. An object is made desirable through the mediation of a third party who inevitably blocks the attainment of the desired object. Rivalry, violence, and chaos would be the result of this triangular and irreconcilable structure of desire. When the situation becomes critical, an arbitrary means is used to restore harmony: a substitute, a scapegoat, is made to bear all the guilt and suffers exile or death (1972).

Girard's discussion of sacrifice has the merit of pinpointing its arbitrary nature, but his writing shows how difficult it is to escape from a sacrificial mode of thinking. He privileges the Gospels as the only originary texts that expose the arbitrary mechanisms of sacrifice. In *The Scapegoat* (1982), he distinguishes between myths and the Bible. The former is unable to offer a critical reading of sacrifice, while the latter demonstrates a resistance to persecution and gives the right interpretation of sacrifice. In terms that suggest immolation, Girard writes that biblical revelation will "spring from the ashes of mythology" (108). For him, Christ's passion is the drama "needed to give birth to the only text that can bring an end to all of mythology" (101). He therefore affirms the necessity of sacrifice and pitches Christianity against myths and against non-Christian cultures and religions. Following his example, Mozina makes a similar distinction between the mythical, what he calls the "traditional" interpretation, and the Christian interpretation of sacrifice, and charts Conrad's move from one to the other. *The Secret Agent* exposes sacrificial mechanisms and yet resists totalizing conclusions, Christian or otherwise.

Conrad privileges neither the Judæo-Christian nor the Græco- Roman representations of sacrifice. Though anthropologists of his day often took the "primitive" Other as the object of study, thus creating a distance between the investigating subject, enlightened and empowered, and the object, passive and benighted, in *The Secret Agent* Conrad focuses on the Christian and Classical leanings towards a sacrificial logic rather than similar rituals among so-called primitive tribes. The chilling fact seems to be that even though attempts have been made to place the civilized upon a higher pedestal, the center of Western civilization portrayed is still controlled by a sacrificial impulse embedded in its religious, political, and social institutions, and rooted in the minds of individuals. If in "Heart of Darkness," the depiction of Western civilization "disturbs imperialist assumptions to the precise degree that it reinforces them" (1978: 135), in *The Secret Agent* the picture is different: the origin of decay springs from the heart of Western civilization. The Professor's background and the comparisons of Ossipon to Apollo illustrate this.

In *The Secret Agent*, Conrad further challenges Western civilization's assumed superiority by one bold brushstroke linking sacrifice to cannibalism. Sacrifice has a sacred aura. No matter how gory the ritual or how violent its implications, the purpose always remains lofty, fully justifying the means. Hence, it is difficult to avoid a sacrificial logic and vocabulary, as in Girard's case. Cannibalism, however, is odious. There were many allusions to man-eating practices in Greek mythology, folk tales, and even the Bible, and references to anthropophagy occur in Herodotus, but the word "cannibalism" was not coined until Europeans encountered the Caribbean in the fifteenth century. To the civilized mind of ascendant modernity, cannibalism was a virtually inconceivable act performed only by the primitive Other, hence the coining of a word that relegates the practice to the Caribs. Despite the surface differences, it is essential to note that sacrifice and cannibalism share a basic characteristic in involving exchange and bartering. In anthropological terms, the ultimate purpose of the ritual killing or offering in sacrifice is to secure benefits. Thus, a bargain is struck between humankind and god, the former's subservience exchanged for the latter's favours. The bargain is succeeded by further bargains when the sacrificer seeks substitutes to avoid pain and loss. In cannibalism, benefit is gained not by exchange with god but by consuming a member of one's own species. Energy in the form of nourishment flows from one to the other in an unfair exchange. Given the essence of exchange shared by both practices, sacrificial rites are often accompanied by acts of cannibalism, literal or symbolic.

This conjoining of a sacred rite with a tabooed abomination has been attested by important voices in various disciplines. Around the turn of the nineteenth century, Frazer gave many examples, particularly in the section "Homeopathic Magic of a Flesh Diet" in *The Golden Bough* (1890, 1922). Several decades later, Theodor Adorno and Max Horkheimer in *Dialectic of Enlightenment* (1944) first call sacrifice a kind of barter and then equate it with cannibalism:

> If barter is the secular form of sacrifice, the latter already appears as the magical pattern of rational exchange. (1997: 49)

> The predominant theory of sacrifice at the present time traces it to the idea of the collective body, the tribe, into which the blood of its slaughtered member would flow back as energy . . . it is hardly possible to make any distinction between human sacrifice and cannibalism. (1997: 52)

More recently, the controversial theologian Burton Mack refers to "the well-known *do ut des*," which he explains as the "formula of exchange, 'I give in order that you may give'" (1987: 2). In "The Problem of Ritual Killing," the anthropologist Walter Burkert cites Theophrastus for having argued that "Phœnician and Greek sacrifice had developed from cannibalism." According to Burkert, not just myths and pre-historic practices show the conjoining of the two, but even religion calls attention to the link: "cannibalistic ideology has even entered religious formulas." Examples are ancient Egyptian pyramid texts, the Gnostic Gospel of Philip, and Burkert adds, "I refrain from quoting the New Testament" (1987: 175).

Conrad perspicaciously sees that sacrifice can simply be a form of violence, even cannibalistic violence. The characters in his novel subscribe to a sacrificial mode of thinking that justifies the means by the ends. Many characters wish to be protectors – Verloc's mission is "the protection of the social mechanism" (17), and even Stevie wants to give Winnie his "manly protection" (131) -- but these protectors turn out to be predators as well. In hoping to strike a bargain by giving up something apparently less valuable in exchange for a "greater good," they end up foregoing their humanity and losing their hold on any promise of social reform or personal salvation. Furthermore, since sacrifice operates through exchange, a substitutionary logic is introduced, triggering an unending series of substitutionary violences that the novel demonstrates.

The novel's plot is built on a sequence of sacrificial acts. Vladimir, sitting in the Russian Embassy, hatches a plan to bomb the Royal Observatory, not to destroy the building but because an attack on a symbol of science can shock the British government into clamping down on anarchist activities. Verloc, unwilling to take the risk himself and unable to get any of his anarchist friends to do the job, targets his half-witted brother-in-law, Stevie. Thus, Stevie becomes embroiled in a political plot whose meaning he hardly understands. He gets blown to bits for what he takes to be a just cause. Winnie, who has sacrificed her happiness by marrying Verloc for Stevie's sake, avenges her brother by stabbing her husband to death. Finally, she is betrayed by Ossipon, who makes off with her money and leaves her alone to die.

Conrad takes care to reveal the violence in the novel as sacrificial and to highlight the mythical and religious background of the sacrificial acts. The novel's most ruthless character, The Professor, is ready to sacrifice the whole world for his ambitions, wanting to exterminate the weak and seeing sacrifice as "the only way of progress" (226). When confronted with Ossipon's sobering question as to what remains, he replies, "I remain – if I am strong enough" (226). Thus, he is ready to sacrifice himself and challenges others to similar acts of desperation. When he meets Inspector Heat, he uses the term "self-sacrifice" (76), daring Heat to arrest him. He confides to Ossipon that he dreams of "a world like shambles" (226), thus bringing to the fore the image of the slaughterhouse. His background alludes to a strain in Christianity that Mack stops short of elaborating. Conrad writes:

> His father, a delicate dark enthusiast with a sloping forehead, had been an itinerant and rousing preacher of some obscure but rigid Christian sect – a man supremely confident in the privileges of his righteousness. In the son, individualist by temperament, once the science of colleges had replaced thoroughly the faith of conventicles, this moral attitude translated itself into a frenzied Puritanism of ambition. He nursed it as something secularly holy. (66)

"Secularly holy" – this describes the force that sanctions sacrifice, whether in the form of religious ritual, social practice, or political aggression.

If The Professor's background hints at Christianity's violent aspect, Ossipon's Apollo-like appearance serves as an ironic comment on Classical virtues. An ex-medical student as well as the author of many F. P. pamphlets, Ossipon is compared to Apollo twice in the final chapter, his head being "Apollo-like in the sunniness of its bush of hair" (230). Apollo, the sun god, represents enlightenment and reason that, in Ossipon's hands, become tools to sacrifice the weak for personal gain. When he and The Professor meet in the last chapter, The Professor challenges him to face the stark reality of his existence:

> "What's the matter with you, Ossipon? You look glum and seek even my company. ... Why? Have you abandoned your collection of women? They are the weak who feed the strong – eh?" (226)

> "Tell me, Ossipon, terrible man, has ever one of your victims killed herself for you – or are your triumphs so far incomplete – for blood alone puts a seal on greatness? Blood. Death. Look at history." (227)

The Silenus Restaurant, the favourite meeting place of the anarchists, gives another clue to the sacrificial rite's Classical root as well as its linkage with cannibalism. The restaurant's frescos show "scenes of the chase" and hunters with their hunting knives (52), pushing the significance of Silenus beyond wine and song. Silenus, foster father of the wine god Dionysus, is fittingly the presiding spirit of a restaurant pub. Through him, however, one reaches further back to a Dionysian cult. In "Culinary Practices and the Spirit of Sacrifice," Marcel Detienne suggests that in Classical Greece there is an "absolute coincidence of meat-eating and sacrificial practice" (1989: 3). He relates the Orphic account of a sacrificial myth, in which the Titans lure and kill the child-god Dionsyus, dismember and roast him, and devour his flesh. Only Zeus's intervention can stop them from gobbling down the heart. Detienne sees this account as the Orphic attempt to "denounce blood sacrifices and turn men away from the cannibalistic practices they unwittingly carry out (by extension) each time they offer an animal victim to the gods" (2). The rite, however, indicates a common practice in Greek civilization in which all consumable meat "comes from ritually slaughtered animals, and the butcher who sheds the animal blood bears the same functional name as the sacrificer posted next to the bloody altar" (3).

It is not, then, coincidental that the novel abounds in references to food and butchers. When Mr Verloc walks to meet Vladimir, Conrad adds the detail of a butcher boy "driving with the noble recklessness of a charioteer at Olympic Games" (17). Winnie is the daughter of a victualler; her former suitor was the son of a butcher; she kills Verloc with a carving knife after he has gorged on roast beef. She is portrayed as having a "full bust" and "broad hips" (10), for, like meat, her body is for sale, exchanged for Verloc's protection of Stevie. Sir Ethelred, at the top of the social ladder, is preoccupied with his Fisheries Bill. The Assistant Commissioner preaches animal cannibalism when he enlightens Toodles as to how to catch a big fish. A sprat, he says, is not only fish to put into a sardine box (packed as a city is) but also bait to catch a dogfish, if not a whale. The city of London itself, which some critics have seen as the novel's true protagonist, is depicted in the "Author's Note" as "a cruel devourer of the world's light" (6). The most shocking image of the whole work, of course, is that of Stevie's remains:

> a heap of rags, scorched and bloodstained, half concealing what might have been an accumulation of raw material for a cannibal feast. (70)
>
> And meantime the Chief Inspector went on peering at the table with a calm face and the slightly anxious attention of an indigent customer bending over what may be called the by-products of a butcher's shop with a view to an inexpensive Sunday dinner. (71)

There are, indeed, characters who claim to fight against oppression and denounce sacrifice, but they cannot extricate themselves from the web of sacrificial logic. Stevie appears to be the most innocent victim. His name reminds one of the first Christian martyr, whose church walls witness the pageantry of Stevie's cab ride. But indignant of the suffering he sees around him during the ride, he feels that "Somebody ... ought to be punished for it – punished with great severity" (132). When he has no money to help the charwoman, again he feels that "somebody should be made to suffer for it" (141). His sympathy for the oppressed amounts to a fanaticism that Verloc manipulates.

The anarchists who denounce sacrifice are, in fact, the high priests of the rite. Perhaps they only parody real revolutionaries, as Conrad explains in the "Author's Note," but they do point to a potential danger of revolutionary ideology. Like Marx who compared human progress to cannibalization and likened capitalism to a vampire sucking out blood (Phillips 1998: 184-87), Michaelis and Yundt denounce sacrifice, which they see as another form of cannibalism. Michaelis talks of the "great capitalists devouring the little capitalists" (43), and Yundt gives a graphic description of the horror: "Do you know how I would call the nature of the present economic conditions? I would call it cannibalistic. That's what it is! They are nourishing their greed on the quivering flesh and the warm blood of the people – nothing else" (44). But the main problem with Michaelis and Yundt is that apart from being ineffectual, they also participate in the act of sacrifice. They both live off women. They totally ignore Stevie, who by sheer physical proximity should be the primary target of their sympathy. Their appearances are also sinister. Michaelis, corpulent like Verloc, has an "enormous stomach" (37). Yundt with his "toothless mouth" declaims:

> "I have always dreamed ... of a band of men absolute in their resolve to discard all scruples in the choice of means, strong enough to give themselves frankly the name of destroyers, and free from the taint of that resigned pessimism which rots the world. No pity for anything on earth, including themselves – and death – enlisted for good and all in the service of humanity – that's what I would have liked to see." (38)

To enlist death for good is the same sacrificial logic the capitalists rely on.

The Secret Agent shows that, in addition to entering religious formulations, sacrificial thinking has entered the moral fibre of individuals and become integral to the ideologies and vocabularies of modernity. If modernity means the collective effort to revitalize the world, one should bear in mind that what is regarded as new may be ancient concepts and ancient rites, and the ancient rite of sacrifice promises rebirth only through death. "The latest ideologies are only versions of the most ancient," Adorno and Horkheimer write in *Dialectic of Enlightenment* (1997-52-53). "The history of civilization is the history of the introversion of sacrifice" (55), they add, for civilized men use reason to dominate nature, sacrificing the latter. Conrad, as in the opening scene of "Heart of Darkness" where industrialized London is indistinguishable from its primitive ghost, constantly reminds his reader of the collusion between progress and regress. But what is the role of literature in this interlocking evolvement of enlightenment and violence? In *The Secret Agent* images of fragmentation through a fragmented narrative re-enact the sacrificial rite. The effect created is nevertheless one of the strongest criticisms of sacrifice possible within the parameters set by a sacrificial society.

Fragmentation is often identified as one of the major characteristics of Modernist literature. Its significance has been variously interpreted, being seen as a reflection of a fragmented modernity, or carrying with it a sense of nostalgia for a lost wholeness and unity. James McFarlane, representing an important position, has written that the Modernist emphasis is initially "on fragmentation, on the breaking up and the progressive disintegration of ... meticulously constructed 'systems' and 'types' and 'absolutes.'" But then the second task of the Modernists is a reintegration, a "re-relating of the fragmented concepts" (1976: 80). This reintegration finds its expression in the mythic order so frequently seen in Modernist literature, for myth "commended itself as a highly effective device for imposing order of a symbolic, even poetic, kind on the chaos of quotidian event" (82). Thus fragmentation is a preliminary stage of breaking up, while the ultimate æsthetic order of the literary work, reinforced by a nostalgic mythic order, promises harmony and unity.

Astradur Eysteinsson has summarized a different approach to fragmentation. He cites, among others, Adorno, Walter Benjamin, and Wolfgang Iser to point out that fragmentation in Modernist literature does not so much reformulate order as rupture it. For Adorno, "the negation of synthesis becomes a principle of form" (1970: 155). Synthesis is denied, because it so often means coercion. Adorno's æsthetics of negativity further sees art as negating the apparent reason and unity of the modern world through non-communication and fragmentation. Modernist literature, by being fragmented, refuses incorporation by an irrational, instrumental reason. Benjamin also writes of the "distinct and the disparate," which he calls the mosaic, that interrupts the apparent continuity of modern existence, resists absorption and incorporation by a fixed structure, and creates spaces and pauses that are conducive to the process of contemplation (1928: 28). Iser explores the idea of spaces or gaps for thought, highlighting the role the reader plays when confronted with a fragmented text: Modernist texts "are often so fragmentary that one's attention is almost exclusively occupied with the search for connections between the fragments" (1974: 280). The quest for meaning starts anew with each new reader, and the meaning created is ever unstill, resisting totalization, negating synthesis.

Neither does Conrad in *The Secret Agent* give any illusory order. In the novel, the mythic order is a sham, sacrifice brings no harmony, and fragmentation leads only to further questionings of instrumental reason. The striking images of fragmentation are pure negation without saving grace: the commingling of Stevie's remains with the roots of trees is a travesty of organic harmony; the boy's remains on a table resemble a cannibal feast; and the apocalyptic image of his decapitated head, amongst a "rainlike fall of mangled limbs" (196) signifies dispersal. Some readers may feel uneasy with the apparent lack of a constructive model, of value. For example, Terry Eagleton writes that "*The Secret Agent* is able to reveal the truth of itself only by that ceaseless process of 'self-detonation' which is irony" and "Value, identified with a despised humanitarianism of which anarchist dreams are an even more degenerate extension, is thus forced beyond the frontiers of the world, exiled beyond articulation" (1978: 140). But when one juxtaposes these remarks with his more recent comments on sacrifice one can better appreciate Conrad's achievement.

Eagleton's thorough study of the tragic bears on the issue of sacrifice, for the origin of tragedy is likely to be the sacrificial rite itself: "The scapegoat or *pharmakos* has a long history in tragic thought. Tragedy means 'goat song,' but it might perhaps be better translated as 'scapegoat song.' It may be that Greek tragedy has some roots in animal sacrifice" (2003: 277-78). Eagleton then proceeds to divide sacrifice into two kinds, characterizing one as "demonic," a mad desire for destruction (The Professor in *The Secret Agent* being an example), and the other as "beneficial": "there are times when something must be dismembered in order to be renewed. If a situation is dire enough, it must be broken to be repaired" (275). In a concluding statement that situates the discussion in a contemporary context, Eagleton re-emphasizes the sacrificial nature of revolution: "The structure of a world increasingly governed by the greed of transnational corporations is one which has to be broken in order to be repaired. If this is the lesson of the *pharmakos*, it is also the faith of political revolution" (296). For Eagleton, sacrifice becomes demonic or beneficial according to the purpose served and the motivations behind it. However, the basic structure of exchange remains, together with the violence, and a crucial question that must be asked is who determines the validity of that purpose and how.

In *The Secret Agent*, Conrad succumbs to no "faith of political revolution." As Avrom Fleishmann has said, *The Secret Agent* gives a "complex political imagination" and is therefore "not reducible to political ideology" (1967: ix). Violence, whether it comes from the demonic Professor, the well-wishing Stevie, or the aggrieved Winnie, provides no solution. Instead of setting up idols and justifying any kind of sacrifice, Conrad arouses the reader's consciousness. Different readers may, of course, respond differently to the novel, although it is commonly agreed that structurally, the fragmentation and complexity of plot distinguish it. These characteristics provide opportunities for the reader to contemplate the human condition depicted, and at the same time guide the reader to a certain response to the sufferings experienced by the characters. The fragmented narrative, in other words, challenges complacency. Apart from instigating the reader to active thinking and a search for meaning, it urges him or her to refrain from a patronizing attitude towards the characters embroiled in their futile acts. When the characters are lost in the maze of the city and of life, can the reader be scornful? The reader must also encounter "sudden holes in space and time" (69) while going through the maze of the novel. At moments, he or she shares the knowledge of the omniscient narrator but at other times partakes of the characters' anxieties. Often the significance of fragments of information can only be understood much later after their initial, impressionistic presentation, a procedure for which Ian Watt coined the term "delayed decoding" (1979: 175). In moving from Chapter III, where the anarchists meet, to the scene at the Silenus Restaurant in Chapter IV, the reader has even less information than characters like Ossipon. The reader is made aware of human vulnerability, and with this awareness comes tolerance and understanding, the beginnings of a hope of regeneration that can look beyond the limitations set by an all-pervasive sacrificial ideology.

"What makes mankind tragic is not that they are the victims of nature, it is that they are conscious of it," Conrad wrote (*CL2* 30). Winnie prefers not to think too much and literally sinks under the burden of her knowledge. She is, then, a tragic figure, understood in the light of this quotation. Yet the reader has a different role, and in writing the novel Conrad implicitly demands consciousness. At the end of the novel, the reader gets this picture of The Professor: "He walked frail, insignificant, shabby, miserable – and terrible in the simplicity of his idea calling madness and despair to the regeneration of the world. Nobody looked at him" (231). The London crowd seems oblivious of the danger among them, but the reader has scrutinized the figure of The Professor, his roots that clutch the past glory of religion, and his revolutionary dream of a world like a shambles. Furthermore, the reader is made conscious of tragic victimizations and can hope to refrain from further victimizations. If the world remains fragmented and the future of humankind uncertain, the reader can keep on adding bits and pieces of information from his or her personal experience to evaluate and re-evaluate the novel as well as what it says about the human condition. The novel takes on further significance after the resurgence of worldwide terrorism. Eagleton has pointed out that certain novels can become "more urgently contemporary than they were on the day of their publication." He adds, "Joseph Conrad's *The Secret Agent* includes the first suicide bomber in English literature, which makes it more relevant now than it was when it first appeared in 1907" (2003). The new insurgence of terrorism and the turn of world events allow readers to re-evaluate *The Secret Agent* and re-judge sacrificial politics.

Works cited

Adorno, Theodor. *Æsthetic Theory* (1970), edited by Gretel Adorno and Rolf Tiedemann, and translated by Robert Hullot-Kentor. London: Continuum, 2002.

—— and Max Horkheimer. *Dialectic of Enlightenment* (1944), translated by John Cumming. London: Verso, 1997.

Benjamin, Walter. *The Origin of German Tragic Drama* (1928), translated by John Osborne. London: Verso, 1985.

Bourdillon, M. F. C. "Introduction." In *Sacrifice*, edited by M. F. C. Bourdillon and Meyer Fortes. 1-15. London: Academic Press, 1980.

Burkert, Walter. "The Problem of Ritual Killing." In *Violent Origins: Walter Burkert, René Girard, and Jonathan Z. Smith on Ritual Killing and Cultural Formation,* edited by Robert G. Hamerton-Kelly. 149-76. Stanford: Stanford University Press, 1987.

Ching, Yuet May. "From Priest to Victim: The Problem of Sacrifice in Allen Upward and Ezra Pound." *Paideuma* 24.1 (1995): 53-69.

Detienne, Marcel. "Culinary Practices and the Spirit of Sacrifice." In *The Cuisine of Sacrifice among the Greeks*, edited by Marcel Detienne and Jean-Pierre Vernaut. 1-20. Chicago: University of Chicago Press, 1989.

Eagleton, Terry. *Criticism and Ideology: A Study in Marxist Literary Theory*. London: Verso, 1978.

——. "Hard Times." *New Statesman*, 7 April 2003 <www.findarticles.com>.

——. *Sweet Violence: The Idea of the Tragic.* Oxford: Blackwell, 2003.

Eysteinsson, Astradur. *The Concept of Modernism.* Ithaca, New York: Cornell University Press, 1990.

Fleishmann, Avrom. *Conrad's Politics: Community and Anarchy in the Fiction of Joseph Conrad.* Baltimore: Johns Hopkins University Press, 1967.

Frazer, Sir James. *The Golden Bough* (1890). Abridged edn. 1922; rpt. London: Chancellor Press, 1994.

Girard, René. *Deceit, Desire, and the Novel* (1961), translated by Yvonne Freccero. Baltimore: John Hopkins University Press, 1976.

_____. *The Scapegoat* (1982), translated by Yvonne Freccero. Baltimore: Johns Hopkins University Press, 1986.

_____. *Violence and the Sacred* (1972), translated by Patrick Gregory. Baltimore: Johns Hopkins University Press, 1977.

Hubert, Henri, and Marcel Mauss. *Sacrifice: Its Nature and Function* (1898), translated by W. D. Halls. Chicago: University of Chicago Press, 1964.

Iser, Wolfgang. *The Implied Reader: Patterns of Communication in Prose Fiction from Bunyan to Beckett.* Baltimore: Johns Hopkins University Press, 1974.

McFarlane, James. "The Mind of Modernism." In *Modernism: A Guide to European Literature, 1890-1930*, edited by Malcolm Bradbury and James McFarlane. 71-93. London: Penguin, 1976.

Mack, Burton. "Introduction: Religion and Ritual." In *Violent Origins: Walter Burkert, René Girard, and Jonathan Z. Smith on Ritual Killing and Cultural Formation*, edited by Robert G. Hamerton-Kelly. 1-70. Stanford: Stanford University Press, 1987.

Mozina, Andrew. *Joseph Conrad and the Art of Sacrifice*. New York: Routledge, 2001.

Phillips, Jerry. "Cannibalism qua Capitalism: The Metaphorics of Accumulation in Marx, Conrad, Shakespeare, and Marlowe." In *Cannibalism and the Colonial World*, edited by Francis Barker, Peter Hulme, and Margaret Iversen. 183-203. Cambridge: Cambridge University Press, 1998.

Smith, William Robertson. *Lectures on the Religion of the Semites.* (1889), edited by John Day. Sheffield: Continuum, 1998.

Tylor, Sir Edward Burnett. *Primitive Culture* (1871). New York: Gordon Press, 1973.

Watson, Garry. "Fundamental Information: *The Secret Agent*, *Billy Budd*, *Sailor* and the Sacrificial Crisis." In *Conrad, James and Other Relations*, edited by Keith Carabine and Owen Knowles with Paul Armstrong. 217-44. Lublin: Maria Curie-Skłodowska University, 1998.

Watt, Ian. *Conrad in the Nineteenth Century*. Berkeley: University of California Press, 1979.

No Escape: Liberation and the Ethics of Self-Governance in *The Secret Agent*

David Prickett
Lockerbie, Scotland

CRITICS HAVE SOMETIMES represented Conrad as oscillating between a relativism arising from his stress on the subjective creation of meaning, and a desire to affirm the existence of objective truths and values.[1] However, instead of constituting a doomed stand against modernity, it is also possible to read his work as an extended attempt to clarify the nature of subjective identity within the conditions of modernity. For Conrad, such a coherent and stable awareness is a crucial aspect of finding ways of carrying on living in a world in which the source of value is no longer certain.

The shift towards the subjective creation of meaning has been portrayed as a moment of crisis in late nineteenth- and early twentieth-century culture, what J. Hillis Miller characterizes as the "gradual exploration of the fact that for modern man nothing exists except as it is seen by someone viewing the world from his own perspective" (1966: 4). Rather than being something that Conrad sets out to "solve," it is this very sense of isolation that functions as the basis for an ethical approach, one concerned with the need to govern the self-interested bias resulting from the isolation of each individual.[2]

Isolation takes many forms in Conrad's work, but is a pervasive theme. Attempts to communicate repeatedly fail, whether between Marlow and Kurtz, Marlow and Jim, Jim and the inhabitants of Patusan, or Razumov and those around him. Similarly Marlow's relationships with his listeners are characterized by failures of understanding. The Assistant Commissioner and Razumov experience aloneness, and in their different ways Winnie, Jim, and Kurtz all die alone and isolated. Many more

---

[1] See, for example, Daphna Erdinast-Vulcan's characterization of Conrad as a "homo duplex" (1991).

[2] The argument that, for Conrad, the subjective creation of meaning produces a bias of self-interest, a condition that may be governed so as to reduce its potential to cause harm, is presented in detail in Prickett (2004).

examples could be given, and it is possible to draw a wide range of inferences from them. For whilst at times it seems as if meaning were something entirely created by the individual and that objective reality does not exist, elsewhere subjectivity is more like a filter between objective reality and the individual.

Even if it is difficult to discern a single version of what constitutes shared reality in Conrad's work, the possibility of communication between characters is often limited. Attempts to overcome this isolation constantly fail, and the fundamental aloneness of subjective identity is not presented as something that may be transcended. This essay suggests that Conrad's recurrent insistence on isolation implies a tendency to self-interest, a condition arising out of the inescapably subjective position of the individual. This is not a prelude to nihilistic despair or irresponsibility; everything may or may not be fundamentally groundless, but apart from those famous passages in which characters like Marlow look into this void, for Conrad the everyday world will carry on much the same, leaving us with the question of how we are to act in it. Conrad's pragmatic concern with the social also means that characters usually engage with the condition of subjective isolation not in abstract metaphysical terms, but through developing an awareness of their specific location in society. Like The French Lieutenant's assertion in *Lord Jim* that all people are cowards, the real question being how one responds to this condition, in these novels the distinction is not between individuals who are totally "good" and those who are "bad," in an inherent or unchanging sense, but between those who are aware of their subjective location and specificity, and those who ignore this subjective bias. Consequently, the absence of an easily identifiable source of value does not mean that it is impossible to make judgements concerning them or their actions.

In *The Secret Agent* most characters ignore or actively occlude the personal genealogies of their beliefs, whereas the Assistant Commissioner has an awareness of the specificity of his position and the effects of his subjective interests. The acknowledgement of one's specific location is also a significant theme in "Heart of Darkness," making it possible to draw a distinction between the characters veiling their actions behind the rhetoric of progress, and Marlow's awareness of its spurious nature. However, his subjective bias means that Marlow still engages in self-justification; work may enable Marlow to sustain himself as an individual, but however he relates to it, his means of survival contributes to the Company's catastrophic activities.

This theme of awareness needs to be located in terms of the wider idea of "seeing." Conrad himself helped to inaugurate this theme when he stated in his Preface to *The Nigger of the "Narcissus"* that "My task which I am trying to achieve is, by the power of the written word, to make you hear, to make you feel – it is, before all, to make you *see*" (x). Critical responses to this assertion have ranged from those that consider it in the context of theories of perception and artistic impressionism to those like John G. Peters, who seek to widen out the meaning of "seeing" to include a consideration of subjective identity and Western civilization. The expansion of this meaning may be further broadened to include ethical action, and in particular how "seeing" one's subjective specificity constitutes an essential prelude to it.

Michael H. Levenson rightly and suggestively argues that for Conrad "words, like events, are in themselves speechless; they depend for their meaning on an animating subjectivity" (2), but the extent to which such meanings may be created autonomously, or that self-creation or liberation from them is possible, needs to be qualified. Consequently, although the societies portrayed in *The Secret Agent* and *Under Western Eyes* might be represented in extremely critical terms, this does not lead to the conclusion that they can be swept away and replaced by something better, as in Miss Haldin's desire for a new dawn, any more than Jim is able to escape his past and start again with a "clean slate" (185).

The Secret Agent is notable for its scathing treatment of the idea of liberation. Speaking nearly eighty years after the publication of Conrad's novel, Michel Foucault expressed a similarly sceptical view. In an interview published as "The Ethics of the Concern for Self as a Practice of Freedom," he observed that it is not enough to declare the desire to be free; the question is how one will act within that freedom. In these terms he distinguishes between processes of liberation and practices of freedom, for whilst an initial struggle for liberation may well be necessary, this is only a beginning, the fundamental question being how one is then to act within these new conditions. Moreover, his assertion of the pervasive nature of power in all social relationships means that liberation can never be conclusive, if it is imagined to be the removal of all power relations so as to reveal or release something occluded by them. Freedom therefore becomes an on-going problematic, something pursued through the constant need to keep power relations open and fluid.

Whilst often thought of as presenting a vision of the individual entrapped within, indeed created by, ever-multiplying spirals of observation and discourse, in his late work Foucault began to be more interested in the active aspects of identity formation. In particular, he examined some historical examples of self-governance from ancient Greece and Rome, most notably the notion of the "care of the self." A widely used term, it could describe activities such as agricultural management and the duties of a monarch or doctor. Foucault notes that in terms of ethics, it "implies complex relationships with others insofar as this ethos of freedom is also a way of caring for others" (1997: 269, 287). In such a practice knowledge does not involve seeking what is regarded as being the true self; rather one needs knowledge so that one can know what can be mastered. This has major social implications, since, in Foucault's account of the Stoics, self-governance of one's desires gave the right to rule others (267).

Some argue that the significance of Foucault's work is limited by the fact that he examines practices that were the preserve of a small male elite.[3] Whilst criticisms concerning the gender bias of his work are important, Foucault himself states that he is not seeking to present the ancient world as an ideal against which to judge modern forms of identity. Instead, such studies are part of his disruption of what he regards as the naturalization of the modern conception of identity, based upon the attempt to uncover and establish the truth of the individual in a positive form, a process through which he or she becomes located within institutional and discursive power.

Much of Foucault's later work is concerned with replacing the generalized notion of liberation with a stress upon specific engagements with power. In similar terms, fictions such as "Heart of Darkness," *Lord Jim*, and *The Secret Agent* suggest that there can only be a limited intervention in the subjective creation of meaning, a self-governance rather than a grand self-creation. Like Kurtz, Jim seeks to be autonomous, to have a "clean slate," and his reading of adventure fiction might be taken to be an attempt at self-formation. However, Jim cannot establish absolute autonomy; indeed the belief that this is possible actually impedes his ability to act, both in the training-ship and on Patusan, whilst his narcissistic daydreams have none of the social concerns evident in the Stoics' accounts of self-awareness.

---

[3] Some feminist criticisms of Foucault's later work are discussed in Ramazanoglu, ed. (1993). More general questions concerning the accuracy of his representation of the Stoics are raised by Hadot (1995).

Both Conrad and Foucault are critical of simple notions of liberation, based on crude divisions between the individual or society to be liberated, and the forces of oppression. For Foucault power is inescapable; thus, rather than the pursuit of an absolute liberation from it, there is a need for its constant governance, and for resistance to institutional attempts to freeze it. This theme of governance informs his observation that the real point about the symbiosis of discourse, power and knowledge is "not that everything is bad, but that everything is dangerous" (1997: 256). This acceptance changes the terms of criticism, in that it allows one to highlight the effects of power, without requiring the Utopian dream of a society free from it.

In *The Secret Agent* Conrad challenges the notion of revolution by revealing the hidden symbiosis of seeming opposites, such as the criminal and the legal, and the subjective genealogies underlying claims to objective analysis or truth. Aware that any posited idea will have grown out of the existing conditions, something that leads to self-contradiction if one is attempting an absolute critique of them, The Professor accuses Ossipon and his fellow revolutionaries of being "the slaves of social convention, which is afraid of you; slaves of it as much as the very police that stands up in the defence of that convention. Clearly you are, since you want to revolutionize it. It governs your thought, of course, and your action, too, and thus neither your thought nor your action can ever be conclusive" (57-58).

A major obstacle to an awareness of this specificity is the blurring of the distinction between the rhetoric of objectivity and the characters' subjective motives. Thus Inspector Heat's personal interests, as seen in his concealment of evidence, override his supposedly neutral bureaucratic role of working for justice. Similarly, much of the Assistant Commissioner's approach to the case is coloured by his concerns regarding what his wife will say if Michaelis is arrested. Conrad emphasizes the effects produced by allowing these hidden relationships to function without question, thereby replicating the existing social conditions. Significantly, whilst The Professor is able to unmask the symbiosis of the police and the anarchists, he is incapable of acknowledging his own subjective genealogy, in which a thwarted ambition has mutated into a longing to destroy the social order he blames for this.

The narrator presents a scathing subjective genealogy of revolutionary belief, in which "the majority of revolutionists are the enemies of discipline and fatigue" (45). However, he does not simply condemn this subjective aspect of belief, commenting that the "way of even the most justifiable revolutions is prepared by personal impulses disguised into creeds" (66). The fundamental commonality of the characters is also indicated in the narrator's observation that "in their own way the most ardent of revolutionaries are perhaps doing no more but seeking for peace in common with the rest of mankind" (67). Throughout *The Secret Agent* there is an emphasis upon the common subjective tendencies of the characters, however much their beliefs differ, and the novel's ethics are based upon the governance of these tendencies, rather than their denouncement. They are all implicated within the conditions of the world represented in the novel, and it is futile to attempt to criticize them from an imaginary position outside of or beyond them.

The Professor expresses contempt for those who "depend on life," which is "a historical fact surrounded by all sorts of restraints and considerations" (57), and his desire for a "clean sweep and clear start for a new conception of life" (61) is a theoretically coherent response to the contradictions ignored by the other revolutionaries. However, like Miss Haldin's abstract notion of a world free from discord, The Professor's rejection of the limitations of meaning and culture is an attempt to deny an aspect of subjective identity. Consequently, whatever the acuity of his insight, it produces an impasse rather than an ethics of self-governance or a practice of freedom.

In works like *The Secret Agent* and "Heart of Darkness," Conrad exposes how the individual subjective bias merges with institutional and socially shared discourses such as bureaucracy, revolutionary ideologies, justice, and progress. Like Foucault, Conrad's response is not to call for a new beginning, but to develop awareness of the functioning of one's existing subjective identity as a means of dismantling the relationships it perpetuates. Even if the irony of Marlow and the Assistant Commissioner seems to have a limited political function, in that the existing social conditions are left in place, awareness of their particular institutional positions allows them to see how their own subjective interests support relationships they find undesirable. Moreover, even if they do little with this knowledge, both are able to carry on functioning socially; Marlow avoids Kurtz's mental disintegration, whilst the Assistant Commissioner is not caught in The Professor's limbo, or Stevie's painful and impotent awareness that it is a "Bad world for poor people" (132).

Besides the hazards of attempting to stand outside of society as it exists, another danger of the concept of liberation is the way in which it tends to valorize a particular group at the expense of others. Conrad does not present a political model predicated upon absolute difference, or simple class distinctions, in which the social critic may speak from one side or the other. Instead, in *The Secret Agent* he seeks to establish the common ground of subjective identity, only then going on to criticize the actions of the characters and their world. His approach highlights how one needs to remain aware that any action is pervaded by subjective bias, and so is, to use Foucault's term, "dangerous." This does not mean that one cannot act, but that one is always liable to replicate the same crimes of self-interest for which one might criticize the "oppressor." Like Stevie's sympathy for both the horse and the cabman, in *The Secret Agent* Conrad consistently avoids ascribing justice to any one group, just as Foucault avoided the Marxist desire to represent a particular class as the wronged, and the locus of justice. Conrad's emphasis upon the need to govern the tendencies of the subjective bias is not a narcissistic retreat into a privatized identity politics, but a way of confronting the dangers inherent in all political programmes.

Conrad's ethics of self-governance is based on the need to see the historically and culturally specific nature of one's identity and society, and also the individual's tendency towards subjective interest. This helps to explain how, rather than being an anarchist or a reactionary, Conrad can be highly critical of the societies he portrays, but also be scathing about those attempting to transform them, if that transformation is pursued without any awareness of subjective bias. He does this through various techniques, in particular by contextualizing statements in such a way that they cannot simply take on the function of objective truth, even if they are also ascribed validity. This refusal to posit an ideal alternative to conditions as they are is expressed by The Professor when he mocks Ossipon's desire to turn the world into "an immense and nice hospital" (225). Yet the specificities of The Professor's own positions and opinions are ruthlessly exposed. Such a universal use of irony does not stem from misanthropy, but constitutes an insistence that the basic conditions of subjective meaning and identity must be seen as clearly as possible if their subsequent effects are to be governed.

The relentless irony of *The Secret Agent*, together with its pervasive atmosphere of self-interest, may negate the possibility of objective truth and disinterested action, but Conrad's concern with the subjective creation of meaning does not preclude developing an ethical position. Unlike the cynical espousal of political ideals by the revolutionaries, or Stevie's disastrously literal acceptance of their words, the Assistant Commissioner experiences "a sudden and alert mistrust of the weapon in his hand" (82). By recognizing that his exercise of the nominally neutral instruments of social order will also constitute an expression of his own subjective interests, he is able to limit the potential abuse of his position. This unambitious concern with the limitation of potentially harmful effects, rather than the judgement of individuals and their actions in relation to an imagined Utopia, is at the ethical heart of the novel.

In an early, but still acute, observation T. S. Eliot suggests that "Mr. Conrad has no ideas, but he has a point of view, a world; it can hardly be defined, but it pervades his work and is unmistakable" (324). Conrad certainly posits no "idea" of an alternative to the world of the "slimy aquarium" (114), but his "view" that all meaning has an inescapably subjective aspect becomes the foundation for a compassionate ethics focussed upon the continual need to govern this all too human tendency.

Acknowledgement

A version of this essay was presented at the 31st Annual International Conference of the Joseph Conrad Society (UK), Amsterdam, July 2005.

Works cited

Eliot, T. S. "Kipling Redivivus." In *Kipling: The Critical Heritage*, edited by Roger Lancelyn Green. 322-26. London: Routledge and Kegan Paul, 1971.

Erdinast-Vulcan, Daphna. *Joseph Conrad and the Modern Temper.* Oxford: Oxford University Press, 1991.

Foucault, Michel. "On the Genealogy of Ethics: An Overview of Work in Progress." In *Ethics:, Subjectivity and Truth: The Essential Works of Michel Foucault*, edited by Paul Rabinow. 1: 253-80. London: Allen Lane, 1997.

———. "The Ethics of the Concern for Self as a Practice of Freedom." In *Ethics: Subjectivity, and Truth: The Essential Works of Michel Foucault.* 1:281-301.

Hadot, Pierre. "Reflections on the Idea of the 'Cultivation of the Self.'" In *Philosophy as a Way of Life: Spiritual Exercises from Socrates to Foucault*, edited by Arnold I. Davidson. 206-13. Oxford: Blackwell, 1995.

Levenson, Michael H. *A Genealogy of Modernism: A Study of English Literary Doctrine, 1908-1922.* Cambridge: Cambridge University Press, 1984.

Miller, J. Hillis. *Poets of Reality: Six Twentieth-Century Writers.* Cambridge, MA: Harvard University Press, 1966.

Peters, John G. *Conrad and Impressionism.* Cambridge: Cambridge University Press, 2001.

Prickett, David. *"To make you see": Subjectivism and Negativity in Four Novels of Joseph Conrad.* PhD thesis, University of Birmingham, 2004.

Ramazanoglu, Caroline, ed. *Up Against Foucault: Explorations of Some Tensions between Foucault and Feminism.* London: Routledge, 1993.

The Female Offender, the New Woman, and Winnie Verloc in *The Secret Agent*

Ellen Burton Harrington
University of South Alabama

"Rarely is a woman wicked, but when she is she surpasses the man."
Italian proverb quoted in Lombroso's *The Female Offender* (1895)

"Lombroso is an ass."
Anarchist Karl Yundt in Conrad's *The Secret Agent* (1907)

THE WORK OF Cesare Lombroso in many ways typifies the concerns of *fin-de-siècle* Britain in attempting a serious study of criminal behaviour in light of Darwinist theories and concerns about atavism. An Italian criminal anthropologist, Lombroso used phrenology, including cranial measurements and the classification of facial features, and contemporary assumptions about atavism and degeneracy in an attempt to develop physical predictors for criminal behaviour.[1] Because he assumed that women in general and certain ethnic groups and individuals were less evolved, his theories supported the racial and sexual biases of late nineteenth-century Britain.[2] As Nicole Hahn Rafter and Mary Gibson,

---

[1] Lombroso gathered a good bit of data from various sources, including, on occasion, novels, and his generalizations are often based on anecdotes and impressions gleaned from photographs.

[2] While Lombroso's ideas remained influential in some circles into the twentieth century, Hunter notes that the 1910 *Encyclopædia Britannica* entry on "criminology" sees Lombroso's work "in a questionable light" and "points to his shortcomings" (1983: 182-83). Rafter and Gibson comment that his theories "dominated criminological discussions in Europe, North and South America, and parts of Asia from the 1880s into the early twentieth century" and also note that "The central idea of the born or genetic criminal continues to attract adherents, and the main legal implication of his work – that some offenders are not fully responsible for their acts – remains key in criminal jurisprudence" (2004: 3).

translators of a new edition of Lombroso's and Guglielmo Ferraro's *La donna delinquente* (1893) note, the work "constitutes perhaps the most extended proof of women's inferiority ever attempted" (2004: 32).[3] Lombroso's assumption that women were less evolved than men had to be reconciled with the fact than his female subjects have fewer anatomical anomalies and women in general a markedly less tendency to commit crime: "The remarkable rarity of anomalies (already revealed by their crania) is not a new phenomenon in the female, nor is it in contradiction to the undoubted fact that atavistically she is nearer her origin than the male, and ought consequently to abound in more anomalies" (Lombroso and Ferraro 2004: 107). Lombroso attributes this lack of anomalies to a "conservative tendency of women in all questions of social order" and a woman's familial duties, because of which she "leads a more sedentary life, and is less exposed than the male to the varying conditions of time and space in her environment" (109). Thus, a woman's domestic duties and limited, "conservative," beliefs prevent the consequences that would likely result from her less evolved state. Examining the causes of women's crime, Lombroso identifies maternal passion among many possible contributing factors, considering the ways in which natural passions like maternal and marital love become twisted into criminal motivation.

Lombroso's theories become the fodder for the dark Darwinism of *The Secret Agent.* Conrad both mocks Lombroso's typologies and easy classification of degenerates and uses his ideas about atavistic throwbacks and criminal types to sketch his central characters. In particular, he invites his readers to look at the unwilling "free woman" at its heart. *The Secret Agent* interrogates discourses about femininity that proliferated in Edwardian England, telling a story that hinges on sympathy for Winnie and the breakdown of her "unfathomable reserve" even as it depicts her as devolving to "the age of caverns" as she takes her revenge (11, 197). Conrad's portrayal of a series of selfish characters acting from their wants and desires becomes a damning picture that offers no hope or relief for the reader, only "Winnie Verloc's story to its anarchistic end of utter desolation, madness, and despair" ("Author's Note," 8). This novel shows the devastating personal consequences of her husband Verloc's

[3] *La donna delinquente, la prostituta e la donna normale* (1893) was published in an English edition as *The Female Offender* in 1895. While Lombroso and Guglielmo Ferrero are listed as co-authors in all editions, Lombroso is generally credited as the intellectual force behind the work with Ferrero's contribution "probably closer to that of a graduate assistant than a true coauthor" (Rafter and Gibson 2004: 33).

political act and the connections between the public and domestic spheres.[4] I argue that Conrad's depiction of Winnie's downfall is self-consciously political, drawing from discourses on female degeneracy from Lombroso and the discourse surrounding the New Woman of the turn of the nineteenth century to comment ironically on women's liberation and dismantle the possibility of a post-Victorian "free" woman. As Conrad notes, Winnie's end is "anarchistic," and, thus, political, even as it presents a portrait of complete, personal devastation, using the botched bombing of the Royal Observatory in part to explore the unravelling of a late-Victorian family in this seedy vision of post-Darwinist London. While Winnie stands out as a pre-eminent example of atavism particularly linked to women and contemporary anxieties about femininity, her portrayal exemplifies Conrad's nihilist vision of a corrupt modern society in which self-interest and degeneracy are endemic.

Conrad's emphasis on "Winnie Verloc' story to its anarchistic end" ("Author's Note," 8) alongside the political plotting it describes marks a particular interest in the heroine, her choices, and options. In *Conrad and Women*, Susan Jones argues that Conrad, who is often construed primarily as an author of masculine sea stories, began to produce novels featuring "prominent female figures" in the early Malay novels and his political works (like *The Secret Agent*), and, by his later fiction, "increasingly turned to the issue of gender, female identity, and, in relation to romance, how women are invited to conform to its conventionalized gestures and plots" (1999: 2). Although *The Secret Agent* comes before this late period, some of these preoccupations are already apparent. After Stevie's death, Winnie tries out a series of "conventionalized" womanly roles, winding up in the familiar tragic role of the fallen woman who commits suicide by drowning. By continually recalling to the reader her position, in particular her newfound one as a "free woman," more so than describing her emotional reaction to the disintegration of her household, Conrad draws attention to the larger, more politicized implications of her personal crisis.

Conrad clearly references contemporary theories about female degeneracy with regard to Winnie, both in her identification with Stevie in his degenerate characteristics, as she seems to regress physically, Hyde-like, after Stevie's death, and in descriptions of Winnie throughout the novel that echo discussions of female criminals and the characteristics of normal women in *The Female Offender*. While Conrad

[4] For a full discussion of this issue, see Soane (2005).

references Lombroso in the novel, it is not clear which of his works Conrad read.[5] Based on the descriptions of Winnie, it seems likely that Conrad had some familiarity with *The Female Offender*, particularly his theories about the effects of maternal passion and the causes of suicide; additionally, Conrad's imagery alludes to Lombroso's repeated characterization of all women as naturally child-like and less evolved.

Conrad is certainly interested in the effect of the intrusion of the politics of the novel and its failed outrage into the closed domestic world of Brett Street, and his characterization of Winnie seems to echo both Lombroso's idea of the potential savagery in someone who is "nearer her origin" and in his conception of "maternal and domestic love" being at the root of some crimes of passion (Lombroso and Ferraro 2004: 107, 253). Although Winnie seems to be a model of restraint, her "ardour of protecting compassion" (49) for her brother Stevie temporarily transforms her into an animated presence, a side of her almost continually repressed. When Winnie realizes the circumstances of her brother's death, she devolves in a matter of moments and stabs Verloc, her murderous blow embodying "the simple ferocity of the age of caverns" (197).

Her breakdown and the subsequent murder of her husband are attributed to her intensity of maternal feeling. In the novel's first pages, Conrad emphasizes her "maternal vigilance" concerning Stevie (14), and her own mother is relieved that the Verlocs have no children because "Winnie found an object of quasi-maternal affection in her brother" (12-13). In the section on crimes of passion, Lombroso notes that an "injury inflicted on the woman's maternal or domestic affections" can be an incentive to crime: "A woman regards her child as a part of herself, providing for him and resenting in her own person the injuries inflicted on him, especially while he is little and cannot provide for himself"

---

[5] Jacobs notes that Conrad seems to reference Lombroso in "Heart of Darkness," *An Outcast of the Islands*, and *Lord Jim*, although *The Secret Agent* is the only Conrad work that specifically addresses Lombroso's theories (1968: 77). He cites Lombroso's *The Man of Genius, Criminal Man, The Female Offender, Crime: Its Causes and Remedies* as possible influences on Conrad. Saveson mentions another possible source, Lombroso's *Les Anarchistes* (1896), as well as four *Blackwood's* editorials about anarchists that Saveson argues "rely" upon Lombroso's classification (1974: 57-58). Hunter examines *The Female Offender, The Man of Genius*, and Havelock Ellis's Lombroso-influenced *The Criminal* in relation to *The Secret Agent*, referring to several other Conrad texts that were possibly influenced by Lombroso, including *Under Western Eyes* and *Lord Jim*.

(2004: 253, 255).[6] Conrad sets up the atavistic regression that will occur in Winnie by emphasizing her similarities to Stevie, who is "delicate and, in a frail way, good-looking too, except for the vacant droop of his lower lip" (13). They have a "pronounced" resemblance to each other as they walk to the bus (131). Conrad characterizes Winnie's life as constantly concerned with her brother and her anxiety to keep him from disturbing Verloc and to restrain his excess of compassionate feeling for the down-trodden. Winnie's excess of compassionate feeling is entirely concentrated on Stevie.

This intensity of feeling, which dates from Winnie's childhood when she protected her brother from her father's abuse, persists in repressed form:

> Winnie after the death of her father found considerable consolation in the feeling that she need no longer tremble for poor Stevie. She could not bear to see the boy hurt. It maddened her. As a little girl she had often faced with blazing eyes the irascible licensed victualler in defence of her brother. Nothing now in Mrs Verloc's appearance could lead one to suppose that she was capable of a passionate demonstration. (34)

When Stevie was "scared, wretched, sore, and miserable" (129) after his father's abuse, Winnie would take him to bed with her, a remedy that he continues to associate with the ultimate in compassion. The potentially incestuous overtones of this "bed of compassion" (129) only serve to intensify the sister's protective feelings. Lombroso notes that, although children are generally well cared for, "Almost the only person against whom they have to be protected or revenged is a bad or careless father, and he fortunately is not a very common phenomenon" (2004: 255). Lombroso's questionable downplaying of the faults of fathers here calls to mind Stevie's poor father figures, his abusive father and then the disregarding Verloc. In this case, Winnie's animosity towards her father and his abuse is transferred to Verloc when he betrays her trust in caring for Stevie; Conrad describes her love for Stevie as a "militant love," a protection of a "fierce and indignant complexion" (186). Winnie had longed that Verloc and Stevie would be like father and son, and, in

---

[6] After the child grows up, "it will no longer excite [his mother] as in his infancy. To a certain degree, in short, she recalls the behavior of female animals who abandon their little ones as soon as they can fly or walk alone" (Lombroso and Ferraro 2004: 255).

Conrad's thoroughgoing irony, that turns out to be all too true. As Winnie's mother comments, "If you had not found such a good husband, my dear … I don't know what would have become of that poor boy" (35).

Assuaging his guilt at the boy's death, Verloc tries to blame Winnie for encouraging him to be close to Stevie. Believing in his centrality as Winnie's husband, he asks, "What would it have been if you had lost me!" (177) to the dazed wife who develops the fixed idea that "He took the boy away from his home to murder him" (186). Fearing she may betray him, Verloc stops Winnie from going out, then calls to her in "the note of wooing" (197). Throughout the scene, the reader watches the desperate, grieving Winnie trying to adjust to Stevie's death, unable to understand or accept Verloc's blame, regrets, and plans. The killing of Stevie both grieves Winnie and destroys her identity, since her role as Verloc's wife is derived from her need to mother Stevie. This depiction might broadly echo Lombroso's theory that women's static existence in the domestic space preserves them from anomalies, since Winnie devolves when Stevie dies and her domestic space is altered by violence. She gradually becomes "cunning" and conceals the carving knife with which the ravenous Verloc has been cutting his meat, then, "As if the homeless soul of Stevie had flown for shelter straight to the breast of his sister, guardian and protector, the resemblance of her face with that of her brother grew at every step, even to the droop of the lower lip, even to the slight divergence of the eyes" (197). Conrad lingers over the death scene, drawing out the actions and the "plunging blow" into which "Mrs Verloc had put all the inheritance of her immemorial and obscure descent" (197). In Conrad's interpretation of Lombrosian regression, Winnie devolves into a primitive past, the spirit of the child-like Stevie overtaking her from their common genetic inheritance: "the offenses [including killing for love] we have detailed prove the likeness between women and children, since they might be described as offenses committed by big children of developed intelligence and passions" (Lombroso and Ferraro 2004: 267).[7]

Winnie's regression passes almost immediately after the crime and leaves her panicked. Her "obscurely prompted blow" (201) seems to

[7] Hunter also notes what seem like echoes of Lombroso at this point in the novel, affirming that Winnie's crime "may well have a great deal to do with her inheritance, and with epilepsy" (1983: 188). He examines Lombroso's discourse on epilepsy in relation to Winnie, a possible connection between *The Female Offender* and *The Secret Agent* not addressed here.

result logically from Verloc's failure to understand her grief and his rapid assertion of his marital rights. In *Joseph Conrad and the Ethics of Darwinism,* Allan Hunter examines *The Female Offender* and other Lombroso works alongside *The Secret Agent*, noting that "Lombroso assumes that 'pure passion' must be incompetent because it cannot know the nature of what it is doing. Conrad shows it as frighteningly competent, since it has cast away the restraint of morality" (1983: 187). *The Secret Agent* has already shown morality to be pretence in a self-interested world, and Winnie's actions seem to be an extension of this characterization. As Hunter comments, even Winnie's apparent altruism results from her self-defined role: "Paradoxically, she has a very rigid identity which includes the trait of acting selflessly, namely, for Stevie" (168). In the degenerate London "aquarium" that Conrad sketches, Winnie responds violently to the loss of her structuring ideals in a culmination of the nihilist sensibility that accrues in the novel.[8]

The Victorian idealization of the figure of the wife-mother creates a dramatic background for Winnie's crime. While there were many sensational portrayals of villainesses in novels of the period, Conrad's gritty post-Victorian vision of Winnie's degeneration after the death of her brother-child possesses an arresting power that also emphasizes larger themes. Conrad's use of Lombroso's ideas about degeneracy goes far beyond the characterization of Winnie, although her developing portrayal serves as a powerful commentary on the atavistic potential of individuals.

In addition to Winnie, the depictions of other characters are indebted to Lombroso. All of the anarchists are marked as degenerate types.[9] The wry presentation of Ossipon's desire to position himself as superior, supposedly a medical man who can set himself above the degenerate Stevie by classifying him, sets the tone for the treatment of Lombrosian theories early by placing them alongside Stevie's chaotic renderings. Thus, Conrad again mocks Lombroso's classifications, even as he uses them to create his vision of London as an evolutionary laboratory in which "the fittest" survive.

Placed alongside Lombroso's classifications and descriptions, his treatment of Winnie remains highly ironic. Near the end of the novel, Comrade Ossipon looks at the murderous Winnie, desperate for his help

---

[8] Conrad alludes to the evolutionary progression to land and the potential for regression: as the Assistant Commissioner enters the investigation, "His descent into the street was like the descent into a slimy aquarium from which the water had been run off. A murky, gloomy dampness enveloped him" (114).

[9] For a full discussion of this topic, see Hampson 1988.

and classifies her as a "murdering type" as he invokes Lombroso "as an Italian peasant recommends himself to his favourite saint" (222). This irreverent application of Lombroso, characterized as prompted by the fear of the crimes that Winnie is capable of committing, turns into another kind of religion rather than the science that Ossipon idealizes. The idea of science as a new religion has been developed earlier by Mr Vladimir, as he assigns Verloc the bombing: "The fetish of today is neither royalty nor religion. Therefore the palace and the church should be left alone," and continues, "The sacro-sanct fetish of to-day is science" (29). By fetishizing science and, by extension, Lombroso, Conrad reveals it to be yet another means of exerting control, using degeneracy rather than immorality as the basis for condemnation. In his consideration of *The Secret Agent*, Ronald Thomas notes the replacement of "what had been a leering sexual attraction for her with an instant diagnosis of her body as a criminal type, satirically signalling how the discourse of criminology was deployed as a form of scapegoating and control more than it was a form of objective knowledge" (1999: 282). This comic depiction of Ossipon's thought process thus further denigrates Lombrosian ideology as another means of setting in place a hierarchy, in this case, one privileging the supposedly scientific observer. Instead of viewing Lombroso's theories as innovative science that allows for greater understanding of criminals and individuals, Conrad pegs them as yet another panicked response to the realization that humans are animalistic at heart, despite the illusory veneer of civilization.

While Conrad seems to allude to Lombroso's model of female degeneracy throughout this section, much of the cast of characters exhibits similar, if less violent, atavistic tendencies. Several characters, including Ossipon and Verloc, respond in a panic when the typical patterns in their lives are disrupted, and Winnie's killing fury seems partly justified by the extent of her loss. Although Winnie comes to exemplify the degeneracy of London, the metropolis that prides itself on civilized local and colonial government, she does not fare much worse than the male characters, entrenched in their solipsistic perspectives. Conrad's atavistic vision is not solely focused on women or *The Female Offender*, and, in some sense, Winnie's regression becomes a reflection of the general character of corruption, even as it elaborates a typology for the female criminal. Thus, Conrad uses Winnie's degeneracy as a measure of contemporary corruption; of course, the sacrosanct space of the Victorian home is prey to those evolutionary urges and corrupt bargains that mark the public space.

As he develops the Lombrosian frame of reference, Conrad introduces another contemporary perspective on femininity. In her interactions with Verloc after she realizes that Stevie has died, Winnie gradually comes to realize that she is a "free woman," a phrase repeated several times in the narrator's description of her that seems to allude to the New Woman of the *fin-de-siècle*.[10] Brian Shaffer argues that this characterization of Winnie is "Conrad's attack on the Victorian New Woman," "the woman who earns her freedom from constraining domestic and matrimonial attachments" in turn-of-the-nineteenth-century fiction (1995: 314). Certainly, Conrad uses language familiar from the debates on the Woman Question, describing the marital bargain that Winnie has transacted with the unaware Verloc for the sake of Stevie. When Stevie dies, Winnie recalls the "seven years' security for Stevie, loyally paid for on her part" (184), fearing that Verloc "would want to keep her for nothing" (192). She has submitted to her husband in accordance with the ideal of Victorian wifehood: feeding him, satisfying him sexually (offering the "usual remedies" for a bad day [48]), and managing the household seamlessly without enquiring about his profession, odd hours, and questionable acquaintances. After her loss, Verloc's murder seems both a misguided part of her grief and an act of monstrous self-assertion. In having Winnie kill her husband to free herself from a marital bargain that no longer has value, Conrad melodramatically stages one of the fears surrounding the consideration of greater rights and equality for women. While the murder itself is sensational, it also poses the question of why women would continue to live as submissive wives and domestic angels following the Victorian ideal if it becomes unnecessary for their livelihood and well-being.

Although she is not an anarchist or a political activist, Winnie talks of slaves at several points, at one rebelliously telling the Chief Inspector investigating the crime, "We ain't downtrodden slaves here" (155).[11] Her

---

[10] The words "free woman" are used to describe Mrs Verloc six times immediately before and after Verloc's stabbing, whereas she is "no longer a free woman" when she appeals to Ossipon for protection (218).

[11] The repetition of the term "slave" in Winnie's dialogue lends emphasis, showing Winnie's internalization of ideology. After Stevie is upset at the rhetoric in the anarchists' meeting, Winnie tells Verloc, "We aren't German slaves here, thank God" (50), relieved that she is not responsible for crises in the larger political sphere. When Verloc poses the idea of emigrating before Winnie is aware of Stevie's death, she responds, "You ain't a slave. No one need be a slave in this country – and don't you make yourself one" (148). By the novel's last

marital bargain and commitment to Stevie do, however, start to read as servitude after Stevie's death. On the surface, Winnie would seem to be free after Stevie's death and Verloc's murder: "Winnie's stab is the one 'free' act of the interlocking pattern of events, the explosion really has provided room in which to move" (Hunter 1983: 178). The murder is clearly an ironic act of liberation, and Conrad seems to be engaging the discourse about women's liberation and the New Woman at the *fin-de-siècle*, representing a "free woman" who does not flee or take advantage of her lack of traditional ties. Like a heroine of Victorian sensation fiction, Winnie is both a sympathetic character and an unacceptable model, her violence too threatening to make her an effective option for frustrated women.

Instead of fleeing, Winnie merely tries to replicate her sexual bargain, attempting to garner a protector in Ossipon, even if it means offering herself sexually. (In yet another jab at bourgeois morality, Winnie has murdered her husband, but is uncomfortable with the moral ramifications of being Ossipon's lover.) Winnie has always found Ossipon attractive in a way that disrupts her sense of herself as a respectable woman,[12] and, making her way alone in the street, she approaches him as a refuge but also as a fulfilment of her long-standing desire, repressed for Verloc's sake. She allows him "to draw her to his breast" and rests against him, later taking his arm herself, and thus cultivating a physical closeness that "startled" Ossipon even as he is plotting to seduce her for her money (203, 204). In her newfound freedom, Winnie, at least superficially, has the qualities of the New Woman: personal and financial autonomy and sexual liberty.

The figure of the New Woman was "first invented as a fictional icon to represent the political woman of the coming century" in *The Woman's Herald* in 1893 (Tusan 1998: 169), but, during and after the 1890s, the term New Woman came to encompass a variety of possibilities, many unflattering to women's liberation: "The New Woman was a seductive temptress and a man-hater, over-educated and empty-headed, mannishly

---

scenes, however, she disregards her own advice, telling Ossipon, "I'll slave for you" (216). The distant political reality of German or Russian "slaves" has become relevant to her immediate personal reality, the subjugation that she comes to see as a kind of salvation.

[12] Earlier, as Winnie discusses Stevie's response to the anarchists' violent rhetoric, the narrator slyly notes: "Of the robust Ossipon, in whose presence she had always felt uneasy behind an attitude of stony reserve, she said nothing whatever" (50).

athletic or languidly anorexic, poised to take over the House of Commons but hysterically unable to decide which necktie to wear" (Mitchell 1999: 583). Conrad's ironic vision of Winnie's liberation does not take on these caricatured traits so much as it effaces the possibility of her liberation from traditional roles. The trance-like Winnie is shocked by the crime that she has committed in stabbing her husband, but Conrad's emphasis on her new status, rather than her emotional state, focuses attention on her role. As a "free woman," she will not escape her domestic role but try to duplicate it on a lower level with Ossipon, as a fallen woman. Conrad makes this repetition apparent in Winnie's interchange with Ossipon after he finds Verloc's body, as she tells him, "Tom, you can't throw me off now" and adds "Not unless you crush my head under your heel" (217). Winnie's role changes as she submits, and the narrator's ironic comment underscores this: "'Where are we going to, Tom?' she asked timidly. Mrs Verloc was no longer a free woman" (218). When he rejects and abandons her, she takes on the familiar Victorian image of the fallen woman, the suicide by drowning. Although Winnie had found Ossipon attractive, he takes advantage of her, robbing rather than seducing her. Winnie's freedom is not a sexual awakening but the same kind of sexual bargain that she has just left. The "respectable girl of the Belgravian mansion" (216) is unequipped to handle this dearly bought freedom.

Both Lombroso's theories and the backlash against the New Woman respond to anxieties about women's changing roles. Conrad seems to dismantle Lombroso's generalized criminal profiles, which easily fell into supporting society's sexual and racial biases, at the same time as he critiques the idealism of the New Woman supporters. The freedom they envision does not seem to have much meaning in a self-interested world structured by traditional roles.

This demonstrates the real complexity of Conrad's depiction of Edwardian London. He acknowledges the baseness and animalistic motivations of his characters in a way that strips Lombroso's categories of their resonance, while using Lombrosian traits to populate his fictional world. At the same time, he refigures the rhetoric of late nineteenth-century New Women further to demonstrate the impossibility of real liberty; in a world driven by self interest, liberty for women and men is subjugated to compulsion and ideology. In the choppy sentences of her stressed mental state, Winnie realizes, "Murderers escaped. They escaped abroad. Spain or California," but these places are "Mere names" and she rests "at the bottom of a black abyss from which no unaided woman could hope to scramble out" (203). In an allusion to the submissive Victorian feminine ideal, a deeply ironic representation after Verloc's murder, she assumes that a woman cannot cope with this situation and must offer herself to another man or kill herself in despair. Winnie cannot be a sensational criminal fleeing the country; she is paralyzed by her perceptions and ideology about crime and punishment. Her suicide is not only an "*act of madness or despair*" (229) but also an acknowledgement that her restraint was only illusory, that human beings possess this inherent atavistic inclination despite our pretences.

Winnie's suicide fits Conrad's vision of unremitting corruption in London, a dark, solipsistic world populated by characters blinded by self-concern and satisfied by the illusory sense of interconnectedness that is made to seem as naïve as Stevie's notion of the police as a "benevolent institution for the suppression of evil" (133) and Verloc's belief that he was loved for himself. Victorian ideals are made to seem absurd and untenable in this Darwinist depiction of the modern city as evolutionary battlefield. Using a Lombrosian typology of the female criminal and a mocking treatment of the New Woman, Conrad draws out the political implications of Winnie's crisis and violence. Shocked by her own actions and ingrained with a traditional moral viewpoint, Winnie is unable to create anything "new" and thus kills herself to avoid the gallows. This bleak ending serves not only as a critique of Victorian values but also, in a properly Lombrosian twist, purposefully explodes any sense of the Edwardians transcending their past.

Acknowledgement

A version of this essay was presented at the 32nd Annual International Conference of the Joseph Conrad Society (UK), London, July 2006.

Works cited

Hampson, Robert. "'If you read Lombroso': Conrad and Criminal Anthropology." In *The Ugo Mursia Memorial Lectures: Papers from the International Conrad Conference, University of Pisa, September 7th-11th, 1983*, edited by Mario Curreli. 317-35. Milan: Mursia International, 1988.

Harrington, Ellen Burton. "The Anarchist's Wife: Joseph Conrad's Debt to Sensation Fiction in *The Secret Agent*." *Conradiana* 36.1-2 (2004): 51-63.

Hunter, Allan. *Joseph Conrad and the Ethics of Darwinism: The Challenges of Science.* London: Croom Helm, 1983.

Jacobs, Robert G. "Comrade Ossipon's Favorite Saint: Lombroso and Conrad." *Nineteenth-Century Fiction* 23.1 (1968): 74-84.

Jones, Susan. *Conrad and Women.* Oxford: Clarendon Press, 1999.

Lombroso, Caesar, and William Ferraro. *The Female Offender*, translated by W. Douglas Morrison. New York: Appleton, 1915.

Mitchell, Sally. "New Woman, Old and New." *Victorian Literature and Culture* 27.2 (1999): 579-88.

Rafter, Nicole Hahn, and Mary Gibson. Editors' Introduction. In *Criminal Woman, the Prostitute, and the Normal Woman,* by Cesare Lombroso and Guglielmo Ferrero. 3-33. Durham: Duke University Press, 2004.

Saveson, John E. "Conrad, *Blackwood's*, and Lombroso." *Conradiana* 6 (1974): 57-62.

Shaffer, Brian W. "*Domestic Ironies*: Housekeeping as Mankeeping in *The Secret Agent*." In *Keeping the Victorian House: A Collection of Essays,* edited by Vanessa D. Dickerson. 313-29. New York: Garland Publishing, 1995.

Soane, Bev. The Colony at the Heart of Empire: Domestic Space in *The Secret Agent*." *The Conradian* 30.1 (2005): 46-58.

Thomas, Ronald R. *Detective Fiction and The Rise of Forensic Science.* Cambridge: Cambridge University Press, 1999.

Tusan, Michelle Elizabeth. "Inventing the New Woman: Print Culture and Identity Politics during the Fin-de-Siècle." *Victorian Periodicals Review* 31.2 (1998): 169-82.

Jews and Degenerates in *The Secret Agent*

Cedric Watts
University of Sussex

> Sometimes a phrenologist … would follow on with a brief phrenological séance, and nothing afforded the comrades more satisfaction than to be informed that their bumps showed undoubted criminal propensities.
>
> Meredith, *A Girl Among the Anarchists* (1903: rpt.1993: 153)

> Menachem Begin, Yassir Arafat, and Nelson Mandela, all once labeled as terrorists, have been rehabilitated as statesmen and awarded the Nobel Peace Prize.
>
> Scanlan, *Plotting Terror* (2001: 6)

ADAM GILLON FOUND "only two" Jews in Conrad's fiction (1994:41).[1] There may, however, be at least nine. In Conrad's *The Secret Agent*, the word "Jew" is not used. Nevertheless, the nomenclature deployed in this novel suggests that, while three Jews are explicitly revolutionary or anarchistic, they are being opposed by two other Jews whose actions bring about the death of innocent Stevie. One political function of this narrative feature is to deflect attention from the historical Irish threat of the 1880s to a threat involving Semitic immigrants. By means of the partly-ironic use of Lombroso's theories, these Jews are also (although not exclusively) associated with criminal degeneracy. In contrast to a probable literary source, the novel *A Girl Among the Anarchists*, however, *The Secret Agent* eschews overt anti-Semitic comments.

Elsewhere, Conrad's attitude to Jews has an ambivalence not unusual in the period. His letters include occasional anti-Semitic phrases. Some are directed against the publishers T. Fisher Unwin (not Jewish) and William Heinemann (an Anglican of Anglo-German descent): the

---

[1] Gillon provides admirable accounts of Yankel and Hirsch.

former being termed "The Patron Jew," the latter "That Israelite" (*CL*1 406, 395). The mission of the magazine *The Outlook* is, Conrad declares, "to make money for a Jew" (*CL2* 34). The crucified Impenitent Thief, admired by both Conrad and Cunninghame Graham, was "no Jew, since he had no eye for the shent-per-shent business the other fellow spotted at once" (*CL2* 5).[2] In *The Inheritors*, of which Conrad claimed joint authorship with Ford Madox Hueffer, a Jewish journalist is regarded with mixed feelings that include patronizing distaste. The journalist is a "good little man," but the hero remarks: "I was not yet so humble in spirit as to relish being called Granger by a stranger of his stamp. I tried to freeze him politely." The "sleek little man" evinces "a pathos that is always present in the type" (105, 102). Granger notes that he frequents a newspaper kiosk "kept by a fellow-Israelite – a snuffy little old woman," "bent nearly double," whose "nose touched her wares as often as not," and comments: "I liked him the better for his solicitude for this forlorn piece of flotsam of his own race" (103, 104).[3]

In "Prince Roman," the "dignified" Jewish innkeeper Yankel is "a Polish patriot," and, by virtue of that patriotism, becomes "one of us," so to speak, like Yankiel in Mickiewicz's *Pan Tadeusz*.[4] In *Nostromo*, Hirsch, though set in a demeaning stereotype (mercenary, complaining, cowardly), breaks free from it when spitting defiantly in the face of his brutal and anti-Semitic captor. Razumov, the gloomy protagonist of *Under Western Eyes*, remarks that his own name "is not Gugenheimer": "I am not a democratic Jew" (208).[5] Later, he spits "violently" at Julius Laspara and mutters "Cursed Jew!" (287). The narrator comments caustically that, although Laspara "might have been a Transylvanian, a Turk, an Andalusian," this is how Razumov (as a Russian Gentile)

---

2 The anti-Semitic phrase "shent-per-shent" (cent. per cent.) here means "profitable." On this and the Impenitent Thief, see Watts, ed. (1969: 62). See also the opening of Gillon's "The Jews in Conrad's Fiction" (1994: 41-44) and Knowles and Moore (2000: 16).

3 Although *The Inheritors* was mostly written by Hueffer, Conrad, as its co-author, obviously shared credit and responsibility for this novel, which has evident political links with "Heart of Darkness" and *Nostromo.*

4 For consistency with "Yankel," I Anglicize and phoneticize here the name of the honest Jew and loyal Pole, Jankiel, described in Adam Mickiewicz's *Pan Tadeusz*, Book 4.

5 Razumov's "Gugenheimer" may clumsily and/or insultingly refer to the dynasty of wealthy industrialists and philanthropists founded by Meyer Guggenheim (1828-1905).

expresses his "hate and contempt" (287). (The comment is historically apt, anti-Semitism being rife in Russia.) Frank Harris once called Conrad a Jew. Conrad replied in a letter which *The New Republic* published in part under the title "Mr. Conrad is Not a Jew" (1918: 109). In that letter, which specified in detail his noble Polish and Catholic ancestry, Conrad diplomatically stated: "Had I been an Israelite I would never have denied being a member of a race occupying such a unique place in the religious history of mankind" (*CL6* 216).

As is well known, *The Secret Agent*'s account of the bomb attempt against Greenwich Observatory was prompted by an actual incident in Greenwich Park in 1894. In that event, the bomb-carrier was a French national, Martial Bourdin, who had travelled in France; his brother-in-law, who had probably supplied the explosive, had a Jewish surname, "Samuels," and was described as having "features of the Jewish type."[6]

Significantly, however, the novel's action takes place not in 1894, the year of the Greenwich outrage, but in 1886. The choice of the latter year is highly significant; and, partly because the impressive Cambridge edition of *The Secret Agent* specifies 1887 as the year (413), I marshal now the evidence that it must be 1886.

When Verloc visits the Russian Embassy, it is late winter, and spring is not far away: "Mr Verloc heard against a window-pane the faint buzzing of a fly – his first fly of the year – heralding better than any number of swallows the approach of spring" (26). The day of the explosion is about a month later. That explosion occurs in the morning, and in the afternoon Ossipon, who had seen Verloc on the day of the latter's visit to the Embassy, says to the Professor: "I hadn't [*sic*] seen him for a month" (62): meaning "I haven't seen him for a month."[7] The commencement of spring is specified by the *Concise Oxford Dictionary* as March in the Northern Hemisphere, and the *Oxford English Dictionary* states that astronomically spring begins at the equinox of 20 March; so a reasonable assumption is that the explosion (a month after the heralding of "the approach of spring") occurs in April. Winnie Verloc's wedding-ring bears the date "24th June 1879"; and the Verlocs, Winnie says on the day before her death, have been married for seven years. Therefore, if she is thinking not of the precise period in years and months but of

---

[6] Nicoll (1897: 8); see also Sherry (1971: 316, 384).

[7] Conrad sometimes uses the past perfect tense (here "hadn't") where the present perfect ("haven't") is correct.

nominal calendar years, or is exaggerating by approximately two months the duration of her unfortunate union, the main action occurs in 1886.

If she is not exaggerating the duration but is thinking of a union that has actually lasted substantially more than seven and a half years, 1887 would be a possible date; but that is firmly ruled out by Chief Inspector Heat. In Chapter 6, this reliable sleuth recalls that he first met Verloc "a little more than seven years ago" (100), three days before the Guildhall Banquet. That banquet, by custom, took place on 9 November, as it did in 1878. Verloc was then unmarried. "Some time later" (101), and evidently seven months later, in June 1879, Verloc married Winnie. Heat's evidence, by showing that Verloc was unmarried seven years and five months prior to the main action, confirms that 1886 is the year of that action.

A politically significant date: in 1886 the claims of Irish Home Rule drastically divided the Liberal Party, so that in June, William Gladstone's government fell and Lord Salisbury's Conservatives gained power. Furthermore, the decade's early years were marked by numerous acts of terrorism in England, usually employing dynamite (invented in 1866 by Alfred Nobel, later the founder of the Nobel prizes). Some attempts were abortive, others horrifyingly destructive. In London alone, for example, in 1883 the locations of attempted bombings included the Local Government Office in Whitehall, the offices of *The Times*, the Metropolitan underground railway between Charing Cross and Westminster Stations, and the same railway near Praed Street Station (where more than sixty people were injured). In 1884, bombs were found at three stations (Charing Cross, Paddington, and Ludgate Hill) and in Trafalgar Square, and there were explosions at Victoria Station (underground), the Junior Carlton Club, the home of Sir Watkin Wynn, Scotland Yard, and London Bridge. During the following year, devices exploded on the Metropolitan Railway near Gower Street, at the House of Commons (where extensive damage was caused), Westminster Hall, the Admiralty, and the Tower of London (*Times*, 5 April 1892: 3c). On 24 April 1886, *The Times*'s leader reported a plan to "explode a dynamite bomb on the table of the House of Commons during their sitting" (9a). Indeed, in April 1885 the magazine *All the Year Round* had remarked that "dynamite outrages … have become a sort of institution in the land" (135). These, however, were attributed not to anarchists or revolutionaries but to Irish nationalists (often termed the "Fenians," forerunners of the "Irish Republican Army") seeking vengeance against England or hoping to coerce the government into granting independence to Ireland.

In *The Secret Agent*, Conrad carefully evades or conceals the Irish problem. Politically, his novel concentrates mainly on a few anarchists or revolutionaries, who are depicted as sordid and futile, and on the manipulation of an informer by a Russian diplomat. Conrad, as a Pole by birth whose parents had been exiled by Poland's Russian overlords, was understandably hostile to the Tsarist autocracy and its agents. By excluding any explicit reference to the Irish campaign for independence, he enables the novel to depict England as a bastion of liberty which provides sanctuary for agitators whom other nations seek to eliminate. Understandably, too, given that in 1886 (the year of the fictional action) Conrad had gladly taken British nationality, relinquishing his Russian legal status, the novel strongly emphasizes (while problematizing) England's liberal tradition of hospitality to exiles. *The Secret Agent* deploys anarchists and the Russian Mr Vladimir in order to occlude Fenians and the Irish leader, Charles Parnell. An obliquely patriotic text results. There is no doubt that Vladimir's embassy is the Russian Embassy. The evidence includes: his name; the association of his methods with "Crim-Tartary"; the Embassy's location in "Chesham Square" (non-existent, but the real Russian Embassy was located in Chesham Place); and the remark that he looks at Europe "from its other end" (172).[8]

A notable feature of the novel is the nomenclature of its villains: "Vladimir," "Verloc," "Yundt," "Ossipon," "Michaelis." There are no Murphys or O'Briens or O'Neills. The names of Conrad's conspirators are distinctively non-British and non-Irish. Furthermore, they could all be Jewish or partly Jewish. The name of the conspiratorial Russian diplomat, "Vladimir," could be that of a Jew or a Gentile. One thinks of, for example, Vladimir Ashkenazy, the celebrated Jewish pianist and conductor, but also of Vladimir the Great (*ca.* 956-1016), Grand Prince of Kiev, the first Christian ruler in that region. The novel, however, strongly suggests that the ambassador is indeed Jewish: "Descended from generations victimised by the instruments of an arbitrary power, he was racially, nationally, and individually afraid of the police. It was an inherited weakness, altogether independent of his judgment, of his reason, of his experience. He was born to it" (169). This passage reminds us that during the centuries of Tsarist autocracy in Russia, anti-Semitism was widespread at all levels of society, from that of the serfs (who

---

[8] Vladimir's predecessor has the German-sounding name "Stott-Wartenheim." When Conrad was writing *The Secret Agent*, the Russian Ambassador to the Court of St James's was of Baltic German ancestry: Count Benckendorff.

inflicted pogroms) to that of the nobility; the police often acquiesced in, or abetted, or even incited such persecution. Prince Urusov warned the Duma of police involvement in pogroms (Trotsky 1972: 132; Urussov [*sic*] 1908: vii, 170-77). In particular, the quoted description's emphasis on *racial* victimization appears to confirm that Vladimir is Jewish. Further corroboration is provided by *A Girl Among the Anarchists* (1903) by "Isabel Meredith" (the pseudonym of Helen and Olivia Rossetti). This work, a probable source of *The Secret Agent*, refers to "the foreign Jews' dread of policemen as omnipotent beings" (1993: 180). Physiological details provide additional support. In *Nostromo*, we are told that Hirsch, the Jew, is "round-cheeked," with a "round face" and a "podgy hand" (200, 202, 205); in *The Secret Agent*, similarly, Mr Vladimir displays "dimples on his round, full face" (the roundness is repeatedly mentioned), and has a "plump hand" (31, 22).

Next: Vladimir's employee, Adolf Verloc, claims to be a British subject. Nevertheless, the name "Adolf " (not the French "Adolphe" or the English "Adolphus") appears to be German. His father, however, was French, and Verloc has moved from France to England on the orders of his Russian paymasters. His wife and mother-in-law profess French ancestry. Certainly "Verloc" sounds French, and is probably intended to sound Jewish, too. Currently the Israeli *Consolidated Jewish Surname Index* (see Avotaynu.com) includes the cognates "Berlock" and "Berlog." To bank his money, he uses the name "Prozor," which is the root of the Russian-Jewish "Prozorov."

The evidence mounts, and a covert plot emerges. "Yundt," like its homophone "Jundt," sounds German (matching the forename "Karl"), and similarly appears in the *Jewish Surname Index*; so this character may be German-Jewish by origin. "Michaelis" is also listed. "Ossipon" has its root in "Osip," meaning "Joseph," and the same index also includes such cognates as "Osipe," "Osvan," "Osban," "Ozban," and "Ozbun." Like the Biblical Joseph, who is his nomenclatural forebear, Ossipon is a devoted interpreter of ominously significant signs. Two named offstage revolutionaries are Latorre, recalling Lassalle, and Moser. Of course, various famous revolutionaries, notably Ferdinand Lassalle, Karl Marx, Emma Goldman, Leon Trotsky, and Rosa Luxemburg, were Jewish. George Woodcock's *Anarchism* states that from the mid-1880s to 1914, Jewish immigrants in East London "provided more recruits to anarchism than the rest of the population of Britain" (1963: 421). There was a Jewish Anarchist Club in Berners Street, and Peter Kropotkin ("the Anarchist Prince") sometimes spoke at the Jubilee Street centre of the

Federation of Jewish Anarchists. Two anarchist journals, *Der Arbeiter Freund* and *Das Freie Wort*, were published in Yiddish versions in London.

In an early letter, Conrad claimed that "England was the only barrier to the pressure of infernal doctrines born in continental back-slums" (*CL*1 16). In *The Secret Agent*, the narrator suggests that various immigrants are sordid advocates of subversion, and the author hints, largely by means of nomenclature, that these conspiratorial figures are Jewish. Verloc, in connivance with Vladimir, seeks to make life harsher for his trusting colleagues who meet at his home, and becomes the agent of the destruction of his own brother-in-law. Thereby he may seem to conform to an ancient stereotype of Jewish treachery. According to the Bible, Cain slew his brother, Abel; Jacob cheated his brother, Esau; Judas betrayed Jesus; and the Jewish multitude insisted to Pontius Pilate that Jesus be crucified. Conrad, criticizing the left-wing ideal of "international fraternity," once remarked to Cunninghame Graham: "Fraternity means nothing unless the Cain–Abel business" (*CL*2 159).

Conrad also said: "as regards the Professor I did not intend to make him despicable. He is incorruptible at any rate" (*CL*3 491).[9] The Professor's name is not specified. He is the atheistic son of an itinerant preacher "of some obscure but rigid Christian sect" and possesses "a frenzied puritanism of ambition" (66). He is not Jewish, it appears; and may not be foreign. He likes the "anarchistic," "lawless" character of Americans,[10] but is "not likely to go and see" the United States (60). The apparent Gallicisms in his dialogue – for example, "slaves of the social convention," "To break up the superstition," and "Conceive you this folly …?" (57, 60, 226) – may be intended to indicate that he is of French origin, but are more likely to be inadvertent solecisms by the author.[11] They may still, of course, be read as such indications.

---

[9] See the annotations to this and the previous letter in Watts, ed. (1969: 121, 171-72).

[10] Anarchism flourished in the United States in the 1880s. In May 1886, the Haymarket Square explosion occurred in Chicago. At a demonstration of workers and anarchists, a bomb exploded and police fired guns into the crowd. Seven policemen and approximately twenty demonstrators died. Eight anarchists were subsequently tried for murder, and four of them were hanged.

[11] The narrator's English contains a sprinkling of Gallicisms, notably: Verloc "concluded to leave it there" (21-22); a composer "in pass of becoming famous" (168); "He ignored [i.e., did not know] how much there was in it" (204); and

If Conrad's Professor is British (which is uncertain) and non-Jewish (which seems virtually certain), he offsets the possibly anti-Semitic and xenophobic implications of other characterizations. Nevertheless, like Ossipon, Michaelis, Yundt, Verloc, Winnie, and Stevie, he could serve as an illustration in Cesare Lombroso's *L'uomo delinquente* (1876). This influential work grew markedly after its first appearance: by 1896-97 it filled three large volumes. Controversially, Lombroso argued that criminals, revolutionaries, anarchists, "idiots," and epileptics were characterized by a number of atavistic mental and physical features: they were "throwbacks," or beings not sufficiently evolved to fit modern society. In their facial, cranial, and psychological features could be detected signs of "inferior races" and of man's bestial ancestry. Conrad's knowledge of Lombroso is more extensive and detailed than Sylvère Monod's Pléiade edition of *The Secret Agent* acknowledges (1990: 1262). Monod suggested that Conrad could have gleaned all he needed from an essay by Anatole France. That essay, however, fails to specify numerous Lombrosian features mentioned in the novel. (France's summary of Lombroso's account of degenerate features does not refer to large and jutting ears, Mongoloid eyes, abnormal ear-lobes, striated or widely-separated teeth, incendiarism, vanity, and sheer sloth.)[12]

Verloc, who denounces the conspirators as "a lazy lot" (45), is amply lazy himself: like the Professor, he likes to lie in bed until noon. The obese Michaelis is sustained by a lady patroness; the scrawny Yundt is dependent on an "indomitable snarling old witch" (45). This tallies with Lombroso's claim that the criminal is characterized by "excessive idleness." He cites a malefactor who said "I would rather die than work" (1897: 390-91). In a conspicuously quotable passage, the novel's narrator tells us: "The majority of revolutionists are the enemies of discipline and fatigue mostly. There are natures too, to whose sense of justice the price exacted looms up monstrously enormous … Those are the fanatics. The remaining portion of social rebels is accounted for by vanity" (45).

Even in its final emphasis on vanity, this chimes with the claims of Lombroso, who alleges that "criminal degenerates" are not only lazy but also display greater vanity than do artists and authors (1896: 448). An

"She had no conscience [i.e., was unaware] of how little she had audibly said" (211).

[12] France's essay is "Les Criminels" (1888). Lombroso's theories are discussed in detail in Hart (1906: 137-38) and more briefly in Meredith (1903; 1993: 187). Hampson (1988) provides a finely discriminating discussion of *The Secret Agent*'s "anthropological" aspects.

obvious irony of *The Secret Agent* is that Ossipon, the disciple of Lombroso, fails to see that he himself, with his "Negroid" and "Mongolic" features, is a classic example of the criminal type as defined by his mentor. Ossipon is described thus:

> A bush of crinkly yellow hair topped his red, freckled face, with a flattened nose and prominent mouth cast in the rough mould of the negro type. His almond-shaped eyes leered languidly over the high cheek bones. … The disdainful pout of Comrade Ossipon's thick lips accentuated the negro type of his face. (39, 43)

Lombroso claims that the facial and cranial features of criminal degenerates often combine features found in Africans and Mongolians. Thus, the nose of the born thief, he asserts, is "of a flattened, negroid character"; violators of women have lips that are "fleshy, swollen and protruding, as in negroes"; swindlers have "curly and woolly hair"; and many congenital criminals also have such "Mongolic" facial features as prominent cheek-bones and oblique eyes or eyelids. The description of Ossipon, even in such details as the "almond-shaped eyes," makes him a Lombrosian case study: visibly a thief, swindler, and violator. Furthermore, Lombroso claims that between 31-40% of anarchists are conspicuously "the criminal type."[13] Ossipon simultaneously confirms and (by being a degenerate advocate) discredits Lombroso. Verloc and his political group are slothful, parasitic, and physically grotesque. Verloc is "very corpulent" (20). Ossipon, although robust in body, is grotesque facially. Michaelis is massively obese, "round like a tub" (37). The aged Yundt is skinny and decrepit. The Professor is very small and puny, wears big round spectacles, and has "flat, large ears" which "departed widely from the sides of his skull" (52). Lombroso says that "many criminals have a restricted field of vision" and that "twenty-eight per cent. of criminals have handle-shaped ears standing out from the face[,] as in the chimpanzee" (1911: 14).[14]

Thus, in an elaborate covert plot, the unsavoury characters in *The Secret Agent* combine traits of criminal degeneracy, as defined by

---

[13] See Lombroso (1891: 337-38; 1896: 126, 278) and Lombroso Ferrero (1911: 14, 15, 16, 18, 305).

[14] In "The Physiognomy of the Anarchists," Lombroso notes that some political criminals had parents who were "very religious" or "religious lunatics." (1891: 339). Conrad's Professor, as noted above, is the son of a fervent sectarian, a "dark enthusiast" who is "an itinerant and rousing preacher" (66).

Lombroso, with a largely Jewish heritage. That the hapless victim, Stevie, and his avenging sister, Winnie, also bear Lombrosian stigmata is another feature that further establishes the dark negativity of this troubling novel. As a fictional work of its time, however, the novel is admirably free from explicitly anti-Semitic descriptions. This, in *A Girl Among the Anarchists*, is a portrait of Jacob Myers, a fictional counterpart of H. B. Samuels, a real-life source for Adolf Verloc:

> The man Myers ... was to all appearances a mean enough type of the East End sartorial Jew. His physiognomy was not that of a fool, but indicated rather that low order of intelligence, cunning and intriguing, which goes to make a good swindler. The low forehead, wideawake, shifty little eyes, the nose of his forefathers, and insolent lock of black hair plastered low on his brow – all these characteristics may frequently be met with in the dock of the "Old Bailey" when some case of petty swindling is being tried. ... It apparently mattered little to this modern Shylock whence came his pound of flesh ...
> (44-45, 50)

In contrast, here is Conrad's description of Verloc:

> Undemonstrative and burly in a fat-pig style, Mr Verloc ... proceeded on his way ... [His] general get up was that of a well to do mechanic in business for himself. He might have been anything from a picture-frame maker to a locksmith; an employer of labour in a small way. But there was also about him an indescribable air which no mechanic could have acquired in the practice of his handicraft however dishonestly exercised: the air common to men who live on he vices, the follies, or the baser fears of mankind; the air of moral nihilism common to keepers of gambling hells and disorderly houses; to private detectives and inquiry agents; to drink sellers and, I should say, to the sellers of invigorating electric belts and to the inventors of patent medicines. But of that last I am not sure, not having carried my investigations so far into the depths. (16)[15]

---

[15] An "invigorating electric belt" of the time was the Pulvermacher Electric Belt, which, when fitted round the waist and abdomen, "assists Nature by a general reinforcement of the vital energy" (according to publicity). This device was advertised repeatedly in *T.P.'s Weekly* when Conrad's *Nostromo* was serialised in it (see, for example, 15 April 1904: 515.) As Conrad knew, a similar device, the Pulvermacher "Hydro-Electric Body-Chain," proved sexually efficacious for Flaubert's Homais (see *Madame Bovary*, Chapter 11). W. C. Hart alleges that

The passage is urbane in its play of irony, satiric in its treatment of Verloc's sordid nature, and sophisticated in its deployment of a disembodied yet strongly characterized narrator. Conrad's description is also liberal in eschewing any anti-Semitic comments of the kind found prominently in *A Girl Among the Anarchists*. In this respect, although *The Secret Agent* is not averse to stereotypes, it resembles a riposte to the Rossetti sisters' novel. Helen and Olivia Rossetti were the cousins of Ford Madox Hueffer, who provided Conrad with information about anarchists; so it is probable that Conrad knew *A Girl Among the Anarchists*, which appeared three years before the commencement and four years before the publication of *The Secret Agent*.

By turning its back on the Irish campaign of the 1880s, and by its depiction of characters with foreign and Jewish names, *The Secret Agent* adopts a strategy that is paradoxically countered by its notable avoidance of explicit anti-Semitism of the kind the Rossettis employed. A cautionary rule therefore emerges. Inferences and interpretations of the political implications of a given literary work strongly depend upon the particular contexts the reader chooses to invoke for purposes of comparison. If we sum it up as "Changing contexts change the contents," we see that it then becomes more than a literary rule: it becomes a rule of history as well. For example, individuals widely regarded as terrorists can, in course of time, become acclaimed winners of the Nobel Peace Prize. As Margaret Scanlan points out (2001: 6), such people include Menachem Begin, Nelson Mandela, and Yassir Arafat, and we may add Yitzhak Rabin (once prominent in the Haganah), who shared the prize with Arafat in 1994, but was assassinated in the following year.

Finally, to be fair to "Isabel Meredith," it should be noted that when, in later life, Olivia Rossetti corresponded with Ezra Pound, she boldly opposed his extreme anti-Semitism, declaring: "I look upon Hitler as a raving homicidal lunatic and am simply filled with disgust at the wholesale massacres of Jews under the most horrible circumstances."[16]

---

numerous self-styled anarchists are "abortionists, professional swindlers … dealers in bogus businesses, medical quacks" (1906: 8-9).

[16] To Pound, 29 September 1951 (Pound 1998: 77). Olivia is mentioned briefly in Pound's 76th and 78th *Cantos*. In a 1948 article, she said: "It was when Mussolini ceased to be guided by his Italian instinct, when he attempted to link up Italy to an aggressive military power, to teach the Italian to feel contempt for the African and hatred for the Jew, that he failed" (*Ibid.*, 9).

Acknowledgements

I wish to acknowledge the gracious cooperation of the late Sylvère Monod and of Robert Hampson.

Works cited

All the Year Round. 23 April 1885: 135.

Conrad, Joseph. "Mr. Conrad is Not a Jew." *The New Republic* (New York), 24 August 1918: 109.

———, and Ford Madox Hueffer. *The Inheritors* (1901). London: Dent, 1923.

France, Anatole. "Les Criminels" (1888). In *La Vie littéraire.* 2: 75-83. Paris: Calmann-Lévy, 1890.

Gillon, Adam. "The Jews in Conrad's Fiction." In *Joseph Conrad: Comparative Essays*, edited by Raymond Brebach. 41-57. Lubbock: Texas Tech University Press, 1994.

Hampson, Robert. "'If you read Lombroso': Conrad and Criminal Anthropology." In *The Ugo Mursia Memorial Lectures: Papers from the International Conrad Conference, University of Pisa, September 7th-11th, 1983*, edited by Mario Curreli. 317-35. Milan: Mursia International, 1988.

Hart, W. C. *Confessions of an Anarchist.* London: Grant Richards, 1906.

Knowles, Owen, and Gene M. Moore. *Oxford Reader's Companion to Conrad.* Oxford: Oxford University Press, 2000.

Lombroso, Cesare. "Criminal Anthropology." *Twentieth-Century Practice*, Vol. 12, edited by T. L. Stedman. London: Sampson Low, Marston, 1897.

———. "Illustrative Studies in Criminal Anthropology. III. The Physiognomy of the Anarchists." *The Monist* 1.3 (April 1891): 336-43.

———. *L'uomo delinquente.* 5th edn. Vol. 1. Turin: Fratelli Bocca, 1896.

Lombroso Ferrero, Gina. *Criminal Man according to the Classification of Cesare Lombroso.* London and New York: Putnam's Sons, 1911.

"Meredith, Isabel" [pseudonym of Helen and Olivia Rossetti]. *A Girl Among the Anarchists* (1903). Lincoln: Nebraska University Press, 1993.

Mickiewicz, Adam. *Pan Tadeusz*, translated by Kenneth R. Mackenzie. London: Polish Cultural Foundation, 1986; rpt. 1990.

Monod, Sylvère, ed. *Conrad: Œuvres.* Bibliothèque de la Pléiade. Vol. 3. Paris: Gallimard, 1990.

Nicoll, David. *The Greenwich Mystery*. Sheffield: Privately printed, 1897.

Pound, Ezra. *"I Cease Not to Yowl": Ezra Pound's Letters to Olivia Rossetti Agresti*, edited by Demetres P. Tryphonopoulos and Leon Surette. Urbana: Illinois University Press, 1998.

Scanlan, Margaret. *Plotting Terror: Novelists and Terrorists in Contemporary Fiction.* Charlottesville: Virginia University Press, 2001.
Sherry, Norman. *Conrad's Western World.* London: Cambridge University Press, 1971.
The Times. Leader. 24 April 1886: 9a.
———. "Dynamite Outrages." 5 April 1892: 3c.
Trotsky, Leon. *1905*, translated by Anya Bostock. London: Allen Lane, 1972.
Urussov, Prince Serge Dmitriyavich. *Memoirs of a Russian Governor*, translated by Herman Rosenthal. London and New York: Harper & Brothers, 1908.
Watts, Cedric. *The Deceptive Text: An Introduction to Covert Plots.* Brighton: Harvester, 1984.
———, ed. *Joseph Conrad's Letters to R. B. Cunninghame Graham.* London: Cambridge University Press, 1969.
Woodcock, George. *Anarchism.* Harmondsworth: Penguin, 1963.

Textualizing Liminality in *The Secret Agent*

Ludmilla Voitkovska, *University of Saskatchewan*
and **Zofia Vorontsova**, *University of Waterloo*

MARKED BY FREQUENT geographic transitions and multiple cultural influences, Conrad's experience positions him in the space between cultural collectives. At the heart of this is the anthropological construct of liminality, an experience rich with ambiguity, uncertainty, and the possibility of creative foment. Its initial and acute phase is marked by disorientation, a loss of identity and control, and a sense of uncertainty about the future. During its second, more adaptive and enduring phase, a person constructs and reconstructs the meaning of his or her experience. In the case of cross-cultural liminality, this phase persists indefinitely, and for some, like Conrad, liminality becomes the sole place one can call "home."

The liminal space between national constituencies – privileged, textual, and discursive – attracts persons predisposed to social and cultural mobility and becomes a hybrid site that witnesses the production of cultural meaning. Since liminality is regarded as a time and place of withdrawal from normal modes of social action, it can become "a period of scrutinization of the central values or axioms of the culture in which it occurs" (Turner 1969: 167). Contemplating liminality as an existential condition, Conrad undertakes an analysis of several issues within his adopted culture. In *The Secret Agent*, he brings the action from exotic and imaginary settings back to England, and populates his London with anarchists, terrorists, revolutionaries, and double agents. His liminal continuum includes persons and principles that fall in the interstices of the social structure, reside on its margins, and occupy the lowest ranks. As a reflection on the perennial opposition between structure and anti-structure, *the* defining aspect of liminal existence, *The Secret Agent*'s liminal aspects mirror the author's ambivalence towards cultural displacement and his efforts to expose living in liminality. His irony is directed against liminality's institutionalization in the Embassy, the police, and criminal activity.

Conrad's characters are complex liminal beings that undergo several transformational stages. Turner describes three transitional phases of liminality: separation, margin, and aggregation. In the first, the individual is detached from a "group either from an earlier fixed point in the social structure, from a set of cultural conditions (a 'state'), or from both." In the next phase, one "passes through a cultural realm that has few or none of the attributes of the past or coming state." Turner suggests that liminal entities are "betwixt and between the positions assigned and arrayed by law, custom, convention, and ceremonial" (94-95). Liminality is a limbo period characterized by ambiguity, humility, seclusion, tests, and sexual uncertainty. Liminal entities often form *communitas*, an unstructured community where all members have equal status. In the third and final phase, reaggregation, the passage is completed, and the individual, who finds relative stability again, has rights to exercise and duties to fulfil. These become clear-cut and "structural," and one is expected to behave in accord with the customs and moral norms that bind all persons in a society or cultural group.

Structured society cannot exist without the presence of a counter-culture. Status is an essential condition of liminality, which presupposes that "the high could not be high unless the low existed" (97). Liminal individuals are "entities in transition, as yet without place or position" (103). Thus, liminality should be considered a space of retreat from the common means of social action – a period of analysis of the values of the new culture being offered to the liminal individual. These individuals experience social life as a "dialectical process that involves successive high and low, *communitas* and structure, homogeneity and differentiation, equality and inequality" (97). Liminal beings are often denied possessions that would distinguish them from one another.

Describing situations that mirror various rites of passage, Conrad analyzes the impact of institutionalized foreign power on the individual's psychological matrix. Verloc's training by the Embassy reads like a rite of passage whereby the initiate is subjected to psychological conditioning intended to prepare him for status elevation. Stripped of his identity, Verloc becomes an agent "so secret that he was never designated otherwise but by the symbol Δ." (26). His meetings with Vladimir are conducted within the liminal space of the Embassy and mix training and mental preparation as he is moulded into an employee who is to be entrusted an important assignment. According to Turner, the behaviour of the liminal persons is "normally passive or humble; they must obey their instructors implicitly and accept arbitrary punishment without complaint" (1969: 95). As becomes someone of lower status, Verloc remains passive during his sessions at the Embassy, his attitude moving sluggishly between "absolute devotion" and "unobtrusive deference" and "proud humility" (20, 18, 23). The height of his emotional expression is a faint smile provoked by imagining himself incorporated into the social structure as a Marshal of France and Member of Parliament, posts that would place him in a dominant position and make him useful to the Embassy.

Vladimir treats Verloc "with a sort of chaffing condescension" (33), not hesitating to demonstrate his power: his "I have been trying to educate you" (31) implies that resisting his power is futile. He humiliates Verloc in order to break his sense of self, thereby allowing him to produce any individual he desires. Vladimir also tells Verloc that he does not appear to be intelligent and is too susceptible, reminding him of his failure as a secret agent at the outset of his career and his five years of confinement in a fortress for stealing French gun designs: "it served you right for letting yourself get caught," says Vladimir. He further establishes his superiority by suggesting that Verloc lacks the mental capacity for his profession: "you wouldn't deceive an idiot" (22). This episode dramatizing the hierarchy of power between Verloc and Vladimir, suggests a rite of passage that should elevate Verloc's status as an Embassy employee.

Verloc's involvement in liminal rituals extends to his exercise of authority over Stevie as he trains him in unconditional obedience. Verloc's household, "hidden in the shades of the sordid street seldom touched by the sun ... the dim shop with its wares of disreputable rubbish" (34), is a typical liminal space, its central element Stevie himself. Stevie is destitute, and Winnie does not want him to have possessions as this would be "tampering with his position of complete dependence" (120). His environment, where he is stripped of possessions in order to foster dependence, mirrors that of a total institution.

According to Erving Goffman, an individual who enters such an institution is "stripped of the support" of previous social arrangements and thus find that "certain roles are lost to him by virtue of the barrier that separates him from the outside world" (1961: 15, 16). Admission rituals also entail the "stripping" of personal possessions, a symbolic phase of "leaving off" involving disposing of property and "important because persons invest personal feelings" in belongings (18). He proposes that once the inmate has been thus deprived, these feelings will be transferred to the institution (for example, standard issue uniforms). An inmate's stay within the institution will be closely monitored by staff, activities "penetrated by constant sanctioning interaction from above, especially during the initial period" (39) before they are internalized and automatic. Individuals in "total" institutions often fail to retain adult-like "self-determination, autonomy and freedom of action" and may consequently become aware of being "radically demoted in the age-grading system" (39, 43).

Stevie, being the youngest of the household, fits Goffman's description of an institutionalized inmate at the bottom of the age ladder. Well behaved, he fears Verloc and unconditionally submits to his authority, remaining "very good and quiet, staring vacantly" (35). All aspects of his life, as in a total institution, are conducted in the same place, under a single authority, each phase of daily life being carried on in his supervisors' company and tightly scheduled. Conrad compares Stevie's life in Verloc's home to that of "an excited animal in a cage" (47). Treated poorly, he can be broken down and indoctrinated into a new world of activity. Verloc extends "as much recognition to Stevie as a man not particularly fond of animals may give to his wife's beloved cat" (35). Not much more, apparently, is expected of Verloc's guests, who, like Ossipon, talk of Stevie "negligently," with "a shade of condescension" and refer to his condition as a "form of degeneracy" (40). Humiliated, Stevie completes his training for his role as suicide bomber: "Never had a sage a more attentive and admiring disciple" (175). However, Stevie's training in Verloc's home, like Verloc's at the Embassy, ends not in status elevation but adds to displacement and the lack of finality.

The same is true of other characters that have undergone training. An "ex-medical student without a degree" (40), Ossipon never left the liminal space of transition. The Lady Patroness, the novel's only non-liminal character, trains Michaelis to become an accepted member of society. Incorporated into the structure by her "splendid" marriage, she is immune from liminality because of her status. At the same time, intelligent and "curious at heart," she uses "the power of her great, almost historical social prestige" to attract within her ken "everything that rose above the dead level of mankind": Royal Highnesses, artists, men of science, young statesmen, and "charlatans of all ages and conditions" (83). She associates with liminals in order to understand "the direction of surface currents" and advance "her own edification" within the structure (84).

The characters reside in spaces bearing liminality's imprint, such as the Embassy, an institution governing relations between cultures and, legally, foreign territory on a national space; gaol, intended to break the cyclical nature of crime; and the police force, a tool of social control and constant reminder of power structure. Several characters have been in correctional facilities where individuals come in as criminals and through various rituals are demoted to equal status and then reformulated into law-abiding citizens. Conrad shows the impact of such "correction" on the psyche as he attributes some aspects of his characters' conduct to their time in prison. Michaelis's habit of talking to himself and his indifference to his listeners' sympathy or hostility, and indeed even to their presence, stems from his captivity. As a result, he is "no good in the discussion" because "the mere fact of hearing another voice disconcerted him painfully, confusing his thoughts at once – these thoughts that for so many years, in a mental solitude more barren that a waterless desert, no living voice had ever combated, commented, or approved" (39).

Having spent five years in "rigorous confinement in a fortress" (21), Verloc possesses all the attributes of liminality: submissiveness, total obedience, silence, sexual continence, sexlessness, suspension of kinship rights and obligations, disregard for personal appearance, heteronomy, foolishness, simplicity, and homogeneity. Of these, the first three are the most salient. He talks to Vladimir in a state resembling "a collapsed coma – a sort of passive insensibility interrupted by slight convulsive starts." His voice during this conversation is reduced to "an uneasy, doglike growl" (31). In fact, Vladimir stifles Verloc's voice, famous for years at open-air meetings and at workmen's assemblies in large halls," the last refuge of his identity, and tells him "'We have no use for your voice. We don't want a voice. We want facts – startling facts – damn you" (25).

Verloc's sexual continence is apparent in the Verlocs' childlessness, Winnie substituting "quasi-maternal affection" for her brother (13). The sexless bedroom scene after the anarchists meet in Verloc's house makes clear that theirs is a marriage of convenience. Discomposed and speechless with the vision of Mr Vladimir, Verloc beholds "his wife re-enter the room and get into bed in a calm, business-like manner which renders him hopelessly lonely in the world" (48).

Whether an object of criticism or as an element of the novel's *genre*, the police are an ever-present super-power in *The Secret Agent*. Goffman's theories on institutional environments may help to understand how the police academy may be used to remove "support provided by … stable social arrangements of [one's] home world" (1961: 14), thus making it a liminal space. As in a prison (or a monastery), the police surrender their individuality to a total institution and are assimilated into its culture by surrendering their previous identity and acquiring new possessions (a gun, badge, uniform). According to Goffman, the demand for conformity is achieved through obedience tests and initiation rituals. Through degradation and embarrassment, "the individual is required to undertake a daily round of life that he considers alien to him – to take on a dis-identifying role" (23).

Conrad's descriptions of Heat's adventures and ruminations are necessary in exposing the police as a liminal institution. This institution is not only liminal in that it provides a place of transition from one world to another but also because it constantly resides between the world of the sacred and the world of the criminal, permanently governing relations between the two. Conrad suggests that Heat is "an old departmental hand," who has his own morality" (110), an indication that his indoctrination is virtually complete. His superior, the Assistant Commissioner has also undergone transformation within the police; as he sets out to question Verloc, he reflects upon his enterprise and seems "to lose some more of his identity" (115).

The Assistant Commissioner repeatedly exercises his higher rank over Heat in order to reiterate institutional hierarchy. He reminds Heat of his lower status, "directing an inquiring gaze at his renowned subordinate," all the while remembering that "He was a loyal servant" (78, 72). Throughout the investigation of the bombing, a considerable, unspoken tension is observed between the two: "'I'll turn him inside out like an old glove,' thought the Assistant Commissioner, with his eyes resting pensively upon the Chief Inspector Heat" (93). However, the Inspector perpetually resists the Commissioner's imposed power *à la* De Certeau through hidden tactics: "'you don't know your place, and your place won't know you very long either, I bet" (97). Equally fascinating is Conrad's placement of the police institution within its own hierarchy of liminal worlds, mediating between society and the criminal world, for nothing seems to compare to "that satisfactory sense of superiority the members of the police force get from the unofficial but intimate side of their intercourse with the criminal classes, by which the vanity of power is soothed, and the vulgar love of domination over our fellow creatures is flattered worthily as it deserves" (96). However, regardless of the superior role the police play among the novel's other liminal spaces, there are strong parallels between the police and criminal worlds in terms of liminal attributes: "he could understand the mind of a burglar, because, as a matter of fact, the mind and the instincts of a burglar are of the same kind as the mind and the instincts of a police officer" (74). In this sense, the two worlds co-exist as mirror opposites, revealing the intrinsically complex nature of structure and anti-structure.

In terms of appearance, the novel's liminal characters do not have to be *dressed* as monsters. Physically revolting, they border on the hideous. Michaelis is a marginal character by virtue of his morbid obesity: "He had come out of a highly hygienic prison round like a tub, with an enormous stomach and distended cheeks of a pale, semi-transparent complexion" (37). In English society individuals are expected to appear tidy and healthy, and his appearance is unacceptable. Yundt, with "faint black grimace of a toothless mouth," is "old and bald, with a narrow, snow-white wisp of a goatee hanging limply from his chin" (38). His energy and spirit defy the image of a terrorist as a driven, relentless, able-bodied man. One would not expect characters so physically worn out to be able to undertake a single terrorist act, nor do they, for Stevie, who is entrusted to carry out the outrage, is similarly unfit for the role: his "back quivered, his thin neck, sunk into a deep hollow at the base of the skull, seemed ready to snap" (40).

During the liminal stage, differences between participants that are normally observed, such as class, are often ignored or de-emphasized. Making a transition between states in the society that is "structured, differentiated, and often [based upon a] hierarchical system of politico-legal-economic positions with many types of evaluations, separating men in terms of 'more' or 'less,'" is defined by Turner as "an unstructured or rudimentarily structured and relatively undifferentiated *comitatus*, community, or even communion of equal individuals who submit together to the general authority of the ritual elders" (1969: 96). A social structure of *communitas* is based on common humanity and equality rather than hierarchy. As "secular distinctions of rank and status disappear or are homogenized, among themselves, neophytes tend to develop an intense comradeship and egalitarianism" (95). The community of anarchists and revolutionaries in *The Secret Agent* has gone beyond what Turner would qualify as an existential or spontaneous *communitas*, which, free from all structural demands, is fully spontaneous and immediate. This community is composed of a combination of normative and ideological *communitas*.

Normative *communitas* is organized into a social system, whereas ideological *communitas* refers to Utopian social models based on existential *communitas*. Situated within the structural realm, the latter arises around the need to mobilize and organize resources, and the necessity for social control among group members in pursuance of these goals. The people brought together directly and by proxy through Verloc are united in their discontent with the structure. Mr Vladimir's desire to bring England into line is predicated on the perception that there is a lack action and insufficient suppression of international crime. He transfers his leadership into the sphere of global ideology by suggesting the blowing up of the first meridian because "the imbecile bourgeoisie of [England] make themselves the accomplices of the very people whose aim is to drive them out of their houses to starve in ditches"; his main purpose is to achieve "universal repressive legislation" (28). The existence and availability of such an ideological *communitas* makes his plans easy to execute. According to Turner, *communitas* emerges where social structure is absent; it "breaks through the interstices of structure, in liminality; at the edges of structure, in marginality; and from beneath the structure, in inferiority" (1969: 128).

Ideological *communitas* eventually develops a strict hierarchy, as does the egalitarian *communitas* of *The Secret Agent*. The role of authority belongs to a professor whose "imagination had been fired early by the tales of men rising from the depths of poverty to positions of authority and affluence" (66). The Professor had been exposed early on to status elevation, a main aspect of liminality: "set before him a goal of power and prestige to be attained without medium of arts, graces, tact, wealth – by sheer weight of merit alone. On that view he considered himself entitled to undisputed success" (66). He believes in his superior status because he does not belong to the normal world: "Their character is built upon conventional morality. It leans on the social order. Mine stands free from everything artificial" (57).

Based upon an examination of Conrad's characters, the hierarchy of his liminal *communitas* is anarchists < thieves and criminals < police < Embassy < The Professor. The Professor believes that he is higher than state authority and society since he holds the ultimate power of destruction through the bomb he carries. He competes both with the revolutionaries (Yundt) and the police: "Revolution, legality – counter moves in the same game; forms of idleness at bottom identical" (58). The revolutionaries accept The Professor as a higher authority and recognize his power, and when talking with him, "big Ossipon" suffers from "a sense of moral and even physical insignificance" (53).

The master clandestine operator, The Professor seemingly conforms to the imposed structure but secretly strives to subvert it. He belongs to two worlds, that of the anarchists and that of law-abiding citizens; secretly carrying explosives, he lives like a normal man. Even though most people know of these explosives, they remain hidden and unseen.

The Professor defiantly brags: "I take care never to part with the last handful of my wares. I've it always by me." To deal with such a man requires "sheer, naked, inglorious heroism" (55). His ability to control the liminal spaces around him ultimately accords him higher status than other liminal characters and normal citizens.

His resistance to social power demonstrates De Certeau's concept of strategic resistance to foreign power imposition. Individuals in liminal spaces are governed by a foreign power and must conform to it if proper training and the building of the new individual are to occur. The conception of power operates either strategically or tactically, and strategies are able "to produce, tabulate, and impose spaces" (1988: 30) that challenge the imposed power structure. De Certeau asserts that hierarchical structures can be manœuvered by an individual with "will and power" (36), with strategies that provide with autonomy. A tactic, on the other hand, is the reply to a forced "law of a foreign power" (37), where one seemingly conforms to the imposed structure, while, at the same time, secretly functioning independently in the available surroundings. Just as strategy is characterized by the "postulation of power," a tactic is determined by its absence (38). Strategies imply a position of strength; tactics illustrate a position of weakness.

Ultimately, De Certeau provides two ways of dealing with imposed power: blatant opposition to the hierarchy within the institution, or quiet conformity and the furtive execution of individual power. The Professor resists conformity: "By exercising his agency with ruthless defiance he procured for himself the appearances of power and personal prestige" (67). Those lacking his will and power experience destructive psychological effect of suspended liminality. Verloc is unhappy in an unfulfilling career as a secret agent since he is not fully part of the normative world, belonging neither to the Embassy nor to the criminal world. Conrad suggests that "there is no occupation that fails a man more completely than that of a secret agent of police" (48). Displaced in his career, Verloc is also is physically and socially marginalized, and the state of dual or even triple liminality adds to his psychological aggravation. The three liminal worlds he belongs to – the Embassy, shady affairs (such as his shop), and the future proletariat society – leave an imprint on his identity: "He trod the pavement heavily with his shiny boots, and his general get-up was that of a well-to-do mechanic in business for himself" (16). Constantly moving between these worlds, he floats in a social limbo between the clean-cut, well dressed world of the Embassy and the dark and shifty world of his shop.

The novel's characters are not made marginal *by* the liminal spaces in which they reside but, rather, are naturally inclined to marginality and thus indefinitely belong to a liminal space. Verloc has "an instinctive leaning towards shady transaction" that "did not take him out of his own sphere – the sphere which is watched by the police" (46). Moreover, should he fail, he does not fear transition into new liminal spaces: "a term of imprisonment, an early release … life abroad somewhere" (178). Besides being predisposed to liminality, no character in the novel is fully incorporated into any structure, and thus there is no aggregation state for them. By giving them the status of permanent liminals, Conrad creates his own category as he institutionalizes liminality as a statement of the impossibility of reaggregation.

Conrad presents liminality as dangerous, inauspicious, and polluting to personæ, objects, events, and relationships not "ritually incorporated into the liminal context" (Turner 1969: 108-09). He seems to suggest that "from the perspectival viewpoint of those concerned with the maintenance of 'structure,' all sustained manifestations of *communitas* must appear as dangerous and anarchical, and have to be hedged around with prescriptions, prohibitions, and conditions" (109). In *The Secret Agent*, that which cannot be clearly classified in terms of the traditional criteria of classification or which falls between the classificatory boundaries of normal existence is presented as polluting and dangerous. In Conrad's liminal world the usual customs and conventions do not apply: Verloc agrees to blow up the Royal Observatory, the symbol of Britain's scientific culture, and, as if devoid of any cultural or family ties and sentiments, unhesitatingly uses his brother-in-law to do so. At the same time, liminal space is critical for empowerment and resistance, as liminality allows an individual to occupy two different worlds, creating what Homi K. Bhabha calls a "Third Space." Verloc develops his own pattern of resistance and empowerment: as double agent, he draws upon and manipulates both worlds, although loyal to neither.

According to Turner, there is a natural cyclical process shifting between separation and reaggregation that entails liminality: "social life is a type of dialectical process that involves successive experience of high and low, *communitas* and structure, homogeneity and differentiation, equality and inequality. The passage from lower to higher status is through a limbo of statelessness" (97). In *The Secret Agent,* this dialectical process is broken. The characters are wedged in a state of liminality, between two or more worlds, never fully part of any one. Stevie is simultaneously child and man; Verloc cannot fulfil the final stage of aggregation into the Embassy or into society. Vladimir dangles the possibility of his acceptance by cultural institutions and at the same time withdraws it by condemning the whole culture: "They dislike finality in this country" (25). His criticism of "this country" in its totality and his discouragement of Englishness suggests that Verloc will remain in the limbo of training, aspiring to become a model employee *and* striving to be English yet never succeeding in either.

Verloc takes a stance of resistance to the social erasure that threatens him. This appears a deliberate response to the experience of being negated as an individual and denied access to the post-liminal state that is his due. For him, the aggregation phase appears to mean passage into a purely criminal world. Once he realizes that he is no longer part of the spy world or the anarchist world, he breaks free from the Embassy and rejects his liminal role: "All the world shall know what I've done for them. I am not afraid. I don't care. Everything'll come out. Every damned thing. Let them look out!" (185). As Conrad's *dénouement* reveals, his characters have only one way out of liminality: death.

Verloc, Winnie, and Stevie are closely bound in life and in death by the events that transpire behind the author's curtain, as they parade the plot and the novel's climax on their shoulders. Stevie, "quite a lad – a weak-minded creature" (165), is the first to escape his liminal existence after he completes his suicide mission, guided by Verloc. Upon realizing that her husband has masterminded her beloved brother's death, Winnie murders Verloc and sets him free from his limbo. When she was younger, she chose not to take a place within the structure to become a butcher's wife. Occupying a calculated state of liminality, this heroine makes a successful bid for release from the romantic plot line's suffocating destiny.

Having escaped the role of romantic heroine, Winnie falls into the trap set by Verloc and enters liminal space, but she first misjudges liminality's dangers and then liberates herself from them by killing her husband. Since there is no structure for her to be reaggregated into, she does not "exactly know what use to make of her freedom. Her personality seemed to have been torn into two pieces" (191). As she leaves the shop, she gains a ravenous freedom she fears yet knows nothing about. Conrad subtly foreshadows her impending full exit from liminality: "She was a woman enjoying her complete irresponsibility and endless leisure, almost in the manner of a corpse" (198). Regardless of her newfound liberty from Verloc's liminality, she understands that "Murderers had friends, relations, helpers – they had knowledge. She had nothing. She was the most lonely of murderers that ever struck a mortal blow" (203) and that she is incapable of residing in liminal space without association to another liminal being.

The Secret Agent shows the high personal and social price that culture must pay for disrupting the dialectic between structure and anti-structure. In a functional social environment, a dialectic relationship between the structure and the *communitas* suggests that "men are released from structure into *communitas* only to return to structure revitalized by their experience of *communitas*." The exaggeration of structure "may well lead to pathological manifestation of *communitas* outside or against 'the law.'" In turn, exaggerating *communitas* "may be speedily followed by despotism, overbureaucratization, or other modes of structural rigidification" (Turner 1969: 129).

Conrad's analysis of British society reads like a criticism of his adoptive culture's failure to maintain a functional balance between structure and the anti-structure. Today, the novel reads as a warning against maximizing *communitas* as this "provokes maximization of structure, which in turn produces revolutionary strivings for renewed *communitas*" (129). Conrad's first-hand experience of the repercussions of existing "betwixt and between" states and cultures drives him to issue a fictional reminder of the dangers inherent in institutionalizing liminality, when several individuals, armed with ideology and discontent with the "limbo of statuslessness" (97) refuse to accept it as their existential condition.

Acknowledgement

A version of this essay was presented at the 32nd Annual International Conference of the Joseph Conrad Society (UK), London, July 2006.

Works cited

De Certeau, Michel. *The Practice of Everyday Life*, translated by Stephen F. Rendall. Los Angeles: University of California Press, 1988.

Goffman, Erving. *Asylum Essays on the Social Situation of Mental Patients and Other Inmates*. Garden City, New York: Doubleday, 1961.

Turner, Victor. *The Ritual Process: Structure and Anti-Structure*. Chicago: Aldine Publishing, 1969.

Van Gennep, Arnold. *The Rites of Passage* (1909), translated by Monika B. Vizedom and Gabrielle L. Caffee. Chicago: University of Chicago Press, 1960.

The Materialist-Scientific World View in *The Secret Agent*

Ludwig Schnauder
Universität Wien

FROM THE BEGINNING of *The Secret Agent* we are made aware of the importance of science in Edwardian society. First Secretary Vladimir of the presumably Russian Embassy tells Verloc that he will lose his job if he does not commit a bomb outrage in order to frighten Britain into passing repressive legislation against foreign anarchists. Vladimir's suggested target is "the sacro-sanct fetish of to-day": science (29). For him this fetishistic belief's symbolic embodiment is the Royal Observatory, Greenwich, and he therefore directs Verloc to "Go for the first meridian" (33). His target is well-chosen. In 1884, Greenwich had been made the keeper of Standard World Time and thereby acquired immense national and international prestige. The bomb outrage, however, gets nowhere near "raising the howl of execration" (32) he desires. The Assistant Commissioner dismisses the affair as "without gravity" and refers to it as "Barefaced audacity amounting to childishness of a peculiar sort" (107). Ten days after it happens, the outrage is already forgotten. If we read this miserable failure metaphorically, we could argue that it supports Vladimir's analysis of the status of science. It and the concomitant materialist-scientific world view have become unassailable and no longer vulnerable to attack. This essay will examine how far the novel as a whole supports such a reading, and to what uses it puts science and the materialist-scientific world view.

Two of the novel's characters can be classified as scientists. An anarchist and "ex-medical student without a degree" (40), Ossipon is a fanatic adherent of the theories of Lombroso, who believed that so-called "'criminal degenerates,' epileptics, and 'idiots' could be recognized and categorized by such physical features as the shape of their ears or lips" (Knowles and Moore 2000: 206).[1] Ossipon appears to have lost the

[1] For a discussion of Conrad's use of Lombrosian theories in the novel, see the essays by Harrington and Watts in the present collection.

ability to view his fellow humans as individuals and regards them in terms of Lombrosian typologies. He identifies Winnie, on the run from the police after killing her husband, as a criminal degenerate: "He gazed at her cheeks, at her nose, at her eyes, at her ears. . . . Bad! . . . Fatal! . . . a murdering type" (222). By reducing Winnie to an object of study, he distances himself emotionally from her and renounces responsibility for abandoning her with all her money in his pocket. He is criticized for the way he fetishizes a specific scientific theory and in invoking Lombroso "as an Italian peasant recommends himself to his favourite saint" (222) has exchanged one set of superstitions for another. His scientific fanaticism is ironically undermined by his vulnerability to his own diagnosis; his physical traits identify him as a Lombrosian degenerate and a congenital criminal: "A bush of crinkly yellow hair topped his red, freckled face, with a flattened nose and prominent mouth cast in the rough mould of the negro type. His almond-shaped eyes leered languidly over the high cheek bones" (39).

The Professor likewise has a scientific background. The "once assistant demonstrator in chemistry at some technical institute," who also worked in a "laboratory of a manufactory of dyes" (62), holds a world view that can be interpreted as an extremist version of Social Darwinism: "Exterminate! ... First the blind, then the deaf and the dumb, then the halt and the lame" (226). When Ossipon anxiously asks him, "And what remains?", his answer is: "I remain – if I am strong enough" (226). The irony undermining this declaration is that physically The Professor is the exact opposite of the Nietzschean superman he believes himself to be: his "physique" is of "lamentable inferiority" (52); he is "frail, insignificant, shabby, miserable" (231) and "unwholesome looking" (68); and he speaks with a weak, rasping voice. The insistence on his large ears, "thin like membranes … standing far out from the sides of his frail skull" (226), suggests that he is a Lombrosian degenerate. If his programme of extermination were implemented, he would be among the first to go. Heat's thoughts take this direction when he contemplates The Professor's appearance: "the physical wretchedness of that being, so obviously not fit to live, was ominous" (76).

These characters can be read as a warning against scientific fanaticism and its dehumanizing tendency; however, their pseudo-science is not an attack upon science as such. It cannot even be claimed that the novel distances itself from the dubious theories of degeneration – after all, the ironic point being made about both is that their physical traits identify them as degenerate and reveal them as potential victims of theories they espouse.

The perspective on the world in *The Secret Agent* is materialist-scientific and informed by concepts associated with Darwin and Darwinism. The novel portrays a social system that seems to reflect the laws of Natural Selection, such as the struggle for survival and the survival of the fittest. These tendencies are reinforced by the values and the workings of capitalism. As Jeremy Hawthorn puts it, in this society "people … treat other people as means to ends, as objects to be manipulated, rather than as fully human individuals" (1979: 74). Vladimir uses Verloc to implement his bombing plan; Verloc, in turn, uses Stevie to carry it out; Karl Yundt and Ossipon exploit their female companions to survive; the Assistant Commissioner uses his wife to gain access to society's highest levels; Winnie has married Verloc to protect her mother and Stevie; Inspector Heat wants to use Michaelis as a scapegoat to bring the investigation into the Greenwich bombing to a quick conclusion; Michaelis himself uses the Lady Patroness to enable him to write his autobiography.

Only the innocent Stevie seems granted insight into this system of mutual exploitation. When he realizes that the cabman whips his decrepit horse *not* because "his soul was cruel and his heart evil" (122) but because he needs to feed himself and his family, he feels "indignation and horror at one sort of wretchedness having to feed upon the anguish of the other" (132). According to Jacques Berthoud, the conclusion Stevie laboriously arrives at – "Bad world for poor people" (132) – shows how he "manages to conceive of the poor as part of a veritable system of suffering, in which the relief of misery requires the infliction of misery" (1978: 140). Berthoud, however, also emphasizes that this "vision of society as some kind of pain generator is clearly not one in terms of which a normal life can be led" (140). This might explain why all the other characters close their eyes to this society's nature and follow Winnie's maxim that "things do not stand much looking into" (136).

The Secret Agent, however, not only suggests that Darwinian forces determine our lives externally but also internally. Darwin insisted that humans are emphatically part of nature and emphasized the close relationship between humanity and our animal ancestors. As Avrom Fleishman summarizes: "The entire society in *The Secret Agent* comes to be seen as a jungle of animal forms obeying the laws of predatory survival. Alien to this world, forced to live in it yet inevitably devoured, men acquire the characters of beasts" (1965: 209).

These creatures are presented as largely controlled by animal instincts barely hidden beneath an ordinary or even elegant exterior, almost in the manner of the creatures in H. G. Wells's *The Island of Dr Moreau* (1896). Verloc, for instance, appears to strangers as if he were a respectable "well to do mechanic," "picture-frame maker" or "locksmith" (16). He seems "thoroughly domesticated," and his mother-in-law believes him to possess a "heavy good nature" and a "kind and generous disposition" (11, 12). His ordinariness is, however, undermined by the fact that he sells his wares "With a firm, steady eyed impudence, which seemed to hold back the threat of some abominable menace" (10). Verloc, we are thus reminded, is not an ordinary shopkeeper but a purveyor of pornography whose own sexual instincts are pronounced. His hardly repressed violence manifests itself in his dreams of revenge on Vladimir and the "Embassy people" (152). He wishes to be let "loose in there with a cudgel for half an hour" and to "keep on hitting till there wasn't a single unbroken bone left amongst the whole lot" (185) and then would "cut their hearts out one after another" (152).

Vladimir, too, veers between the civilized and the instinctual-animalistic. His sensitive and cultivated looks and his "drawing room reputation as an agreeable and entertaining man" (20) contrast starkly with his talk of murder, butchery, destruction, and bombing campaigns. He is able to switch with perfect ease between a refined and a savage mode of speaking and behaving, at one moment speaking French or "idiomatic English without the slightest trace of a foreign accent" (21), at another availing himself of "an amazingly guttural intonation not only utterly un-English, but absolutely un-European" (24). During part of the interview he is "Lying far back in the deep armchair, with squarely spread elbows … throwing one leg over a thick knee" (21); later he "advanced into the room with such determination that the very ends of his quaintly old-fashioned bow-necktie seemed to bristle with unspeakable menaces" (24).

Winnie most powerfully illustrates how closely the ordinary and the savage may be intertwined. In the novel's first half she is a taciturn housewife who cares for her weak-minded brother and fulfils her wifely duties. What could, however, make us suspect early on that her "unfathomable indifference" (10) and "stony reserve" (50) are a mere façade is that her "temperament" is described as "maternal and *violent*" (182; emphasis added) and that her "militant love" (186) for Stevie is said to have "the unerring nature and the force of an instinct" (137). When her brother is killed, she regards her marital contract with Verloc ended and momentarily feels like "a free woman" (189). Shortly afterwards, however, her instincts take control of her and she kills, becoming what Ossipon calls a "savage woman" (216). Into her "plunging blow" (197), she puts "the simple ferocity of the age of caverns, and the unbalanced nervous fury of the age of barrooms" (197).

Although Winnie's atavistic transformation is an extreme example of the way the bestial may at any time break through the surface of the ordinary – in the way that in Stevenson's *The Strange Case of Dr Jekyll and Mr Hyde* (1886) the brute and the savage overpower the normative – the novel in general insists that *all* characters are to some extent controlled by animal instincts. Particularly pernicious and pervasive is egoism, which can be seen as a variant of the survival instinct. The investigation into the bombing, for instance, reveals how professional decisions can be based upon private self-interest. Among the reasons why Chief Inspector Heat wants to turn Michaelis into a scapegoat are his desire to protect his informer Verloc, his aversion to "meddle with the desperate ferocity of The Professor" (96), and his vindictive desire to get even with him for having been released on ticket-of-leave due to journalists who exploited "the sentimental aspect of his imprisonment either for purposes of their own or for no intelligible purpose" (85). In general, the anarchist's arrest would be the most convenient way of proceeding as it would bring the investigation to a rapid and satisfactory conclusion. As Heat knows, "the rules of the game did not so much protect Michaelis" as other individuals whose arrest would be "a more complicated matter" (95).

Although the Assistant Commissioner is superior in more than a hierarchical sense to his Chief Inspector, his intercession in Michaelis's favour has not much to do with ideas of legality, the fear of a possible miscarriage of justice, or saving an innocent man from imprisonment. It is mainly due to his "instinct of self preservation" (89) – he wants to safeguard his domestic peace. Michaelis, after all, enjoys the favour of an aristocratic society hostess who has an excellent influence on his petulant wife. He knows that the Lady Patroness's "arbitrary kindness would not brook patiently any interference with Michaelis' freedom" (87) which, in turn, would make his married life more difficult. He therefore comes to a conclusion "extremely unbecoming his official position without being really creditable to his humanity. 'If the fellow is laid hold of again … she will never forgive me'" (89). From this moment on he proceeds to turn the Chief Inspector "inside out like an old glove" (93) and – due to the unexpected information he divulges – succumbs "to a fascinating temptation" (103) to take on the case himself. Once again this resolution, grounded in egoism, smacks of self-indulgence. After all, he is not only unhappy in his marriage but also in his job. Annoyed with his dependence "on too many subordinates and too many masters" (80), he finds the "desk work" he is forced to do "the bane of his existence because of its confined nature and apparent lack of reality" (104). "A born detective" (92) possessing "an adventurous disposition" (89), he cannot resist the chance to escape the "futility of office work" (80) and "do some real work for his salary" (93) for the first time since taking up his appointment.

The Darwinian perspective is so consistently deployed in *The Secret Agent* that even concepts of morality and altruism are ambiguous. For instance, when Heat contemplates Stevie's mangled remains, he is so affected by what he sees that he rises "by the force of sympathy, which is a form of fear, above the vulgar conceptions of time" (71). This would mean that altruistic feelings or actions arise from anxiety for one's own well-being and are therefore informed by egoism. Similar scepticism pervades the portrayal of Stevie's compassion. Although critics have seen him as the novel's moral centre, a variant of the "holy idiot,"[2] he is not exempt from the narrator's Darwinian perspective, and the animal imagery so frequent in the novel is also used for him.

His moral qualities are not informed by "turning the other cheek" but are part of a chain of instinctive, uncontrollable reflexes: "The anguish of immoderate compassion was succeeded by the pain of an innocent but pitiless rage" (130). Pushed to extremes, this blind rage might even drive him to homicide.[3] John Lyon adds that Stevie's compassion is "not straightforwardly altruistic since it is so intensely and narrowly bound up with his own 'morbid horror and dread of physical pain'" (2004: xii). It is also suggested that Stevie's moral notions are merely the result of conditioning. Thus his belief that Mr Verloc is "*good*" (135) is an "ethical fact" "established, erected, consecrated … behind Mr Verloc's back, for reasons that had nothing to do with abstract morality" (135). The narrator also tells us that the "main sanctions of Stevie's self restraint" have been his "father's anger, the irritability of gentlemen lodgers, and Mr Verloc's predisposition to immoderate grief" (135). The narrative's relentless Darwinism not only undermines the moral value of Stevie's compassion but also that of Winnie's and her mother's sacrifices for him. As Allan Hunter argues: "It seems they are inherently – genetically –

---

[2] For instance, Berthoud (1978: 141) and Fleishman (1965: 204).

[3] Hearing of cruelty in the German army, Stevie flies into such a rage that Winnie takes the carving knife from him. According to her, "he would have stuck that officer like a pig if he had seen him then" (51).

predisposed towards acts of abnegation that Conrad saw as typical of women. ... If natural selection has made sure that the two women are likely to act that way, then their altruism is instinctive, not really conscious. Can it therefore *be* altruism?" (1983: 176). Although Winnie and her mother are forced into "acts of abnegation" at least as much by economic necessity as by predisposition, it is true that Winnie's and her mother's devotion to Stevie is frequently described in instinctual terms.

Even more troubling than the idea that their love for Stevie might be "mere" instinct is that their sacrifices initiate a tragic chain of cause and effect that inexorably leads to the destruction of the very person they mean to save. The first link in this chain is Winnie's mother's decision to retire to an almshouse in order to strengthen Stevie's "moral claim" (125) on her daughter and son-in-law. This "move of deep policy" (125) is tragically successful. Even though Stevie has been "the unconscious presiding genius" (183) over Winnie's life, too, now that their mother is gone, her "quasi-maternal affection" (13) for her brother is intensified. She redoubles her efforts to recommend his usefulness and devotion to her husband and even tells him that "*You* could do anything with that boy" (140).

Verloc, who has hitherto "extended as much recognition to Stevie as a man not particularly fond of animals may give to his wife's beloved cat" (35), starts to feel flattered by "the extraordinary character of the influence he apparently has over Stevie" (178) and even agrees to let him come along on his walks. While Winnie believes that "the supreme illusion of her life" (184) is about to be realized – namely, that Verloc should behave like the loving father Stevie never had – the reader already knows that Verloc's kindness is irresponsible selfishness. Made desperate by Vladimir, he has decided to use Stevie as an unwitting accomplice in the bomb plot. When he later tries to justify his action he puts his finger upon a painful truth: "Strike me dead if I ever would have thought of the lad for that purpose. It was you who kept on shoving him in my way" (193). According to Aaron Fogel, altruism is at the root of the tragic course of events that leads to Stevie's destruction: "the Euripidean plot … [sharpens] the sense of causality, to realize the idea that sympathy itself causes the tragedy: it is the effective cause and not only the permeating affect. As mænads of pity and charity, Winnie and her mother involuntarily help to kill Stevie, driven not by intoxication but by pity" (1996: 188).

This subversion of traditional morality raises the question whether the novel implies that in a materialist-scientific world ethical principles are obsolete. If the answer is "Yes," then *The Secret Agent* aligns itself with Nietzsche's radical materialism as expressed in *The Twilight of the Gods* (1889):

> Christianity is a system, a consistently thought out and *complete* view of things. If one breaks out of it a fundamental idea, the belief in God, one thereby breaks the whole thing to pieces: one has nothing of any consequence left in one's hands… Christian morality is a command: its origin is transcendental … it possesses truth only if God is truth – it stands or falls with the belief in God.
>
> (translated by Hollingdale 2003: 80-81)

The Secret Agent, however, does not go so far. Showing that altruism is to some extent informed by egoism or that well-meant moral actions *may* have disastrous consequences does not invalidate morality. Nowhere is it implied that Winnie and her mother should not have sacrificed themselves for Stevie, or that the latter's compassion is worthless.

Some critics have argued that even though the novel does not have characters such as Emilia Gould, Monygham, or Marlow who vindicate moral principles against all odds by deliberately basing their actions upon them, we can attribute a moral quality to the narrator despite his lofty position and his relentless irony. J. Hillis Miller explains the function of these characteristics as follows:

> To describe this town London from the point of view of someone blindly enclosed in it would be no way out of the darkness. The nature of the collective dream is invisible to the dreamers because it determines what is seen and how it is judged. If society is to be exposed there must be a withdrawal to some vantage point outside it. (1966: 44)

This is why a detached point of view becomes necessary. Although he does not explicitly say so, the terms Miller uses imply a comparison between Conrad's narrator and aspects of Schopenhauer's philosophy.[4] According to the latter, we are relentlessly subject to the will, which manifests itself in the world and in our bodies; however, Schopenhauer recognizes special moments of contemplation during which the

---

[4] In philosophical terms Schopenhauer, of course, is not a materialist. Nevertheless, his emphasis on the power of the instincts and his critique of Christian morality anticipate Darwinian and Nietzschean ideas.

"miserable pressure of the will" is lifted and we are free to view and gain insight into "the universal spectacle of the will" (Safranski 1989: 216).

In *The Secret Agent*, the narrator's disillusioned but clear-sighted perspective might be regarded as the extended realization of such a moment. What is more, Schopenhauer's moments of contemplation are characterized by "non-participatory viewing, without being involved in blinding seriousness" (Safranski 1989: 339). Again, this seems an apt description of the narrator whose irony frequently makes for grim comedy. Arguably, the novel's effect upon the reader is similar to that of Schopenhauer's "will-less" moments and can thus be described as cathartic.[5] Schopenhauer apart, the narrator's commitment to reveal the truth about the human condition in a materialist-scientific universe also reminds us of Conrad's view of the writer's task in the "Preface" to *The Nigger of the "Narcissus"*: "By the power of the written word, to make you hear, to make you feel … before all, to make you *see*" (x). To achieve this moral duty Conrad needed to create a narrator who "would enable me to say all I felt I would have to say *in scorn as well as in pity*" (7; emphasis added). The complex ways in which pity originates in the novel, whether despite or because of this scorn, have been the subject of debate. John Lyon argues that

> moments of local intensity, fully dramatized, overcome the structural ironies in the course of the experience of reading, while such moments are further overlaid by a narrative commentary which … can at once distance and entangle the reader. The security of ironic withdrawal is itself ironically unmasked for the reader: it dissolves in the face of the absorbing, if melodramatic, immediacy of the "scenic present."
>
> (2004: xxxvi)

Hugh Epstein similarly claims that "the novel does retrieve moments in which words are held to express a significance that resists the irony that crowds upon them" (1993: xiii). Such instants occur during the scenes featuring Winnie, her mother, and Stevie. The achronological structure informs the reader in advance that the two women's attempts to secure Stevie's future are doomed; however, because of the "immediacy and cinematic precision" (Lyon 2004: xxxvi) with which the characters' suffering is rendered we are made to experience a pity that "constitutes a

---

[5] Such an interpretation is also suggested by Fogel's analysis quoted above in which he compares the plot to a Euripidean tragedy.

rebuttal of the sentimentalism and patronage that characterizes well-bred sympathy" (Berthoud 1996: 114).

Out of context, Stevie's remark about the nature of society – "Bad world for poor people" (132) – appears banal and trivial; however, the effort it costs him to reach this conclusion and to verbalize it "stands as the index of a moral responsiveness greater than the words themselves and remains active in unresolved opposition to the almost excessive authority of the narration" (Epstein 1993: xiii). This analysis also holds true for Winnie's reply to his insight that "Nobody can help that" or the cabman's "This ain't an easy world" (132, 129). These utterances all express "the lament of poor humanity, rich in suffering and indigent in words" and contain "the very cry of truth" that is "found in a worn and artificial shape picked up somewhere among the phrases of sham sentiment" (223).

As we have seen, *The Secret Agent* consistently employs a materialist-scientific world view and, in contrast to its Victorian forebears, rejects any compromise with the remnants of the theological one. The novel therefore asks its readers to readjust their view of themselves, of the species, and of human institutions and thus of their conceptions of morality and altruism. Nevertheless, this is not a novel without morality; indeed, the narrator's commitment "to make us *see*" may be interpreted as a subtle moral affirmation. As a consequence, the narrator may be said to speak, implicitly at least, "to the latent feeling of fellowship with all creation – and to the subtle but invincible, conviction of solidarity that knits together the loneliness of innumerable hearts" ("Preface": viii).

Acknowledgement

A version of this essay was presented at the 32nd Annual International Conference of the Joseph Conrad Society (UK), London, July 2006.

Works cited

Berthoud, Jacques. *Joseph Conrad: The Major Phase.* Cambridge: Cambridge University Press, 1978.

——. "*The Secret Agent.*" In *The Cambridge Companion to Joseph Conrad*, edited by J. H. Stape. 100-21. Cambridge: Cambridge University Press, 1996.

Epstein, Hugh. "Introduction." Conrad, *The Secret Agent*, edited by Hugh Epstein. vii-xxiii. Wordsworth Classics. Ware: Wordsworth, 1993.

Fleishman, Avrom. "The Symbolic World of *The Secret Agent.*" *English Literary History* 32 (1965): 196-219.

Fogel, Aaron. "The Fragmentation of Sympathy in *The Secret Agent.*" In *New Casebooks: Joseph Conrad*, edited by Elaine Jordan. 168-92. Basingstoke: Macmillan, 1996.

Hawthorn, Jeremy. *Joseph Conrad: Language and Fictional Self-Consciousness.* London: Edward Arnold, 1979.

Hillis Miller, J. *Poets of Reality: Six Twentieth-Century Writers.* Cambridge, Massachusetts: Harvard University Press, 1966.

Hunter, Allan. *Joseph Conrad and the Ethics of Darwinism.* London: Croom Helm, 1983.

Knowles, Owen, and Gene M. Moore. *Oxford Reader's Companion to Conrad.* Oxford: Oxford University Press, 2000.

Lyon, John. "Introduction." Conrad, *The Secret Agent*, edited by John Lyon. xi-xxxix. Oxford World's Classics. Oxford: Oxford University Press, 2004.

Nietzsche, Friedrich. *Twilight of the Idols and The Anti-Christ*, translated by R. J. Hollingdale. London: Penguin, 2003.

Safranski, Rüdiger. *Schopenhauer and the Wild Years of Philosophy.* London: Weidenfeld and Nicolson, 1989.

Sarah Bernhardt in the title-role of Victorien Sardou's *La Tosca*, photographed by Félix Nadar (Bibliothèque Nationale de France: ICO PER 2369 [14])

Tosca's Kiss: Sardou, Puccini, and *The Secret Agent*

J. H. Stape and Allan H. Simmons
Research Fellow and Reader in
St Mary's College, Strawberry Hill

Questo è il bacio di Tosca![1]
– Floria Tosca upon stabbing Baron Scarpia, Puccini, *Tosca*, II.v

CONRAD'S KNOWLEDGE and use of opera has been the focus of several discussions, and as Laurence Davies has stated, "Conrad knew enough about nineteenth-century opera to refer to its techniques, and even to adapt them to his own purposes" (forthcoming).[2] Our intention here is to extend the range to which Davies refers to include Giacomo Puccini's *Tosca* (1900), based upon the French play from which his librettists Giuseppe Giacosa and Luigi Illica drew their libretto, and Victorien Sardou's *La Tosca* (1887), written as a vehicle for Sarah Bernhardt. We wish to suggest that this work – in both its forms – may influence not only the technique but also the themes, plotting, and characterization of the murder scene and its aftermath in *The Secret Agent.*

The Play and Opera in London

Did Conrad ever see *Tosca* or *La Tosca*? His correspondence provides no evidence that he saw either or both works. It would, however, have been scarcely possible for anyone with a passing interest in the London theatre of the 1890s and the early twentieth century to be unaware of the play or the opera. Conrad had several opportunities to see the former with Bernhardt herself in the title-role and to hear what Bernard Shaw famously called Puccini's "shabby little shocker." It was Shaw, too, who coined the term "Sardoodledom" to describe plays where action dwarfs character (Carner 1985: 1). For his part, Conrad described Sardou as a "good mechanic" when advising Edward Garnett to learn playcraft from him (*CL4* 428).

---

[1] Translation: "*This* is Tosca's kiss!"

[2] On Conrad's interest in opera, see Baldanza (1980), Knowles and Moore (2000), and Davies (forthcoming).

Bernhardt's triumphant London début in the role occurred in July 1888, the first performances having taken place at the Théâtre de Porte St-Martin, Paris, the previous November. During the play's first London run Conrad was in the Antipodes, but Bernhardt returned in *La Tosca* in the summers of 1889, 1890, and 1892, annually during the London seasons of 1894-99, and again in the summers of 1901-03 (Wearing 1976 and 1981).[3] December 1889 saw an English language version of the play at the Garrick Theatre (*Times*), and a parody, *Tra-la-la Tosca, or The High-Toned Soprano and the Villain Bass*, "A Perversion of *Tosca*" by F. C. Burnard with music by "Florian Pascal," ran for 45 performances at the Royalty Theatre in January and February 1890.[4]

The accolades during Bernhardt's second season in the play were even warmer than those for the first. *The Times* reviewer commented that "Never, indeed, has she played with greater witchery, charm, or emotional power" (19 July 1889: 4). She thereafter toured the play, a staple of her annual repertoire (in French), in Canada and the United States as well as in South America. The American novelist and short-story writer Willa Cather, who travelled to Omaha, Nebraska, to see it (Funda and Andersen 2004: 10), was so struck by Bernhardt's acting and famous "*voix d'or*" that she vividly (if with slight inaccuracy), recalls the play in her first short story, "Peter" (1892):

> Once, a French woman came and played for weeks, he did not remember her name now. He did not remember her face very well either, for it changed so, it was never twice the same. But the beauty of it, and the great hunger men felt at the sight of it, that he remembered. Most of all he remembered her voice. He did not know French, and could not understand a word she said, but it seemed to him that she must be talking the music of Chopin. And her voice, he thought he should know that in the other world. The last night she played a play in which a man touched her arm, and she stabbed him. (1970: 542)

The opera based on the play was first performed in England by the Royal Opera, Covent Garden, with the composer in attendance, on 12

[3] For a discussion of Bernhardt's London career, which began with *Phèdre* with the Comedie Française in 1879, see Stokes (2005).

[4] *The Times* reviewer slated the performers but thought additional rehearsal time would render the burlesque more enjoyable. In this send-up, after Tosca murders Scarpia with a playbill, she covers his face with a dish-cloth; Cavaradossi is executed by a phalanx of photographers (*Times*, 10 January 1890: 10).

July 1900, not long after the Roman première at the Teatro Costanzi of 14 January and the La Scala première, under Arturo Toscanini, of 17 March.[5] It was reprised in London in June 1901 (with Bernhardt appearing in the play shortly thereafter and thus giving theatre-goers the opportunity of seeing both versions of the work in rapid succession). It re-entered the repertory in the autumn seasons of 1904 and 1905, and the summers of 1906 and 1907, the June performances of the latter year with a cast headed by Enrico Caruso as Mario Cavaradossi and Antonio Scotti as the villain, Baron Scarpia (*The Times*, 15 June 1907: 10). Conrad also had the opportunity to refresh his memory of *Tosca* in Montpellier between his arrival on 18 December 1906 and the opera's last performance for the season on 3 January 1907, after which a strike closed the opera house (situated in the Place de la Comédie across from the Hôtel Riche et Continental where the Conrads were staying) for the duration of his sojourn (*Le Petit Méridional*, 3-4 January 1907).

During Caruso's appearances in the opera in June 1907, the Conrads were temporarily resident in Kensington for Jessie Conrad's confinement, where the delivery of her second son occurred in August, with Conrad writing Chapters 4-5 and much of Chapter 6 during this period (Harkness and Reid 1990: 280). He "completed" the novel in early November, although he returned to it for extensive revisions and expansion in the spring and summer of 1907, in particular of the murder scene and the ending, with final revision in proof being made in August, shortly before the book's publication by Methuen on 12 September.

From *La Tosca* to *Tosca*

Intrigue surrounds Puccini's involvement in *La Tosca*, which had been a dramatic success for almost a decade before he showed a serious interest in it. He twice saw Bernhardt in the title-role, in 1890 in Milan and in 1895 in Florence. The play's operatic potential, with an opera singer as its heroine, is obvious, and was noted by the 83-year-old Verdi, who declared that he would have attempted the work had he been young. (George Bernard Shaw commented in his review of *Manon Lescaut*'s Covent Garden première in May 1894: "Puccini looks to me more like the heir of Verdi than any of his rivals" [Anon., 1992: 1405].)

---

[5] The libretto (in Italian only) and a history of first performances are conveniently available at Stanford University's *Opera Glass* website. Quotations from the libretto are from this source.

Transformed into a libretto by Giuseppe Illica, Sardou's play had originally attracted Alberto Franchetti (1860-1942), "the Meyerbeer of Italy," a wealthy aristocrat who dabbled in operatic composition and had to his credit *Asrael* (1888) and *Cristoforo Colombo* (1892). Giovanni Ricordi, the music publisher, and Illica convinced him that an operatic version of *La Tosca* would fail, both because of its brutal subject matter, involving scenes of torture, attempted rape, murder, and suicide, and because of its contentious political and historical background: Republicans against Royalists; Austria at war with Italy; Bonaparte against Melas; and so on. The day after Franchetti relinquished his claims, Ricordi presented Puccini with Illica's draft libretto and a contract. Giacosa was called in as Illica's collaborator, and Sardou reportedly found their work better than his original.

Examples of how the "holy trinity," as Ricordi called them, of Puccini, Giacosa, and Illica – a partnership responsible for *La bohème* (1896), *Tosca* (1900), and *Madama Butterfly* (1904) – improved on Sardou are not hard to find. For instance, looking at Scarpia lying dead on the floor, Tosca reflects: "*È avanti a lui tremava tutta Roma!*" [And before him all Rome trembled!]. Sardou's original is: "*Et c'est devant ça que tremblait toute une ville!*" [And before *that* a whole city trembled (148)]. The operatic version is at once more politically precise and expansive. Whereas the play suggests that the city has been wrong to fear such a figure, whose insignificance is signalled by the contemptuous "*ça*," Puccini's version conveys the horror of Scarpia's reign. As a student of the composer notes, it "justifies Tosca's killing of him not as the act of a woman defending her honour but as a blow struck in the cause of liberty against a man who had terrorized not just vaguely 'a whole city' but the Eternal City itself!" (Hughes 1959: 103).

Used as a lever to persuade Franchetti, the opera's political dimension exerted a contemporary *frisson*. In Paris in May 1896 to supervise the French première of *La bohème* (Carner 1985: 17), Puccini missed the uprisings in Italy, that included bomb-throwing and the massacre of rioters in Milan. Four years later the opera's first night in Rome was touched by a strained political atmosphere and coloured by rumours of an assassination plot to blow up the Queen in the royal box, with the conductor primed to strike up the national anthem should anything untoward occur during the performance.

Floria Tosca and Winnie Verloc

Set in Rome on the day of the Battle of Marengo,[6] the play's Napoleonic backdrop is important to its plot and characterization. Tosca's lover, the painter Mario Cavaradossi, an ardent Bonapartist, stands opposed to the supporter and instrument of tyranny, Baron Scarpia, Rome's feared and autocratic chief of police who relies on a system of spies, informers, and torture to maintain an ideological panopticon over the city's Napoleonic sympathizers. The direct confrontation between Cavaradossi and Scarpia in the famous torture scene pits the painter's libertarian and "modern" values against Scarpia, the embodiment of reactionary forces, decadent aristocratic privilege, and political repression.

Although the play's political dimensions might have had an immediate appeal to Conrad – a keen student of things Napoleonic – the real interest in placing the play and the opera in juxtaposition with *The Secret Agent* lies in their possible influence on structure, pacing, incident, and character in the novel's murder scene and in Winnie's suicide.

In one of the play's most dramatic scenes, greatly heightened by Puccini's musical treatment, Tosca is offered the devil's choice of either allowing her lover, Cavaradossi, whose torture by Scarpia she has already overheard, to die, or to bestow her favours upon the corrupt aristocrat. She feigns the surrender of her person, and then, surreptitiously taking a knife from a nearby dining-table, stabs Scarpia to death at the very moment he opens his arms to claim his prize, uttering the harrowing words to her would-be rapist: "*This* is Tosca's kiss!"[7] Facing the continuation of her erotic servitude, Winnie Verloc, in a similar victim position, no less dramatically liberates herself from it, stabbing Verloc to death with the same carving knife that he has used to serve himself to roast

---

[6] Napoleon triumphed over Austria's forces under Lieutenant General Michael Melas in the brief but crucial battle fought on 14 June 1800. For a useful summary of the event, see "Marengo Revisited: A Bicentennial Review" (2006).

[7] In Conrad's "The Idiots" and *Victory*, knives, stabbing, and suicide play a central role. In the early story, Susan Bacadou stabs her husband with a pair of scissors to free herself from a marriage of sexual servitude, and, in *Victory*, Lena famously views her acquisition of Ricardo's knife as capturing the "very sting of death" (399), an association that reworks an idea adumbrated in *The Secret Agent* where Ossipon views Winnie as "twined round him like a snake, not to be shaken off. She was not deadly. She was death itself – the companion of life" (217). (It is worth noting that in "The Idiots," Susan, like Tosca, leaps to her death after stabbing her sexual torturer to death.)

beef, that quintessential symbol of English middle-class domesticity.[8] Winnie's choice, made long ago, resembles that faced by Tosca: to trade her favours for the well-being of someone she loves and protects. In Winnie's case, she bargains her feeling and body to save Stevie from the world's utter indifference to his welfare; Tosca saves her lover from the barbarous Scarpia, who would put him to death for his political allegiances and as a display of power.

Winnie and Tosca both leap to their deaths upon learning that the freedom they have obtained from committing murder proves illusory and after becoming the victims of elaborate deceptions. Mrs Verloc, "the free woman," finds herself dependent once more upon a man, becoming, as it were, a "fallen woman," again negotiating her security via male power and in trading her favours this time with Ossipon whose intention to deceive and rob her takes shape the more she becomes reliant upon him. Bearing a safe-conduct out of Rome from Scarpia for herself and Cavaradossi, Tosca is the victim of a more elaborate deception. Scarpia takes his revenge even in death as the painter's mock execution at the Castel Sant'Angelo turns out to be a real one, moments after Tosca announces his "freedom" ("*Sei libero!*") to her lover, reveals how she killed their oppressor, and begs him to act his part convincingly after he is shot, when they will flee Rome by sea. The motifs of illusory liberty, deception, and suicide structure the conclusion of *La Tosca / Tosca* and *The Secret Agent* as the women victims are lured into a trap that contains the classical element of surprise (Ossipon's jumping from the moving train with Winnie's money and Scarpia's providing a safe-conduct that proves, in fact, to be a death warrant).

---

8 Food, eroticism, and death similarly figure in *La Tosca/Tosca*. The opera singer's presence interrupts Scarpia's repast and, in a symbolic chain of association, his oral/gustatory gratification is displaced onto Tosca herself. In Sardou, the beast-of-prey motif is explicit on three occasions: Tosca twice characterizes Scarpia as a "*tigre*" (120, 159) and once as a "*bête feroce*" (147). In Giacosa and Illica's libretto, Scarpia's self-comparison to "an agile leopard" ("*Agil qual leopardo ti avvinghiasti all'amante*") attacking its prey makes explicit the consumption cycle of food, sex, death. Although the motif of predation and the beast imagery in *The Secret Agent* have been subject to considerable critical comment, it may be worth recalling that in the lead-up to the murder this chain of association includes "brute," "venomous beast," and "swine" (180); the image of Verloc baring his teeth "wolfishly" (185); his snarling; and his appearance as a "reflective beast … gloomier than a seal" (193).

The nexus of money, sex, and male power operates chillingly in both works to reveal the essentially predatory nature of the societies they portray, for even after Verloc's and Scarpia's deaths the women they have victimized are humiliated, constrained, and defeated, and their only recourse to power over their own lives is, ironically, the taking of them. Tosca at the very moment she does so is unable to escape fully, dying with her torturer's name upon her lips as she leaps from the parapet: "*O Scarpia, avanti a dio!*" [O Scarpia, we meet before God].[9]

Parallels: Sardou / Puccini / Conrad

If murder followed by suicide provides the most obvious parallel in incident between *La Tosca, Tosca*, and *The Secret Agent*, this pattern is reinforced by several shared conceptual, structural, and thematic elements as well as by a fundamentally dramatic modelling of the action, from which Conrad later carved out a stage play. The sinister musical phrase that opens the opera announces the theme of evil embodied in Scarpia and recurs throughout, even after his death at the close of Act 2. In *The Secret Agent*, Verloc's indolent self-centredness serves the same purpose, ultimately rendering him incapable even of understanding Winnie's devastation over Stevie's death, when such utterances as "What would it have been if you had lost me!" (177) appear heartlessly unaware. Scarpia's perfidious obsession and Verloc's self-absorption lead to the same end, providing two extremes of male treatment of women.

Detection, surveillance, torture – physical and emotional – and mis-recognition are crucial to both plots, which further share such motifs as thwarted dreams of a life in exile, gallows-references, and the domestication of violence that ensures collision of the public and private spheres. For example, the Assistant Commissioner's designation of the Greenwich affair as "a domestic drama" (222) recalls correspondences between worlds of state and the individual in *Tosca*, evident not only in the broader tragedy in which Cavaradossi and Tosca are implicated – "*L'uno al capestro, | l'altra fra le mie braccia*" [The one to the gallows, | the other to my arms] as Scarpia promises himself – but also subtly in the shepherd boy's folk lament at the opening of Act 3, itself disturbed by

---

[9] The operatic version is dramatically superior to the original in which Tosca, cornered by Spoletta and Scarpia's other henchmen responds to Spoletta's "*Je t'enverrai rejoindre ton amant!*" [I shall send you to rejoin your lover!] by jumping from the parapet with the words "*J'y vais canailles!*" [I'm going there, villains!] (161).

the Scarpia theme and sung against the backdrop of church bells ringing for matins.

Structurally, too, the works depend upon displaced action that subordinates dramatized violence in favour of its emotional and psychological consequences. Thus, the distanced presentation of Stevie's dismemberment has its counterpart in Cavaradossi's off-stage torture, his head slowly crushed by the grimly parodic "crown of thorns" as his screams add to the emotional torture of Tosca by Scarpia, who clearly appreciates the moment sadistically in a voyeurism that has an aural component, as he relishes his rivals screams and gloats over Tosca's agony. This does not mean that the moment of Verloc's death, presented as a shadow-play, is denuded of drama, but rather that Conrad's dramatic action is fashioned in terms that approximate to the condition of opera. The novel's climactic scene is punctuated by references to "harmonising," "tenor," and "tone" (188, 189) when presenting the Verlocs' contrasted emotions and perspectives, the musical register serving as an ironic emphasis of their discordance and culminating in the metronomic "Tic, tic, tic" of Verloc's blood (198).

Perhaps the most striking structural parallel is Conrad's orchestration of Verloc's stabbing, with the rise to climax and gradual diminution of intensity followed by silence, a pattern common to both Sardou and Puccini. After the stabbing, Tosca first gloats over Scarpia's body – as Winnie specifically does not: "She adopted that easy attitude not in order to watch or gloat over the body of Mr Verloc" (198) – then calmly and ceremoniously places candles at his sides and a crucifix on his breast, leaving the room gradually. After her initial "immobility and silence" (198) Winnie panics, but Conrad closes his chapter in a prose equivalent of what Puccini does musically, in a fade-out focussing upon the seemingly trivial detail of Verloc's hat, the ironic symbol of his social respectability and ordinariness: "Then all became still. Mrs Verloc on reaching the door had stopped. A round hat disclosed in the middle of the floor by the moving of the table rocked slightly on its crown in the wind of her flight" (199).

The case for Conrad's knowledge of either Sardou or Puccini is by necessity circumstantial, relying on probability, and thus a matter of echoes, delicate shades, and shared concerns, what Cavaradossi in his first aria calls "*Recondita armonia*" [Hidden harmony]. Winnie's archetypal and mythic significance is enlarged by placing her in contiguity with Floria Tosca; eminently Continental works in conception, *La Tosca* and *Tosca* enter the debate then raging in England about the New Woman, partly through Conrad; and Conrad's art in *The Secret Agent* is illuminated by a focus on its operatic qualities. Sardou, a minor writer, provided major artists with incomparably rich raw materials, and Winnie and Tosca, a century after their creation, remain vivid, tragic figures identified by means of æsthetic and cultural palimpsest.

Acknowledgements

We should like to thank Laurence Davies for sharing his forthcoming essay on Conrad and opera with us and for encouraging us to explore this topic, and are grateful to Owen Knowles for comments on a draft of this essay.

The photograph of Sarah Bernhardt as Tosca is in the public domain.

Works cited

Books and articles

Anon. *The Great Composers and Their Music.* London: Marshall Cavendish, 1993.

Baldanza, Frank. "Opera in Conrad: 'More Real Than Anything in Life.'" *Studies in the Literary Imagination* 13 (1980): 1-16.

Carner, Mosco. *Giacomo Puccini: "Tosca."* Cambridge Opera Handbooks. Cambridge: Cambridge University Press, 1985.

Cather, Willa. "Peter" (1892). In *Willa Cather's Collected Short Fiction, 1892-1912*, edited by Virginia Faulkner. 541-43. Rev. edn. Lincoln: University of Nebraska Press, 1970.

Davies, Laurence. "Conrad in the Operatic Mode." In *Joseph Conrad and the Performing Arts*, edited by Richard J. Hand and Katherine Isobel Baxter (forthcoming).

Funda, Evelyn I., and Susan Andersen. "Predicting Willa Cather: Using 'Peter' and 'The Opinions, Tastes, and Fancies of William Cather, M.D.' as Introduction." *Teaching Cather* 4.2 (2004): 4-12.

Harkness, Bruce, and S. W. Reid. "The Texts." In Conrad, *The Secret Agent*, edited by Bruce Harkness and S. W. Reid. 235-327. The Cambridge Edition of the Works of Joseph Conrad. Cambridge: Cambridge University Press, 1990.

Hughes, Spike. *Famous Puccini Operas.* London: Robert Hale, 1959.

Knowles, Owen, and Gene M. Moore. "Opera." In *The Oxford Reader's Companion to Conrad.* 261-63. Oxford: Oxford University Press, 2000.

"Marengo Revisited: A Bicentennial Review." *War Times Journal* <www.wtj.com/articles/Marengo>. Accessed: October 2006.

Opera Glass. Stanford University <opera.stanford.edu>. Accessed: October 2006.

Sardou, Victorien. *La Tosca*. In *Théâtre complet*. 15 vols. 1: 1-161. Paris: Albin Michel, 1934-61.

Stokes, John. *The French Actress and her English Audience*. Cambridge: Cambridge University Press, 2005.

Wearing, J. P. *The London Stage: A Calendar of Plays and Players, 1890-1899*. 2 vols. Metuchen, New Jersey: Scarecrow Press, 1976.

———. *A Calendar of Plays and Players, 1900-1909*. 2 vols. Metuchen, New Jersey: Scarecrow Press, 1981.

Newspapers

Le Petit Méridional (Montpellier), December 1906-January 1907.

"Lyceum Theatre" [Rev. of British première of Sardou's *La Tosca*]. *The Times*, 10 July 1888: 5.

"Opera Comique Theatre" [Rev. of second London season of Sardou's *La Tosca*]. *The Times*, 19 July 1889: 4.

"Royal Opera" [Rev. of Enrico Caruso's performance in *Tosca*]. *The Times*, 15 June 1907: 10.

"Royalty Theatre." *The Times*, 10 January 1890: 10.

An Analogous Art: *The Secret Agent* and John Virtue's *London Paintings and Drawings*

Hugh Epstein
London

THOSE LUCKY ENOUGH to have seen the exhibition of John Virtue's *London Paintings* at The National Gallery in London, 9 March – 5 June 2005,[1] and the accompanying exhibition *London Drawings* at The Courtauld Institute, saw in the twelve huge canvasses (the largest ever hung by The National Gallery) and the hundred A4-size drawings surely the only visual images that can creatively be set alongside Conrad's depiction of a dissolving London, "cruel devourer of the world's light" ("Author's Note," 6), an "enormous town slumbering monstrously on a carpet of mud under a veil of raw mist" (224).

The London of *The Secret Agent* has attracted several pictorial re-imaginings: the films, whether for the cinema or television, always disappoint, their stolid realism at odds with the dark expressionism with which Conrad's writing inhabits London locations in order primarily to render them as textures that overpower small gestures of human connectedness. We read London not in the multifarious human commerce of its streets but, somewhat as Verloc does, through "a fragile film of glass stretched between him and the enormity of cold, black, wet, muddy, inhospitable accumulation of bricks, slates, and stones, things in themselves unlovely and unfriendly to man" (48).

Even Hitchcock's *Sabotage* (1936) entirely loses this sense of threatening encroachment after its brilliant opening frames. Editors fare only a little better in their attempts to find visual equivalents in paintings. Wordsworth Classics went for an architecturally exact depiction of the Houses of Parliament and Westminster Bridge by John MacVicar Anderson (1835-1915) for the cover of their 1993 edition, only to replace this in 2000 by John O'Connor's (1830-89) *St Pancras Hotel and Station from Pentonville Road*, a painting now popularly marketed under the title *Sunset*, which gives some indication of how the warm light it casts upon its tram- and carriage-thronged thoroughfare would give the prospective reader little sense of the London that emerges in the pages to follow.

---

[1] The exhibition received the South Bank Show Exhibition of the Year Award 2005.

Both Oxford World's Classics and Penguin Modern Classics more sensibly went for the significant John Atkinson Grimshaw (1836-93) for their respective 1983 and 1982 editions. Grimshaw was celebrated for his night scenes of cities, in which his palette was touched by the black glamour of smoke pollution and fog, somewhat in the manner of Whistler or of Monet's 1899 early morning sequence. Yet even here there is something too persistently representational in *Battersea Bridge by Moonlight* (1885) or *Hampstead Hill* (1883) to convey Conrad's vision of insulation and damp disintegration visited upon human consciousness by the edifices with which London buries in darkness its "five millions of lives" (6). Degas' *Interior* (1868-69), more recently known as *The Rape*, and Sickert's *Ennui* both offer a psychologized domestic interior space full of the unarticulated tensions of Brett Street, yet there is too insistent a narrative, too definite a set of relations, to make such pictures, contemporary though they are with the novel, fully suitable correspondences to Conrad's evocation of urban occlusion.

To turn from nineteenth-century impressionism and twentieth-century film realism to John Virtue's twenty-first-century expressionism is to experience an access of visual power and scope adequate to the disconcerting strangeness and the reach of *The Secret Agent.* Virtue's canvasses are overwhelming. Painted entirely in acrylic, black ink, and shellac, huge and with a tempestuously active surface of horizontals and verticals, rushes and swabs of black, of drips and spatterings on Turner-esque white gleams, Virtue's creation of London is as exhilarating and frightening as Conrad's. Greenwich, Somerset House, St Paul's, the NatWest Tower, the "Gherkin," Blackfriar's Bridge are all discernible, yet these canvasses are at their best when at their most abstract, when London is resolved into an accumulation of eroding presences bearing the accretions and depredations of time, soot, and human endeavour from which the human has all but disappeared.

Most obviously, in terms of *The Secret Agent*, one thinks of Chapter VII, in which the Assistant Commissioner ventures into the London night:

> His descent into the street was like the descent into a slimy aquarium from which the water had been run off. A murky, gloomy dampness enveloped him. The walls of the houses were wet, the mud of the roadway glistened with an effect of phosphorescence, and when he emerged into the Strand out of a narrow street by the side of Charing Cross Station the genius of the locality assimilated him. (114)

Landscape No. 709: Acrylic, black ink, and shellac on canvas (2003-04)

In Virtue's *London Paintings*, this sense of assimilation is achieved by the washes, the rubbings, the layering of various blacks worked over meticulously observed details of buildings, bridges, and river, turning topography into landscape. (Each of Virtue's works is a numbered "Landscape.") Equally, Conrad offers the atmosphere of a landscape rather than the exactitude of topography:

> A pleasurable feeling of independence possessed him when he heard the glass doors swing to behind his back with a sort of imperfect baffled thud. He advanced at once into an immensity of greasy slime and damp plaster interspersed with lamps, and enveloped, oppressed, penetrated, choked, and suffocated by the blackness of a wet London night, which is composed of soot and drops of water. (116)

That composition can be read directly from the surfaces of Virtue's canvasses, where spray paint and splatterings, sponges and J-cloths combine to produce all sorts of shadings and stipples that carry the history of the city's ceaseless erosion and rebuilding. But it is in Conrad's taking the Assistant Commissioner into a semi-abstract "immensity" that he is most like Virtue, or Virtue most like Conrad. So, later, Winnie Verloc's sense of her solitude as a "free woman" represents itself to her in terms that would find a mirror in the scope of Virtue's re-imagining of London: "the whole town of marvels and mud, with its maze of streets and mass of lights, was sunk in a hopeless night, rested at the bottom of a black abyss from which no unaided woman could hope to scramble out" (203).

Simon Schama has called Virtue's grand, dynamic landscapes "not a visual document of London … so much as an overwhelming *embodiment* of London" (2005: 21). In a rather over-excited appreciation – "Virtue's vision is the real London eye. Instead of detachment there is smashmouth contact ... the whipsaw excitement of the city; its rain-sodden, dirt-caked, foul-tempered, beery-eyed, jack-hammered, traffic-jammed nervy exhilaration" – Schama nevertheless finds in Virtue's works a prompting to meditate the same questions that have exercised Conrad's critics since the publication of the Preface to *The Nigger of the "Narcissus"*:

> By picturing I mean not just the attachment to description (for evidently that is not John Virtue's thing), but the evocation through the brush of something *about* a seen place, person or object … rather than a retinal report. So that we might well say that what John Virtue depicts is not London at all, but an idea of London, a sense of London (though not, I think, an *impression* of London).

This, surely, is part of the same discussion as "to hold up … the rescued fragment before all eyes in the light of a sincere mood" (x). But in the dismissal of the "retinal report" it must not be forgotten that Virtue's huge canvasses have been supported by two years of a very different sort of contributory activity – the hundreds of pencil drawings, observations of buildings grouped around the river, that Virtue undertook almost every morning between 2002 and 2004 from four precise locations. These spare, swiftly executed A4-drawings are the bare data of observations achieved under the conditions of space and time (as Virtue says, "You will not have that day again"): always the lines of roofs, upper storeys and their ranged windows; the Oxo Tower, Canary Wharf, the "Gherkin," St Paul's, Big Ben, Nelson's Column; always verticals and horizontals and the sense of the river, rarely depicted but washing through the foreground; a blank foreground, so much omitted yet to be inferred. Like Conrad's London and unlike Dickens's, this is a depopulated city, seeping away into its damp foundations even as it raises new lines for the eye on its horizons.

Study from roof of Somerset House, looking east

These are not visual equivalents for anything we could point to directly in *The Secret Agent*, but they are products of a similar sense of the city having its own life, an indifferent activity of rising and falling like the beast "slumbering monstrously on a carpet of mud under a veil of raw mist" where "the robust form" of Comrade Ossipon

> was seen crossing the streets without life or sound, or diminishing in the interminable straight perspectives of shadowy houses bordering empty roadways lined by strings of gas lamps. He walked through Squares, Places, Ovals, Commons, through monotonous streets with unknown names where the dust of humanity settles inert and hopeless out of the stream of life. (224)

Landscape No. 710: Acrylic, black ink and shellac, (2003-04) (and facing page)

To achieve this sort of writing, Conrad has reduced topographical detail to a geometric denotation deliberately removed from its sources in human endeavours, hopes, and fancies; so in his observational drawings, Virtue summarizes and simplifies the city into distant lines and foregrounds of suggestive but uncharted blankness. "What he describes as its abstract, visual pattern," as Charles Saumarez Smith has said (2005: 11).

The most obvious suggestion for *London Paintings* in Conrad's work would probably be Marlow's "And this also … has been one of the dark places of the earth" (*Youth* 48). There can, however, be no suggestion that Virtue worked with any illustrative intent or consciousness of Conrad's writings. While we know that he read Peter Ackroyd's *London:*

The Biography with close attention throughout the period of working on these paintings, Virtue has written to me quite explicitly that, although he has been an avid reader of Dickens since he was fourteen, "Joseph Conrad is not someone I think about in connection with my work." Despite this authoritative dissociation, the correspondence in the vision of the two artists is immediately striking, but what is really more remarkable and productive of critical reflection is the similarity that can be found in their processes of composition, even though the medium for their expression is so different.

In his essay "In the Midst of Life: John Virtue's Images of London," Paul Moorhouse relates the way in which collecting observations while walking and standing in particular spots, over and over again, has been central to Virtue's art since 1978. Writing of an earlier sequence, he says:

> at the end of each walk he would return home armed with the drawings he had made earlier that day. These would then be worked on further, the pencil or charcoal structure he had established on the spot being progressively covered by a dense thicket of cross-hatched lines, using pen and ink mixed with shellac. At the end of this subsequent stage, the appearance of the drawings would be entirely transformed, the pencil marks embodying direct observation now buried beneath a new surface of marks, made reflectively and at a remove from the initial experience. This method is significant for it attests the complex relationship between the primacy of looking and then progressive *withdrawal* from topographical detail that stands at the heart of Virtue's work. (2005: 38, 41)

For the reader of *The Secret Agent* this irresistibly brings to mind Conrad's account in his "Author's Note" of how the initial visual data for his "monstrous town" had been gathered ready for transformation in a process startlingly similar to Virtue's:

> I had to fight hard to keep at arms-length the memories of my solitary and nocturnal walks all over London in my early days, lest they should rush in and overwhelm each page of the story as these emerged one after another from a mood as sincere in feeling and thought as any in which I ever wrote a line. (7)

Both writer and painter deliberately overpaint those first impressions with a "mood" produced in a deliberate removal from them, one which in both cases will produce a "vision" (although, I agree with Schama, not an *impression*) of London stark, indifferent, oppressive. So "strange forms, sharp in outline but imperfectly apprehended appeared and claimed attention as crystals will do by their bizarre and unexpected shapes … Then the vision of an enormous town presented itself, of a monstrous town" (6). This is the second or subsequent stage in the movement towards composition, not the notation of the topography itself, but the artistic reaction to those original sensations that will throw a unifying colour upon the totality of the work to be written What Paul Moorhouse says of Virtue could be said of Conrad too: "Virtue's paintings of London arise from daily contact with a metropolis humming with life, experienced directly and at its centre. But the finished paintings are the outcome of a protracted, solitary, studio-based process of accretion and reflection" (2005: 47). Dickens's written London bears directly the print of his daily walking and social contact; Conrad's bears the muffled sense of an encounter recalled through a medium darkened yet clarified by loneliness.[2]

A vital layer in that medium was, of course, a written one: not only Dickens himself but, nearer the surface as it were, Ford Madox Hueffer's *The Soul of London* (1905), which renders exactly the quality that both Conrad and Virtue apply to their finished works. Writing of the young provincial newly arrived to take up residence in the capital, Hueffer says: "For, sooner or later, the sense of impersonality, of the abstraction that London is, will become one of the most intimate factors of his daily life" (6). So, in *The Secret Agent,* even where the writing seeks momentarily to embrace London's vigorous, populated world of social relations, phrase by phrase the description resolves into the impersonal abstraction of Hueffer's intuition. In Chapter V, Conrad's Professor is assailed by a sense of things only too well known to his creator:

> after a while he became disagreeably affected by the sight of the roadway thronged with vehicles and of the pavement crowded with men and women. He was in a long, straight street, peopled by a mere fraction of an immense multitude; but all round him, on and on, even to the limits of the horizon hidden by the enormous piles of bricks, he felt the mass of mankind mighty in its numbers. They swarmed numerous like locusts, industrious like ants, thoughtless like a natural force, pushing on blind and orderly and absorbed, impervious to sentiment, to logic, to terror too perhaps. (67)

In Conrad's London, as in Virtue's, the human is diminished (more than it ever is by the sea); the edifices, lines, spaces, vistas, silences even are rendered as having a force independent from and greater than the human energies that (in a different account of the generation of the city) would logically have brought them into being. Even where, at the opening of Chapter II, the picture of London offered is apparently one of a benign concourse of civilized social activity, what happens as we read is the progressive evaporation of human relations under the stare of

---

[2] Two very interesting essays are immediately relevant to this discussion of how Conrad (and Dickens) was penetrated by his urban surroundings, and the ways in which he used this experience artistically: see Hampson and Kirschner in *Conrad's Cities* (1992).

the sun, and the dissolution of London and Mr Verloc himself into surfaces of rich yet depthless colour:

> And a peculiarly London sun – against which nothing could be said except that it looked bloodshot – glorified all this by its stare. It hung at a moderate elevation above Hyde Park Corner with an air of punctual and benign vigilance. The very pavement under Mr Verloc's feet had an old gold tinge in that diffused light, in which neither wall, nor tree, nor beast, nor man cast a shadow. Mr Verloc was going westward through a town without shadows in an atmosphere of powdered old gold. There were red, coppery gleams on the roofs of houses, on the corners of walls, on the panels of carriages, on the very coats of the horses, and on the broad back of Mr Verloc's overcoat, where they produced a dull effect of rustiness. (15)[3]

The ironies remain obscure but penetrating. It is surely inadequate to say that the passage is a projection of Mr Verloc's comfortable self-deception about the fitness of things and his own comfortable place in them. There is a separate, non-human creating and disintegrating force being invoked here, even as the sun is complacently co-opted as servant protector of the *haute bourgeoisie*. Oddly, perhaps, I find illumination about

[3] This is clearly a recollection of the staring sun at the opening of *Little Dorrit*, now ironically gentrified and diminished in intensity for its London appearance. I am grateful to Katherine Isobel Baxter for finding a closer parallel passage, in every sense except that of artistic intention, in the following from Willa Cather:

> The beautiful surfaces and the beautiful life of London lie from Trafalgar Square westward through St. James's Park, along Piccadilly, through to Kensington to Hammersmith. From Trafalgar westward the very colour of the city changes; the grimy blackness of the smoke-laden town grows to a splendid grey about the National Gallery and St Martin-in-the Fields, and from there the colour runs gradually into a higher and higher key, into the glorious greens of the parks and the bold white of the club houses along Piccadilly, and finally in the broad asphalts of Kensington that are covered, or rather dusted, with yellow sand that catches the sunlight like gold powder, lying bright between their lines of elm and plane trees. (*Nebraska State Journal*, 17 August 1902)

In contrast, Conrad's use of similar visual material is beguilingly surreal, an effect arising from the "eidetic" quality of his memory, a term acutely coined by Paul Kirschner.

this passage, in a way that takes us straight back to Virtue and his artistic practice, from one of Conrad's most gifted admirers, Iain Sinclair.[4] In his latest novel, *Dining On Stones* (2004) – dedicated to Conrad – his fictional surrogate Andrew Morton, musing about photography and writing, says: "The prose I contrived from these snapshots would be more provocative, so I hoped, than the awkward blocks of verbless sentences 'inspired' by the many thousands of diary-images I'd gathered during the years of my compulsive logging of London and the river" (25). And a little later he is thinking about a film he had left in a camera now lost: "an abandoned essay … The film, lost in the bilges, was busy in my memory. Soft evidence transformed into fiction. The image you don't have, mislaid by chemist, stolen camera, retains its malignancy. It is unappeased" (27). And that is exactly the word for Conrad's London and for Virtue's: Verloc and the denizens of Kensington are shown in the passage above to be incapable of an awareness that this is a city and a world whose dismaying solitudes cannot be placated by wealth, by the comfortable sense of proprietorship, or the easy assumptions that rob existence of its strangeness. And the art of Conrad and of Virtue lies not in reproduction of the impressions immediately before the senses (although they have played their part in constructing written and visual images) but in seeking and confronting the image that they *don't* have simply to hand from observation, the malignant and unappeased sense of things that lies just beyond the grasp of realism.

I hope that some future edition of *The Secret Agent* (or even, more tellingly, of "Heart of Darkness") will dare to have a reproduction of one of Virtue's *London Paintings* on its cover. It would lend vivid support to Conrad's statement to Barrett H. Clark in 1918: "a work of art is very seldom limited to one exclusive meaning and not necessarily tending to a definite conclusion. And this for the reason that the nearer it approaches art the more it acquires a symbolic character" (*CL6* 210-11).

John Virtue's great, restless, and dissatisfied canvasses mostly conceal or obscure with veils of black the relentless observation of architectural detail upon which they are built, but they do not dispense with it. Discussing this aspect of his work in a video made for The National Gallery, he says: "Observing these things, persisting with exactitude and precision – and *then*, it might be *released* into this painting" (transcription and emphasis mine). This has much to tell us about the achievement of "symbolic character" in Conrad's works, as well as in Virtue's own.

---

[4] For a discussion of Conrad and Iain Sinclair, see Hampson (2006).

Acknowledgement

The illustrations are reproduced by kind permission of John Virtue. Special thanks are also due to Colin Wiggins, The National Gallery, London.

Works cited

Cather, Willa. *Willa Cather in Europe: Her Own Story of the First Journey*. 1902; rpt. New York: Knopf, 1956.

Conrad, Joseph. *The Secret Agent* (1907), edited by Roger Tennant. Oxford: Oxford World's Classics, 1983.

——. *The Secret Agent* (1907). Harmondsworth: Penguin, 1982.

——. *The Secret Agent* (1907), edited by Hugh Epstein. Ware: Wordsworth Classics, 2000.

Hampson, Robert. "Spatial Stories: Conrad and Iain Sinclair." *The Conradian* 31.1 (2005): 52-71.

——. "Topographical Mysteries: Conrad and London." In *Conrad's Cities: Essays for Hans van Marle*, edited by Gene M. Moore. 159-74. Amsterdam: Rodopi, 1992.

Hueffer, Ford Madox. *The Soul of London*. London: Alston Rivers, 1905.

Kirschner, Paul. "Topodialogic Narrative in *Under Western Eyes* and the Rasoumoffs of 'La Petite Russie.'" In *Conrad's Cities*, 223-54.

Moorhouse, Paul. In *John Virtue: London Paintings*. 35-50. London: The National Gallery, 2005.

Schama, Simon. "John Virtue: The Epic of Paint." In *John Virtue: London Paintings*. 13-31. London: The National Gallery, 2005.

Sinclair, Iain. *Dining on Stones*. London: Hamish Hamilton, 2004.

Smith, Charles Saumarez. Introduction to *John Virtue: London Paintings*. 9-11. London: The National Gallery, 2005.

Wiggins, Colin. "John Virtue: London Paintings." In *John Virtue: London Paintings*. 59-86. London: The National Gallery, 2005.

Four Notes on *The Secret Agent*: Sir William Harcourt, Ford and Helen Rossetti, Bourdin's Relations, and a Warning Against Δ

Michael Newton
Universiteit Leiden

I. Sir William Harcourt

AMONG CRITICS and editors of *The Secret Agent*, the identification of Sir Ethelred with Sir William Harcourt (1827-1904) amounts to an accepted fact. This rests on Conrad's testimony that he read Robert Anderson's *Sidelights on the Home Rule Movement* (1906), in which Harcourt figures prominently, and his mention of Harcourt by name in the 1920 "Author's Note" to the novel. In *Conrad's Western World* (1971), Norman Sherry sketches points of resemblance: Harcourt was fat, and so is Sir Ethelred; both required police protection (which Home Secretary has not?); both had weak eyes. He also notes that Harcourt's political activities around 1894 show some kinship with Sir Ethelred's.

Attentive readers in 1907 need not have waited for Conrad's clue of 1920 to guess that Sir Ethelred was a caricature of Harcourt. Indeed, it is from caricature that one element of Conrad's representation of Harcourt derives. At two moments in the novel he refers to Sir Ethelred's crusader ancestry (his name is, of course, in this novel of cosmopolitans and immigrants pure Tennysonian English) and implicitly presents the minister as a knight fighting foreign and pagan forces, whether Crim-Tartars, Turks, or the "paynim." This image, made ludicrous by Sir Ethelred's obesity, possibly alludes in the first instance to a cartoon in *The Westminster Gazette* of 5 March 1904 by F. C. Gould of Harcourt as "The Old Crusader," which depicts him as a rather melancholy mediæval knight. The picture comments on Harcourt's recent resignation from politics. The wistful caricature itself refers to an earlier drawing by John Tenniel, its fame part of Harcourt's public image. Titled "*À Outrance*," it appeared in *Punch* in October 1879 and depicted Harcourt as an Arthurian knight setting out to joust.

This version of Harcourt as a lordly crusader should be placed alongside his popular image at the time of the Greenwich Outrage. In January and February 1894, the Commons and Lords were doing battle over the Parish Councils Bill and the Employers' Liability Bill. The perception among Liberal supporters was that the Lords were ready to savage these bills. Harcourt responded militantly, raging at the Lords in a speech: "'We had been too long,' he said, 'a peer-ridden nation, and time was at hand when the issue as to whether the Commons or the Lords should be tried, and he had no doubt about the result. … Are you going to be governed by yourselves or will you submit to an oligarchy which is the mere accident of birth?'" (Gardiner 1923: 2:255).

To his foes, this displayed a new, uncharacteristic, and perhaps opportunistic Radicalism. As his political enemy, Joseph Chamberlain was happy to point out, the now-radical Harcourt had even once flirted with serving under his friend Disraeli. Yet this accusation misrepresented Harcourt, who had long been something of a radical, and in 1873 had even feebly resisted the knighthood associated with his new post of Solicitor-General. He was notably conciliatory in his dealings with Ireland, a reason perhaps for the fiercely Unionist Robert Anderson to keep his Home Secretary "in the dark" about anti-Fenian espionage. Harcourt indeed ended up a supporter of Home Rule; he was also firmly anti-Imperialist. Moreover his claim that "We are all Socialists now," made in August 1887, was striking enough to become instantly famous and usually contested – by both left and right. Conrad alludes to the statement in his 1904 review of Anatole France's *Crainquebille*: "as an illustrious statesman now no more, a great prince too, with an ironic mind and a literary gift, has sarcastically remarked in one of his public speeches: 'We are all socialists now'" (*Notes on Life and Letters*, 33-34).

At the time when Conrad first arrived in England, Harcourt's patrician radicalism was making news. On 14 February 1894, he delivered an inflammatory speech against the Lords. A cursory reading of newspapers of the time would show the Greenwich and Paris outrages juxtaposed with Harcourt's Liberal fury with the aristocrats and churchmen who ran the House of Lords. Harcourt combined membership of the political élite with a radical tendency to question conservative traditions. This aspect of his politics seems most central to Conrad's depiction of Sir Ethelred, where the ambiguous relationship between authority and those who would overthrow it forms a significant element. Just as the apparent anarchists' plot is an Embassy conspiracy, and as police and thieves stand together in connection, so the seat of Parliament appears a revolutionary institution, the home of another kind of sham, whether named Toodles or Sir Ethelred.

II. Ford and Helen Rossetti

If readers would almost certainly have picked up that Sir Ethelred alluded to Harcourt, they could also easily infer that the novel was "based" on the actual Greenwich Park explosion. As A. N. Monkhouse, *The Manchester Guardian*'s reviewer, remarked: "With his accident in Greenwich Park we come to the surface of common knowledge, for most of us can recall that curious, alarming incident" (Sherry, ed., 1973: 183). *The Secret Agent* was using a story familiar to many. Yet when he started to write the novel, Conrad had the good fortune to come to this well-known event with a little secret information. References in his letters and, more importantly, the "Author's Note" present us with indications of a confidential understanding of the events behind the Greenwich Bombing. Outside the realm of open discourse, this was "inside knowledge" emerging haphazardly from the underground of Anarchism itself.

Clues to the nature of this clandestine information occur in a letter to Conrad's publisher, and an inscribed a copy of the novel. On 7 November 1906, Conrad wrote to Algernon Methuen: "it is based on the inside knowledge of a certain event in the history of active anarchism. But otherwise it is *purely a work of imagination*. It has no social or philosophical intention" (*CL3* 371). What this knowledge was precisely is revealed in Thomas J. Wise's copy of *The Secret Agent* (Ashley 466, British Library): "this novel was based on two pieces of information, one that the perpetrator of the attempt on the Greenwich Observatory was a half-witted youth, and the other that his sister committed suicide some time afterwards." As it happens, both pieces of covert data were entirely wrong.

Conrad's public declaration of insider information as it occurs in the "Author's Note" is a familiar aspect of the Jamesian preface, as imitated by Conrad, that the moment of inspiration should seem slight: the artist catches hold of something that others would miss. In a judicious account of the novel's sources, Stephen Arata points out that in Conrad's account the "stimulating" words are Harcourt's: "All that's very well. But your idea of secrecy over there seems to consist of keeping the Home Secretary in the dark," while a friend's fragment of knowledge ("Oh, that fellow was half an idiot. His sister committed suicide afterwards") was the passive illumination that Harcourt's offhand comment brings to imaginative life (1999: 173).

Conrad describes this second source as an "ominiscient" friend and, Conradians concur, this means Ford Madox Ford. The friend's knowledge was not, however, the "Author's Note" concedes, great but picked up anyhow from a random conversation with someone not himself an anarchist. Where did this knowledge come from, and how should we regard its factual basis?

At first, Ford might seem an excellent candidate for providing secret insight into the dark world of anarchism. His cousins Olive, Helena, and Arthur Rossetti were teenage anarchists in the 1890s, and wrote, edited, and printed a key anarchist journal, *The Torch*. However, much of what Ford wrote concerning Bourdin and his fellow anarchists is confused at best and misleading nonsense at worst.

His acquaintance with anarchists probably extended no further than his cousins and Prince Peter Kropotkin, a leading anarchist theorist. In later reminiscences, Ford liked to portray himself as implicitly having had an anarchist phase. Evidence from his letters and memoirs and from Olive Garnett's diaries strongly suggests that the young Rossettis and Ford did not meet often, perhaps did not particularly get on, and were poles apart politically. Similarly, while Ford knew Stepniak (who moved on the fringes of anarchist circles) and Kropotkin, he was far from being especially intimate with either or at any time an anarchist himself. In retrospect, the air of danger around early 1890s anarchism imaginatively appealed to Ford as a form of *nostalgie de la boue*, but his involvement in the anarchist milieu in the 1890s, let alone later, was predominantly a matter of acquaintance with a few people who were more directly involved. His friend Olive Garnett was far closer to the Rossettis and to Kropotkin and more intrigued by anarchist ideas. Ford's sister, Juliet Soskice (née Hueffer), lived with the Rossettis during their *Torch* period, but, like her brother, her view of their activities was sceptical and comically tinged. In her memoirs, she depicts them as teenage poseurs, possibly the case but not something preventing *The Torch* from being a significant anarchist publication.

Ford's reminiscences of his anarchist involvement reveal him as particularly unreliable. In *Ancient Lights* (1911), for instance, he implies that he attended Bourdin's funeral, seeing one of the largest crowds of anarchist sympathizers he had ever seen and counting himself one such. If so, his experience of "crowds" was limited: contemporary observers put numbers at the funeral around 500-600 at most. A letter to Sir Edward Bradford from Asquith shows that the largest crowd at the event were probably the police, who, from other evidence, did all they could to prevent a full procession, violence *against* the anarchists, and graveside speeches (Garnett 1993: 39; *The Commonweal*, 10 March 1894, p. 2; *Daily Graphic*, 24 February 1894, p. 1; HO144/257/A55660; see Burgoyne in this collection).

The difficulty in considering the extent of what Ford could have told Conrad arises from the fact that Ford wrote nothing on anarchism before the publication of *The Secret Agent*, and nothing about his being a source for that novel before Conrad's "Author's Note." The latter silence may be gentlemanliness on his part, but once Conrad had mentioned the fact in print, Ford set about appropriating the anecdote, gaining credit for Conrad's story, and turning himself into the novel's "onlie begetter." Similarly, his claim that he wrote a little of *The Secret Agent* is unproveable – particularly that he added "details about policemen and anarchists" (Saunders 1996: 1:221). This seems another example of Ford's boast that these were topics in which he might be considered an expert. He even claimed to have been "in the same room with Vaillant if not with Ravachol on more than one occasion," an extremely improbable acquaintance, however remote, with a would-be assassin and anarchist murderer (Ford 1999: 85).

In later reminiscences, Ford revised the nature of the conversation Conrad described in his "Author's Note":

> what the writer really did say to Conrad was: "Oh that fellow was half an idiot! His sister murdered her husband afterwards and was allowed to escape by the police. I remember the funeral. . . ." The suicide was invented by Conrad. And the writer knew – and Conrad knew that the writer knew – a great many anarchists of the Goodge Street group, as well as a great many of the police who watched them. The writer had provided Conrad with Anarchist literature, with memoirs, with introductions to at least one anarchist young lady who figures in the *Secret Agent*. . . . (1924: 231)

The new version of what Ford "really did say" derives from knowledge of the novel's contents after the fact and mixing-up "The Informer" with it. At heart it is an attempt to make the book seem even more derivative of Ford's omniscience, the central element in all of Ford's post-1920 discussions of the novel.

This omniscience is compromised by the fact that neither bit of information Ford claims to have told Conrad was true. There was no "Goodge Street Group," and the *Torch* was never printed there, although issues of the journal were sold in the street at E. Lapie's (Johnson 1993: 260). It is possible that Ford provided Conrad with anarchist literature and memoirs. The latter, if they existed, would probably have been Kropotkin's and those of the Rossetti sisters, *A Girl Among the Anarchists* (1903). The only certainty about what Ford says is that the introduction to "at least one anarchist young lady" did occur with Conrad meeting Helen Rossetti once or twice, probably in 1903-04. In doing so, the novelist was indeed getting a step closer to "inside knowledge" of events.

Yet how "inside" was her knowledge? The Rossetti sisters were in Italy nursing their consumptive mother at the time of the Greenwich Bombing. There was, however, speculation that their brother Arthur was involved with Bourdin's act or planned to follow his example.[1] What Helen Rossetti told Conrad is unknown; however, some critics have guessed at the impression she made on him from the evidence of "The Informer," which offers unsympathetic "portraits" of her and Ford. If this is the case, the irony of this portrayal deepens if we consider that in one sense they both supposedly acted as "informers" for Conrad, filling him in on anarchism and the Greenwich Outrage.

Other than reading her novel, the inside information Conrad would most likely have picked up from Helen Rossetti might have been David Nicoll's view of events. Nicoll (1859-1919) edited the anarchist paper *The Commonweal* during 1890-92 and later edited a journal called *The Anarchist*. His view, published in two pamphlets that Conrad could have read, was that Bourdin was betrayed by H(enry) B(enjamin) Samuels, a fellow anarchist with whom Bourdin was intimate. He accuses Samuels of acting as an *agent provocateur* for the police and intending to entrap Bourdin. Also possibly involved was another notorious spy, August Coulon. In describing this plot, Nicoll saw a repetition of a previous conspiracy in which a group of Walsall anarchists, entrapped by Coulon, ended up with heavy prison sentences despite very likely being innocent.

It is certain that the Rossettis looked on Nicoll favourably. He was sentenced to jail for eighteen months in 1892 for incitement to murder the judge and policeman involved in prosecuting the Walsall anarchists. In his absence, the Rossetti sisters "took over the premises and printing press of *The Commonweal*" (Tryphonopoulos and Surette, ed., 1998: xiii). Olivia Rossetti declared that she had been inspired to become an anarchist both by childhood reading – Plutarch, Corneille, histories of the French Revolution – and more immediately by hearing Nicoll speak in Regent's Park (Ibid., xiii). Garnett reports in a diary entry for May 1893 that on

---

[1] The evidence is thin, consisting of worry expressed in the 26 February 1894 entry in Olive Garnett's diary that Arthur might study explosives on behalf of his anarchist friends (1993: 43-44). Oliver Hueffer passed on information that it had been reported in the press that Arthur Rossetti might be making bombs and that the police apparently suspected him of complicity with Bourdin (Garnett 1993: 59; Moser 1980: 17; I have been unable to trace the press report.)

learning that they will have to travel abroad with their sick mother, "Helen [Rossetti] weeps to think that she will not see Nicholl when he comes out of prison. But they intend … to correspond regularly with their friends" (Garnett 1989: 184-85).

As Nicoll's line on events was to demonize Samuels as the villain of the Greenwich Outrage, it is also interesting to note that the Rossetti sisters' early relationship with Samuels was often uncomfortable. In April 1893, Samuels had begun attempting to visit them at their home, a transgression of the divide between anarchist activism and their domestic lives that left the sisters ill at ease (*Ibid.*, 181). Samuels's rejection of anarchism shortly after the Greenwich Bombing and his defection to the ILP marked him out as a traitor for the Rossettis and many in the movement. Their final view of him appears in their *A Girl among the Anarchists*, in which Bourdin becomes "Augustin Myers" and Samuels, significantly, his ghastly brother, "Jacob," depicted in blatantly anti-Semitic terms:

> a mean enough type of the East End sartorial Jew. His physiognomy was not that of a fool, but indicated rather that low order of intelligence, cunning and intriguing, which goes to make a good swindler. The low forehead, wideawake, shifty little eyes, the nose of his forefathers, and insolent lock of black hair plastered low on his brow – all these characteristics may frequently be met with in the dock of the "Old Bailey" when some of case of petty swindling is being tried. (Rossetti 1903: 45)

Jacob's brother, like Bourdin, is French, but why an "East End sartorial Jew" should have a Frenchman for a brother is never explained, and Jacob, "a modern Shylock," is certainly more East End than French (Rossetti 1903: 50). Although Nicoll also accused Dr Fauset MacDonald of complicity in the plot against Bourdin, the Rossetti sisters' opprobrium is reserved entirely for Samuels/"Myers." The Rossettis were close to MacDonald (or Dr Armitage as he is named in their book), and their autobiographical novel is at pains to exonerate him.

Conrad may have gathered ideas from *A Girl Among the Anarchists*. Like *The Secret Agent*, this novel depicts the anarchists as grotesques; certain details provide a context for Ossipon's philandering and the embarrassment of Verloc's marriage; the laziness of Short, a character in the Rossettis' novel, may have contributed to Verloc's indolence. However, all this is speculation: such things could have been easily found elsewhere or simply invented.

Given the circumstances of their dislike of Samuels, their admiration for Nicoll, and the evidence of their novel, it appears probable that Helen Rossetti took on trust that part of Nicoll's public attack insofar as it condemned Samuels as a police spy who had manipulated Bourdin.[2] On the other hand, their refusal to countenance the involvement of MacDonald (the man who had perhaps supplied Bourdin with sulphuric acid for the explosives) makes their story distinct from Nicoll's. Given this difference, it may be significant that there is no equivalent to Dr MacDonald in Conrad's novel; at least, the character who does supply the explosives (The Professor) is very far indeed from either the real Dr MacDonald or the fictional Dr Armitage. If Conrad did borrow from Nicoll's account, the story he used was, it seems, refracted through what we know of Helen Rossetti's view of events and could have been passed on either in conversation or a putative reading of the Rossettis' novel.

III. Bourdin's Relations

It is difficult to trace the impact, if any, that Nicoll had on Conrad. While it is true that Nicoll's conspiracy theory resembles *The Secret Agent*'s plot, the novel differs in several essential respects. Most interestingly, Nicoll also says nothing of the family connection between Samuels and Bourdin. He begins by saying that Samuels boasts of an intimacy with Bourdin, and then declares that the two men were indeed intimate, without ever asserting that theirs was a familial link (1897: 6). Nicoll's version of events (like the Rossettis') makes no mention of Bourdin's sister, central to the novel's conception as described in the "Author's Note."

Similarly both versions of what Ford said to Conrad leave out the vital detail of the brother-in-law's being the betrayer. In the first case, we have merely the sister's suicide; in the second, the murder of her husband, and then her being allowed to escape by the police. The crucial matter regarding the possible "source" for the story therefore becomes the question of why a story about Samuels as Bourdin's betrayer should turn into a story about a sister who avenges her dead brother. Where

[2] As Hermia Oliver has suggested, there may have been personal motives for Nicoll's attack. While Nicoll was in prison from 1892-93, Samuels apparently acted as temporary editor of *The Commonweal*. In 1893, on his release, for reasons perhaps due to his mental instability, Nicoll did not resume the editorship. That Nicoll resented Samuels' continued editorship of *The Commonweal* is clear from a letter of April 1897 to Max Nettlau, as well as from the tenor of everything he wrote subsequent to his release (Nettlau Archive, IISG 212).

might Conrad have heard of a familial relationship between Samuels and Bourdin? He appears simply to have read it in the papers. Sherry (1971) contends that Verloc was an amalgam of two of the men who entrapped Bourdin: Samuels and Coulon. From Coulon, Conrad took the peculiarly *bourgeois* manner of being a police spy and his foreign origin (Coulon was Belgian while Verloc is half-French).[3] What Conrad took from Samuels was, Sherry maintains, his treachery and his family connection to Bourdin. The press reports of the Greenwich Bombing are quite clear on the matter: Samuels was Bourdin's brother-in-law. But this identification is doubtful.

Martial Bourdin's family relations have yet to be exhaustively investigated. We know that he was living in London at the invitation of his brother, Henri. Martial had been born in Tours, Henri at Sancerre, but the family lived in Paris. In interviews at the time of the Greenwich Bombing, Henri was at pains to state that he knew nothing of his brother's anarchist activities. It is highly probable that he was lying. As Mary Burgoyne mentions in this collection, we know from Hermia Oliver that Henri Bourdin was (some years before at least) himself an active anarchist and was numbered among those studying Marx with the anarchist, Charlotte Wilson in 1884 at the Hampstead Marx Circle or Proudhon Society. He attended the readings with August Bordes, a member of the Autonomie Club. Despite their shared interest in anarchism, Henri declares that his brother was incorrigibly taciturn, a habit of silence made to account for his family's ignorance of his politics. But we also hear, from other witnesses, that Bourdin, famously forthright in his views, was keen to declare them to everyone. The man who served him lunch knew he was an anarchist, but his brother claims he did not. The possibility that his own brother should not know of Martial's anarchism, while himself moving in anarchist circles, acquainted with members of the Club Autonomie (in which Martial was an active member), and related by marriage to a prominent Anarchist like Samuels stretches belief. Given the heavy sentences meted out to those even remotely connected to the Walsall anarchists, it would seem that Henri Bourdin was covering his tracks. Mary Burgoyne's intriguing discovery of the arrest of Bourdin's father could cut two ways: either it shows that Henri did well to lie low, for it is entirely possible that Étienne Bourdin

[3] Coulon was well-known (Helen Rossetti and Bourdin were acquainted with him), and his fame must have made him a peculiarly ineffective spy; a famous *agent provocateur* is something of an oxymoron. If Coulon was watching Bourdin, then Bourdin must have known about it.

was arrested simply for being Martial's father, or it reveals that the Bourdin family's interest in anarchism extended beyond the two brothers.

Martial and Henri Bourdin worked together as ladies' tailors at 18 Great Titchfield Street, with Henri's wife, Kate, and his wife's sister-in-law, Louisa Sullivan. From her own testimony, we know that Louisa Sullivan was English, could not understand much French, and, like Henri Bourdin, knew nothing of Martial's anarchism.

H. B. Samuels (1860-1933), Martial Bourdin's supposed brother-in-law, was also a tailor. Born in Hull, he had spent time in the United States, but returned to Britain in 1885, where he involved himself in the Socialist League as an agitator and writer. Among the English anarchists, he was one of the most vocal supporters of "propaganda by the deed" and has been described as "simply an advocate of violence – by others" (Oliver 1983: 59). A letter from William Morris to Samuels has the air of someone endeavouring not to humour a fanatic (Letter 1516 in *The Collected Letters of William Morris*, dated August 20 [1888]).

What was Samuels's relation to Bourdin? The interview conducted with Samuels for *The Morning Leader*, 19 February 1894, designates Samuels as Bourdin's brother-in-law. Samuels describes having lunch on the day of the explosion with Martial Bourdin, but does not mention that Henri, according to other evidence, was also there. Similarly, *The Kentish Mercury* of 23 February 1894 states, concerning Bourdin's inquest: "Mr. H. B. Samuels, the brother-in-law of the deceased, and the editor of the anarchist publication, the *Commonweal*, arrived, accompanied by other members of the Autonomie Club. Relatives of the deceased, including his brother, Henri Bourdin, who was the first witness called, were also present." Samuels is both marked out as a brother-in-law and yet distinguished from the "relatives of the deceased."

This seems fairly incontrovertible evidence of the relationship and would probably have continued to stand were it not for the National Censuses of 1891 and 1901, which allow the tracking of Samuels. He was indeed married, the father of five in 1891 and of seven by 1901, supporting them as a "ladies tailor." In 1891, he resided at 11 Mabledon Place, St Pancras, one of five families in the building (RG12/119 (47), p. 5). In 1901, he lived at 19 Oxford Road, Leyton, with another large family in the same house (RG13/110 (71), p. 30). His wife, Mary, three years younger than he, was born in Marylebone in 1864. Clearly, the notion that Samuels was married to Bourdin's sister, a Frenchwoman and that this was the truth revealed to Conrad as "inside knowledge" can no longer hold. Other evidence – such as no one's remarking on Samuels's wife being French (in the Rossettis' novel she is a cockney harridan) and her being reported as being unmoved by Bourdin's death – would support this assumption.

Census records and birth, marriage, and death certificates produce the solution to these mysteries. Henry Samuels and Mary Sullivan married on 13 December 1879 in a church service (Oct–Dec 1879 St Saviour's Southwark, London 1d/165). The marriage certificate indicates that Henry was employed as a tailor. His wife, the daughter of Daniel Sullivan, had no occupation, and the couple were already living together at 5 Marshall Street, London. Both Henry and Mary lied about their ages. Mary gave hers as 19 (she was 16, but by only six days); Henry declared himself to be 20, whilst, born on 7 April 1860, he was 19.[4]

In his obituary of Bourdin for *The Commonweal*, Samuels talks of Bourdin's coming from a family of eight, although he also asserts that Bourdin's father and mother, neither interested in politics, were nearly ninety. This is implausible: Bourdin was twenty-six. He and Henri (only two years older) were either adopted or Samuels was mistaken. It would, however, be an odd mistake for a brother-in-law. Samuels appears confused, then, on the subject of Bourdin's family. Yet he claims: "Martial was a relative of mine, but there was hardly any affection between us on that score." A "relative" is, of course, a broader category than "brother-in-law."

The 1891 Census (RG12/1045 (111), p. 42) shows Henri Bourdin (aged 27) living in Willesden with E(mmeline) Kate Bourdin (aged 24) and their three children, Adele (aged 5) and Henry (aged 3). The youngest (aged 1) is named "Spartacus M(artial)," a likely indication that Henri had not yet abandoned revolutionary politics. Kate's birthplace and that of the two older children was given as Marylebone; Spartacus was born in Willesden. Henri's profession – his name appears as Henry – is given as "Ladies Tailor."

Henri and Kate Bourdin's marriage certificate (Oct–Dec 1886 Westminster 1a/1003) reveals more details. Married in December 1886, the date suggests that they "had to," as it is highly likely that Kate was either already heavily pregnant with her first child or was already a mother. They were also already co-habiting at 12 Noel Street, St James's. The choice of a Registry Office and the absence of a religious service, like Henri's decision to affirm rather than swear on the Bible at his brother's inquest (the coroner explained this to himself on the basis that Bourdin was a foreigner) also suggests the persistence of "radical" views. Kate's

---

[4] Mary Sullivan was born on 7 December 1863 and baptized in St Pancras Workhouse Chapel ten days later (personal communication, Mark Samuels).

father, Daniel Sullivan, is noted as deceased, and the witnesses were her brother, Daniel, and her sister Mary Samuels.

This provides enough clues to locate the family of Kate Bourdin and Mary Samuels. The 1871 Census shows resident in Marylebone, London-born Daniel Sullivan (aged 37), a plasterer, and his wife, Mary (aged 32) (RG10/150 (81), p. 78). They had five children: Henry (aged 12); Daniel (aged 10); Mary, the future Mrs Samuels (aged 7); Katherine (or Emmeline Kate), the future Mrs Bourdin (aged 5); and Margaret (aged 4). Another child, Louisa, was born in 1873 or 1874.[5] This family picture fits neatly with other evidence provided by the Census and the above-mentioned marriage certificates. By the 1881 Census, the father was dead, as, it seems, was Margaret, and Henry had left home (RG11/144 (58), p. 56). Mary, of course, was by now married to Henry Samuels. Although only fifteen, Kate was employed as a dressmaker.

Press talk of the Bourdin dressmaking concern has it consisting of four members: Henri, Martial, Kate Bourdin, and her "sister" Louisa. The absence of a Louisa Sullivan from the family is explained by the fact that she was not Kate's sister but her sister-in-law, married to her brother, Daniel Sullivan. The 1891 Census shows Sullivan, now a plasterer like his father, married to Louisa, born in the parish of the Strand, and with two children, named Daniel and Louisa (RG12/217 (91), p. 21).

Therefore Samuels was not Martial Bourdin's but Henri Bourdin's brother-in-law. If Martial Bourdin had a sister, she does not appear in connection to the events of the bombing, the anarchist milieu, or his extended family in London. If her "suicide" or "murder of her husband" did provide inspiration for Conrad, the context for these putative deeds would be entirely French. The Bourdin, Sullivan, and Samuels families were connected by marriage, profession, and politics. The fact that two of the Sullivan daughters married anarchists seems more than simple coincidence; possibly both women had some connection with political radicalism. That Samuels and Henri Bourdin continued to be on friendly terms after the bombing shows both their family connection and that Samuels had done nothing to sour the relationship – such as being responsible for Henri's brother's death.

The press seem consistently to have tidied up these complex relationships into something more readily understandable and intimate.

[5] See 1891 RG11/90 (117), p. 63. She married a Danish shoemaker, Frederick Hans Gundersen, in Jul–Sep 1894 Marylebone 1a/1373. The 1901 Census lists him as Hann Fred[erick] Gundersen (RG13/3 (119), p. 23).

Louisa Sullivan is described as Kate Bourdin's "sister," Samuels as Martial's "brother-in-law." In this way, journalists heightened the sense of loss and more firmly placed the strange and unfamiliar anarchist in the comfortable context of the English family. Much as Conrad does in *The Secret Agent*, the alien world of foreign anarchism becomes something much closer to a domestic tragedy.

Why was Samuels's actual relationship to Martial Bourdin felt to matter in the first place? Conrad original discussion of his sources says nothing about brothers or brothers-in-law but is instead interested in idiocy, sisters, suicide, and Home Secretaries declaring that secrecy means their being kept in the dark. It is as though, dissatisfied with these clues or with the experience of the novel as fiction, critics have sought out a real betrayal. Inspired by Nicoll with his paranoid fears of conspiracy, and indeed sharing a kinship with his methods and fantasies, critics have sought out a secret, have looked, too, for some "inside knowledge" of their own. It is a researcher's quest to construct the hidden, just as Conrad's novel itself offers us the concealed world of anarchism, of Soho, shady wares, and the interior life that does not bear too much looking into. What seems hidden was always in plain view: no one needed to be informed of the true story behind Conrad's novel. Meanwhile the critical reading sought out an occluded factual situation for which the novel could act as an analogue, as though the novel itself could penetrate the permeable boundaries of reality.

IV. A Warning Against Δ

The archives of the Royal Observatory Greenwich in Cambridge University Library (File RGO 7/58) reveal much of interest to the student of Conrad. In 1880, for instance, the Observatory had been examined in order to consider how safe it was from dynamite explosion; in 1885, in the midst of the Fenian bombing campaign, correspondence between the Observatory and the Home Office on the same subject concluded that the building was vulnerable to attack from outside. Clearly prior to Bourdin's death, the building was already considered a possible target. Only a month before the explosion itself, a break-in at the Museum prompted requests from the Astronomer Royal, Sir William Christie, for better protection. The only loophole was that no park keeper could be made available between 4.15 pm to 5.30 pm. This, perhaps coincidentally, was precisely the time at which Bourdin was to approach the Observatory. For conspiracy theorists, this could prove a pregnant discovery.

The file also contains written reports from the Observatory's workers describing events on the evening the bomb exploded. Poignantly, one man momentarily thought that Bourdin's body was that of a crouching child, so diminutive and slight was the bomber. Following the outrage, Christie received letters of condolence and relief. One Isabella Watson wrote to tell him that she had saved the Observatory by the power of prayer: "your telescope intercepted by spiritual means." The Blackheath Camera Club sent a vote of congratulations. Filed with these letters is a "letter card" of a more arresting kind. It is difficult to decipher, for the writer, having filled out the card vertically, turned it and wrote more on the other horizontal side. Postmarked "Shepherd's Bush, W, 16 [Feb] [18]94," the message is as follows on one side of the card:

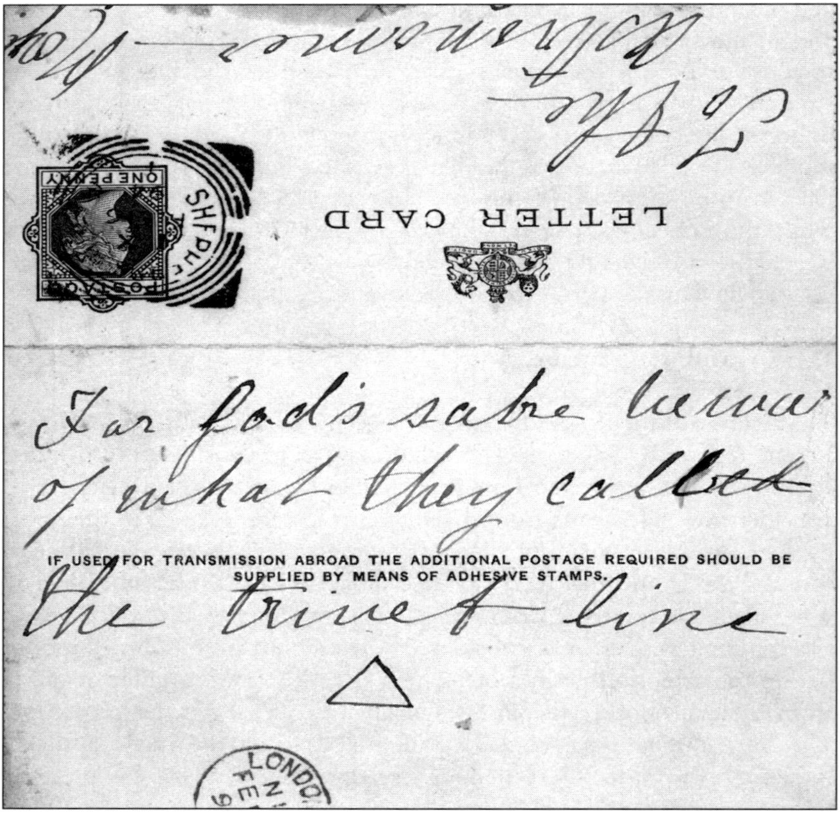

To the Astronomer Royal
For God's sake bewar of what they call~~ed~~ the trivet line

Δ

The verso reads:

Feb 16th /94

To the
Chief Astronomer
Sir

beware of the ~~stop~~ night through the blacks and take care of a man called Matei electrician I think. Regent street intensely bad, try and put down all such chemical experiments as Professor Dewar's etc and men who care for *chemistry only*, take care of the black cross X. *Please*

Agnes Henritte Jones Loinsworth
Freethinker

intensely bad, try and
put down all such
chemical experiments
as Professor Dewar's, etc
and men who care
for chemistry only take
care of the black cross X. Please
Agnes Henritte Jones Loinsworth
Freethinker

"Professor Dewar" is the prominent chemist and physicist Sir James Dewar (1842-1923), co-inventor in 1890 of cordite, the basis of the high explosives used by the army.[6] "Matei" is likely Count Cesare Mattei (1809-96), the Italian inventor of electrohomeopathy, a treatment for illness "invented" in 1865 and based on herbal principles only. His *The Principles of Electro-homeopathy: A New Science* (1883) circulated in translation in Britain and America and attracted considerable international attention.[7]

Sherry traces the novel's use of the triangle to Clan-na-Gael, part of what he saw as the book's Irish context (one more pressing and obvious at the start of the Troubles) (1971: 323). The Cambridge editors of *The Secret Agent* note: "Although the executive of the Clan-na-Gael were known as the triangle (see Sherry) and a contributor to *Blackwood's* (David Macbeth Moir) signed himself 'Delta,' the delta probably derives from forces internal to the novel. Throughout the manuscript the symbol is **B**. Conrad's change to the delta, or triangle, is thematic" (1990: 417). The editors' response seems right, invoking the work of art, not a series of abstruse allusions to "facts" waiting to be uncovered. Rather the novel becomes an interweaving of discourses. As the editors state, Conrad did not settle on Δ to stand for Verloc until rewriting the book for Methuen. Verloc had earlier been represented by "B" and then, in *Ridgway's* by "β." In other words, Conrad always thought of Verloc as suitably represented by a Greek letter. Was he thinking of Fenian politics or Classical learning, the symbols of revolution or of algebra?

For those who take their Sherry straight, one reading of this card might have Conrad visiting the Royal Observatory or meeting with Sir William Christie on the subject of the bombing, with mention being made of the mysterious card from Agnes Loinsworth. Clearly the matter need not go so far: Was she alluding to Clan-na-Gael or to some other revolutionary body? Was she sharing in the significances Sherry uncovered? Is a letter from Nicoll to Slaughter in The Socialist League's archive (IISG 2347) that has the word "triangle" scrawled on it among a series of street names similarly evidence of a deepening mystery? Rather, perhaps, there is only the coincidence thrown up by the archive, something in the novel

---

[6] Interviewed about the bombing (*Daily Graphic*, 19 February 1894), Dewar made the point that although it looked as if Bourdin were about to deploy his bomb immediately, an attack on the Observatory was unlikely given the explosion's size, for the bomb was too small to do more than scar the walls or, if thrown through a window, to wound one or two people.

[7] By the turn of the twentieth century some one hundred publications and three journals were devoted to Mattei's system, which had adherents in France, Germany, Italy, Britain, and the United States. For a full discussion, see Baylen (1969).

suddenly permeated by something from outside and *vice versa*, a connection created by the activity of research, always involved in the making of connections between seemingly discrete worlds, the uncovering of the clandestine, the stumbling upon a little "inside knowledge."

Acknowledgements

Aside from the contemporary newspaper reports of the Greenwich Bombing read at The Newspaper Library, Colindale, this article relies on The Archives of the Royal Observatory, Greenwich, held at Cambridge University Library; online materials by the Internationaal Instituut voor Sociale Geschiedenis (IISG), Amsterdam; The National Archives; and The University of British Columbia Library. The images are reproduced by permission of the Particle Physics and Astronomy Research Council and the Syndics of Cambridge University Library.

I offer thanks to Adam Perkins of Cambridge University Library, and should like to acknowledge the hospitality and generosity of Mrs Caroline White in allowing me access to Olive Garnett's diaries and other papers, and to Gene M. Moore for help in transcribing the Loinsworth letter card. I owe a special debt to Mark Samuels, who most generously shared information about his great-grandfather and his family, and to J. H. Stape, who made available his editorial and sleuthing skills and immense Conradian knowledge without stint.

Works cited

Ancestry.co.uk <www.ancestry.co.uk>. Accessed: November 2006.

Anderson, Sir Robert. *Sidelights on the Home Rule Movement.* London: John Murray, 1906.

Arata, Stephen. "*The Secret Agent.*" In *A Joseph Conrad Companion*, edited by Leonard Orr and Ted Billy. 165-94. Westport, Connecticut: Greenwood Press, 1999.

Baylen, Joseph O. "The Mattei Cancer Cure: A Victorian Nostrom." *Proceedings of the American Philosophical Society* 113.2 (1969): 149-76.

Ford, Ford Madox. *Ancient Lights and Certain New Reflections.* London: Chapman and Hall, 1911.

———. *Joseph Conrad: A Personal Remembrance.* London: Duckworth, 1924.

———. *Letters of Ford Madox Ford*, edited by Richard M. Ludwig. Princeton: Princeton University Press, 1965.

———. *Return From Yesterday* (1931). London: Carcanet Press, 1991.

Gardiner, A. G. *The Life of Sir William Harcourt.* 2 vols. London: Constable, 1923.

Garnett, Olive. *Tea and Anarchy! The Bloomsbury Diary of Olive Garnett, 1890-1893*, edited by Barry C. Johnson. London: Bartletts Press, 1989.

———. *Olive and Stepniak: The Bloomsbury Diary of Olive Garnett, 1893-1895*, edited by Barry C. Johnson. Birmingham: Bartletts Press, 1993.

Harkness, Bruce, and S. W. Reid. "Notes." *The Secret Agent.* 413-27. Cambridge: Cambridge University Press, 1990.

Macnaghten, Sir Melville L. *Days of My Years.* London: Edward Arnold, 1914.

"Meredith, Isabel" (Olivia and Helen Rossetti). *A Girl Among the Anarchists.* London: Duckworth, 1903.

Morris, William. *The Collected Letters of William Morris*, edited by Norman Kelvin. 3 vols. Princeton: Princeton University Press, 1996.

Moser, Thomas C. "An English Context for Conrad's Russian Characters: Sergey Stepniak and the Diary of Olive Garnett" *Journal of Modern Literature* 11.1 (1984): 3-44.

———.*The Life in the Fiction of Ford Madox Ford.* Princeton: Princeton University Press, 1980.

Nicoll, David. *The Greenwich Mystery.* Sheffield: David Nicoll, 1897.

———. *The Greenwich Mystery: Letters from the Dead.* Sheffield: David Nicoll, 1898.

Oliver, Hermia. *The International Anarchist Movement in Late Victorian London.* London: St Martin's Press, 1983.

Pound, Ezra. *"I Cease Not To Yowl": Ezra Pound's Letters to Olivia Rossetti Agresti.*, edited by Demetre P. Tryphonopolous and Leon Surette. Urbana: University of Illinois Press, 1998.

Quaill, John. *The Slow Burning Fuse.* London: Paladin, 1978.

Saunders, Max. *Ford Madox Ford: A Dual Life.* 2 vols. Oxford: Oxford University Press, 1996.

Sherry, Norman. *Conrad's Western World.* Cambridge: Cambridge University Press, 1971; rpt. 1980.

———, ed. *Conrad: The Critical Heritage.* London: Routledge & Kegan Paul, 1973.

Soskice, Juliet M. *Chapters from Childhood. Reminiscences of an Artist's Granddaughter.* London: Selwyn & Blount, 1921.

Thompson, E. P. *William Morris: Romantic to Revolutionary.* London: Lawrence & Wishart, 1955.

Conrad among the Anarchists: Documents on Martial Bourdin and the Greenwich Bombing

Mary Burgoyne, editor and compiler
St Mary's College, Strawberry Hill

"No doubt a wicked attempt to blow up the Observatory, they say. H'm. That's hardly credible." (59)

SUCH WAS THE UBIQUITY of anarchist activities throughout Europe in the nineteenth century's final decades that Conrad, in an effort both to amuse and indeed flatter his "aunt," described a farcical scenario wherein he was accused of being an anarchist. Within days of his arrival in the *Adowa* in Rouen, on 4 December 1893, an anarchist attack was perpetrated against the Chamber of Deputies. Writing to Marguerite Poradowska in January 1894 whilst still in Rouen, Conrad constructed an account of the confusion that ensued at the railway station when he attempted to collect the eagerly anticipated copy of her latest novel, *Le Mariage du fils Grandsire*. For purposes of identification the package had been allocated a number and, feigning indignation that "such a work of art" should be so prosaically labelled, he informed the hapless clerk that this is "An outrage. You are bourgeois scoundrels," to which the clerk countered "you are an anarchist, that's what you are! Where is your bomb?" The farce continued, with Conrad recounting his supposed flight from the summoned police who were "thirsting" for his blood (*CL*1 143).

This final detail is prescient. Despite the fact that the bomb thrown by the perpetrator of the Chamber of Deputies outrage, Auguste Vaillant, caused minimal damage and no fatalities, he was none the less tried, found guilty, and sentenced to death, at just one sitting of the court on 10 January, the day the *Adowa* set sail for London. The following month, Émile Henry threw a bomb into the crowded café of the Hôtel Terminus in Paris,[1] killing one and injuring twenty, and would thus become the

[1] According to Sherry (1971: 425 n. 7), "Conrad probably had [the Hôtel Terminus] incident in mind when he has Vladimir lecture Verloc on the uselessness of such attacks: 'A murderous attempt on a restaurant ... would suffer ... from the suggestion of non-political passion'" (29).

third French anarchist, after Vaillant and Ravachol,[2] to be executed for engaging in what is known as "propaganda of the deed."[3]

On 15 February 1894, just three days after the café outrage in Paris, Martial Bourdin died from injuries sustained from what was presumed to be the premature explosion of his own bomb, a short distance from the Royal Observatory in Greenwich Park, London. Bourdin's Death Certificate (Fig. 1) cites as his Cause of Death: "Felo de se," literally, a felon of himself or self-murder. Despite initial reports to the contrary, evidence given by the government's Inspector of Explosives, Colonel Majendie, at the inquest into Bourdin's death, confirmed the official view that the Royal Observatory was the anarchist's intended target (see *The Weekly Times and Echo* report and extracts from *Liberty* [Refs. 6 and 18]). Early in 1906, this incident provided Conrad, with the genesis of the short story, "provisionally called *Verloc*" (*CL3* 316), which would eventually be published as *The Secret Agent.*

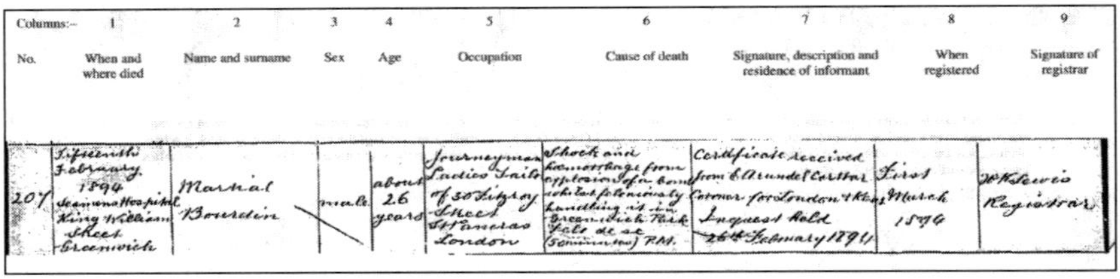

Columns:–	1	2	3	4	5	6	7	8	9
No.	When and where died	Name and surname	Sex	Age	Occupation	Cause of death	Signature, description and residence of informant	When registered	Signature of registrar
207	Fifteenth February 1894 Seamens Hospital King William Street Greenwich	Martial Bourdin	male	about 26 years	Journeyman Ladies Tailor of 30 Fitzroy Street St Pancras London	Shock and hemorrhage from explosion of a bomb [illegible] feloniously handling it in Greenwich Park Felo de se ([illegible]) P.M.	Certificate received from E Arundel Carttar Coroner for London & Kent Inquest held 26th February 1894	First March 1894	[illegible] Registrar

Fig. 1. Entry for Martial Bourdin in The Register of Deaths, Greenwich North.

In his 1920 "Author's Note" to the novel, Conrad writes that "the tale … came to me in the shape of a few words uttered by a friend in

[2] Born François Köningstein (1859-1892), Ravachol adopted his mother's maiden name. A proponent of propaganda of the deed, his acts were both political and criminal, and this proved divisive within the movement. On 11 and 30 March 1892, he bombed the homes of the judge and prosecutor involved in the trial of the Clichy Levallois anarchists. Only the buildings were damaged, but he received a life sentence. Three months later he was tried and found guilty of murdering a hermit, and guillotined on 11 July 1892.

[3] The phrase was popularized by the French anarchist Paul Brousse (1844-1912). In an article published under this title in the August 1877 *Bulletin of the Jura Federation*, he cited as examples of "propaganda of the deed" the 1871 Paris Commune, a workers' demonstration in Berne provocatively using the socialist red flag, and the Benevento uprising in Italy (<en.wikipedia.org> Accessed October 2006).

casual conversation about anarchists or rather anarchist activities ... we recalled the already old story of the attempt to blow up the Greenwich Observatory" (4-5). Alluding to the incident's futility, he continues: "one remained faced by the fact of a man blown to bits for nothing even most remotely resembling an idea, anarchistic or other" (5). Much has been made of Conrad's retraction in 1923 when he stated that "I never knew anything of what was called ... the 'Greenwich Bomb Outrage.' I was out of England when it happened, and thus I never read what was printed in the newspapers at the time" (cited in Sherry 1971: 228-29). However, this claim has been disproved by the meticulous scholarship undertaken by Norman Sherry (1971) and Ian Watt (1973), who also suggest several potential sources for *The Secret Agent.* To Sherry, these include contemporary press accounts and anarchist publications, including pamphlets, among them David Nicoll's *The Greenwich Mystery* (1897; rpt. in Sherry, 379-94). Ian Watt, however, felt that Conrad's denial of any "detailed knowledge either of the explosion itself or of anarchism in general" was more legitimate than Sherry allowed (1973: 230) and placed greater emphasis on Conrad's references to Sir Robert Anderson's "summary recollections"[4] and the "few words uttered by a friend," Ford Madox Ford.

Ford's throwaway remark, ostensibly referring to Martial Bourdin, "Oh, that fellow was half an idiot. His sister committed suicide afterwards" ("Author's Note," 5), forms the basis for the Verlocs' domestic arrangements in *The Secret Agent.* Ford revised this account somewhat in his memoir of Conrad stating that "Oh that fellow was half an idiot: *His sister murdered her husband afterwards and was allowed to escape by the police*" (1924: 231; emphasis added). Ford is renowned as "an apologist of the school of Imaginative Reminiscences" (1993: vii),[5] and there is no evidence to support the veracity of these statements other than that of the sibling relationship, and, of course, there is no neat "escape" for Winnie Veloc in the novel. Although Sherry indicates the correspondences and contradictions between the reported historical events and those in the tale, it is worth recalling Conrad's comments on his art in conversation with G. Jean-Aubry: "As you know, I do not write history, but fiction, and I am therefore entitled to choose as I please what is most suitable in regard to characters and particulars to help me in the general impression

[4] Sir Robert Anderson, *Sidelights on the Home Rule Movement* (1906).

[5] Jennifer Shaddock, Introduction to *A Girl Among the Anarchists* by "Isabel Meredith" (the pseudonym of Helen and Olivia Rossetti).

I wish to produce" (Jean-Aubry, ed., 1927: 1:77). As Watt and others have further demonstrated, Conrad did not confine himself to the inspiration provided by the Greenwich Outrage itself, and introduced elements drawn not only from the Fenian terror campaigns in the preceding decades but also some details from the activities of the Russian secret police, as he suggested in a letter to Cunninghame Graham (*CL3* 491).

In this footnote to extant research on the Greenwich Outrage I draw upon less rehearsed contemporary reports and reactions to the outrage from both the popular and the anarchist press. These documents are collected at the end of this introduction. The Freedom of Information Act (2000) has resulted in some hitherto closed Home Office files being opened, including some relevant to the Outrage.

The breaking news reports of the bomb blast were characterized by an almost ghoulish delight in the graphic descriptions of Bourdin's injuries (see Ref. 6). This finds an echo in Conrad's disdain for writings that "elaborate mere ugliness … to shock" ("Author's Note," 4). It was noted in *The Sheffield Daily Telegraph* (Ref. 2) that much of the initial reporting was provided by the Central News Agency, with supplementary information taken from other news wires such as Reuters and Dalziel. Hence, the front page of *The Weekly Times and Echo* of 18 February 1894 (Ref. 6) contains contradictions and inconsistencies, a recurring feature in coverage of the Greenwich Affair.

There is little verifiable information regarding Martial Bourdin, and much of what was reported in the bombing's aftermath was based upon speculation and hearsay. Alarmist reporting implicated the victim in concurrent outrages throughout Europe, identifying him as one of the anarchists' "most zealous workers" (*Pall Mall Gazette*, 16 February 1894: 7). Thus it is surprising that reports of the arrest of Bourdin's father on charges of anarchism in Paris received no attention (then as now); coming as it did only three weeks after the Greenwich Outrage, it should surely have been grist to the mill of the popular press (Ref. 16). Only scant details can be derived from the evidence presented at the inquest, which is also marked by contradictions (Ref. 13), and from interviews given by Bourdin's brother, Henri (Ref. 17), and his purported brother-in-law, H. B. Samuels,[6] who, as *The Commonweal*'s editor, also wrote the

[6] Samuels was born Levi Herris Wilchinski (Apr–Jun 1860 Hull 9d/171); his name was changed in 1863 (personal communication, Mark Samuels). The 1861 Census finds him living (as Herris Levi) with his Prussian-born Polish uncle and aunt in Hull (RG9/3590 (124), pp. 16-17). On his relation to Bourdin, see Newton in the present collection. "His [Samuels's] marriage to a sister of the

front-page obituary published on 10 March 1894 (Ref. 6; see Fig. 3).

Samuels's interview given to *The Morning Leader* (rpt. in Sherry 1971: 238) is of interest as he is the last person on record as having spoken to Bourdin, just hours before he died. These accounts, however, reveal little, other than that Bourdin had a *Wanderlust* and kept his own counsel, but whether or not these were connected to anarchist activities has not been proved conclusively.[7] Yet Henri Bourdin's reticence about his brother's life can be understood as a determined effort not to be associated publicly with the anarchist movement.[8] Such caution was clearly advisable as, within days of the Outrage, letters and postcards were delivered to Henri's rented workshop premises threatening "to blow it up," and his landlady was considering taking action against "several daily newspapers, in which it had been suggested that her house contained explosives" (*Morning Leader*, 20 February 1894: 5). Similar threats were also received at the Autonomie Club, frequented by Martial Bourdin and the *Commonweal* group (Ref. 12).

Henri Bourdin is listed in 1884 as one of "three anarchists" invited to join a society formed by Mrs Charlotte Wilson to discuss the French translation of Karl Marx's *Das Kapital*, as this edition "was more comprehensible."[9] However, Henri's marriage in 1886 was perhaps the prelude

---

French anarchist tailor, Henri Bourdin, may … have occurred in America. It was apparently not registered in London" (Oliver 1983: 59). See also Samuels's claim that "Martial was a relative of mine" (Ref. 17).

[7] Bourdin goes unmentioned in Jean Maitrons's definitive *Dictionnaire biographique du mouvement ouvrier français* (1964-90) and *Le Mouvement anarchiste en France* (1975), as confirmed by Mitch Abidor, historian of French anarchism, and Mme Agnès Renou, on behalf of "le SINDBAD," Département Philosophie, histoire, sciences de l'homme, Bibliothèque nationale de France. Accordingly, there is no record that Bourdin was a member of the militant association L'Aiguille (referred to as the "Needles" in "His Life in Paris" in *Weekly Times & Echo* [Ref. 6], and as reported in *The Morning Leader*, 19 February 1894: 5).

[8] The name of Henri's son, Spartacus Martial Bourdin (b. 1890), perhaps not only pays homage to his uncle but may also provocatively suggest his father's political beliefs (Registration of Birth: Jan–Mar 1890 Hendon 3a/212). The gladiator-slave who allegedly became leader of an unsuccessful uprising against the Roman Republic, Spartacus is often perceived as a symbol of oppressed people fighting for their freedom against a powerful state.

[9] As noted in Oliver (1983: 29). Wilson (1854-1944), a former Fabian turned anarchist, was editor of *Freedom* and instrumental in Peter Kropotkin's coming to England in 1886.

to his embourgeoisement as suggested by his domestic details entered in the 1891 Census returns, and an oblique testimony to Vladimir's assertion that "Anarchists don't marry" (33). The Census confirms his occupation as a ladies tailor, and he is named as head of a household in Willesden – distinct from his workshop in Great Titchfield Street in London's West End – that included his wife Kate, their three young children, and a "general domestic servant." As Henri had stated, his brother is not recorded as living at this address.[10]

England and its liberal traditions had historically provided asylum for political refugees and noted expatriate anarchists such as Peter Kropotkin, Enrico Malatesta, and Communard Louise Michel were free to preach their own brand of political activism (see Fig. 2). The escalation of terrorism on the continent was met there by the exercise of powers already in place "to expel and conduct to the frontier any person whose presence is considered dangerous to the commonwealth."[11] However, as was noted in various reports (see Ref. 3), successive outrages resulted in an increase of anarchist sympathizers leaving under their own volition and pre-empting the inevitable expulsion. Thus, England's liberal traditions were being severely strained by the steady influx of what Colonel Howard Vincent termed as "the refuse population of Europe" (Ref. 4). On 15 February 1894, Home Secretary Asquith, in response to questions raised in the Commons on the freedoms enjoyed by the more vociferous domiciled anarchists, stated the Government's position that "the Anarchists are best treated by being left alone and allowed to blow off steam" (Ref. 1). Just a few hours later, Martial Bourdin blew himself up in Greenwich Park.

The mounting antipathy towards "the right of asylum" (*Ibid.*) as sanctioned by England was now given free rein both at home and abroad. What had been merely suggested pre-Bourdin was now becoming open criticism of England's supposed laxity in dealing with anarchists.

---

[10] 1891 Census details for 45 Victoria Road, Willsden (RG12/1045 (111), p. 42). It had been erroneously assumed that Martial Bourdin lived at his brother's workshop address in Great Titchfield Street, as he had Henri's business card on him when he died. Under the anglicized name Henry, Henri Bourdin continued to do business as a ladies' tailor, listed in the London telephone directory at 36 Upper Berkley Street in 1904. In 1940, he is listed as "H. Bourdin, Tlr" at 18 Noel Street, W1.

[11] From a question tabled by Colonel Howard Vincent in the Commons and extract from *The Times*, 20 February 1894 (Ref. 4). HO 144 545 A55176/12 (File opened 2006).

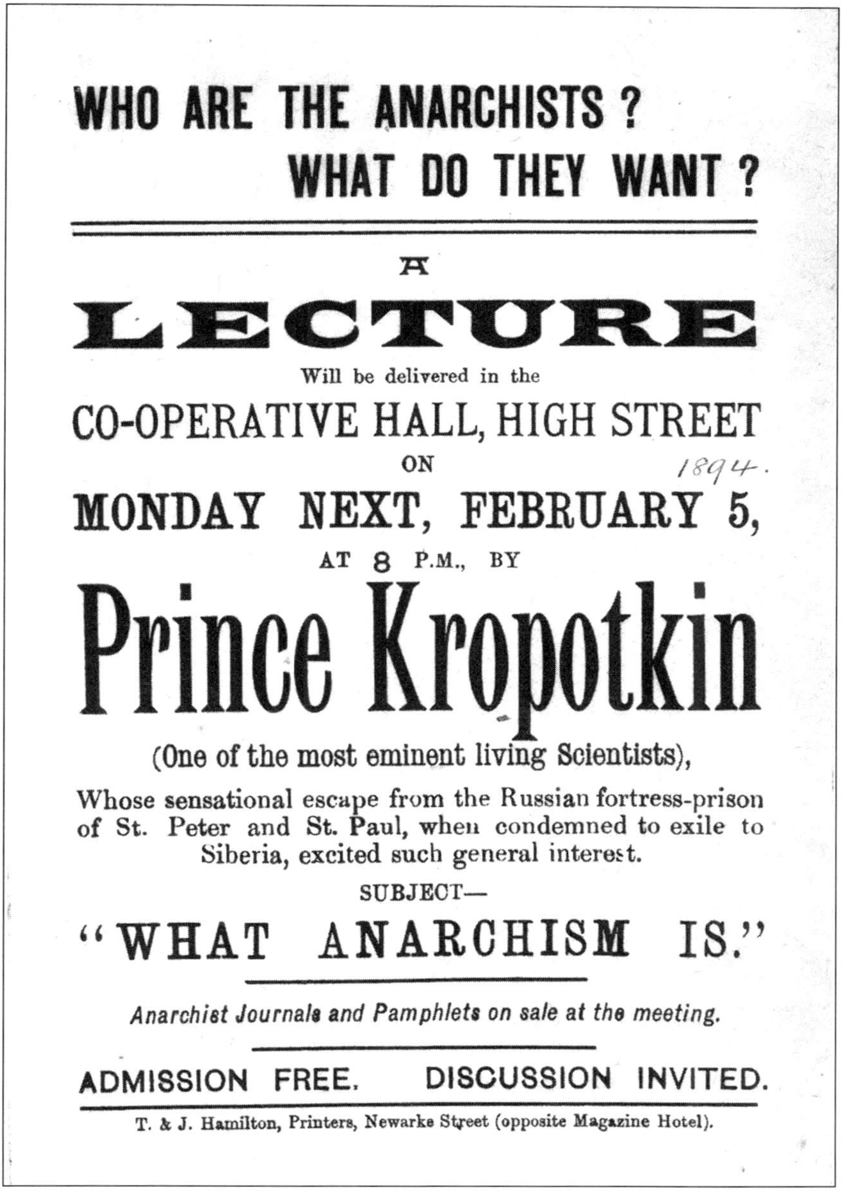
WHO ARE THE ANARCHISTS ?
WHAT DO THEY WANT ?

A
LECTURE
Will be delivered in the
CO-OPERATIVE HALL, HIGH STREET
ON 1894.
MONDAY NEXT, FEBRUARY 5,
AT 8 P.M., BY
Prince Kropotkin
(One of the most eminent living Scientists),
Whose sensational escape from the Russian fortress-prison of St. Peter and St. Paul, when condemned to exile to Siberia, excited such general interest.
SUBJECT—
"WHAT ANARCHISM IS."

Anarchist Journals and Pamphlets on sale at the meeting.

ADMISSION FREE. DISCUSSION INVITED.

T. & J. Hamilton, Printers, Newarke Street (opposite Magazine Hotel).

Fig. 2. Kropotkin poster (Special Collections, University Library, University of Leicester)

THE COMMONWEAL

A REVOLUTIONARY JOURNAL OF

Anarchist-Communism.

VOL. 2, No. 23 NEW SERIES, SATURDAY MARCH 10, 1894. FORTNIGHTLY, ONE PENNY.

IN MEMORIAM.

MARTIAL BOURDIN. DIED FEB. 15, 1894.

AGED 26 YEARS.

Spurning the name of a slave,
Fearless of gaol or of grave,
Fighting for Freedom he gave
His life in the Revolution.

Time shall not rob him of fame ;
Hating the Tyrant, and game
In the spirit that rings in his name
He died for the Revolution.

Our noble comrade lies now beneath the sod. At an early age he risked his future chances of comfort, pleasure, and life itself, for the benefit of suffering humanity,—ignorant, brutish, suffering humanity,—that greeted his funeral cortege with derision, contempt, and hatred, bred from their brutalizing surroundings and prejudices which enable the classes, who "toil not, neither do they spin," to live in splendour and voluptuousness upon the degradations and miseries to which the workers are condemned by the present capitalist system, which Martial Bourdin labored to destroy and for which he sacrificed his life. He was not one of the poorest, the most wretched, the most exploited or oppressed ; he earned a tolerably comfortable livelihood, but he had seen enough of the cruelties and injustices inflicted upon the class to which he belonged—the workers—in France, in America, and in London, to make him determined to throw himself entirely into the struggle of the workers against the shirkers.

He was no writer, he had not any oratorical ability ; so he contented himself with working in a quieter and more effective way as he considered, rather than do nothing except criticize and waste his time in bickerings and unmanly actions, as some do. His old father and mother, nearly ninety years of age, still obliged to work and still in poverty after working their whole lives and rearing a family of eight to be useful workers in this rotten society : seeing that this is the end that we must, nearly all of us, reach if we are fortunate enough to escape disease, starvation, or the workhouse, he threw himself into the struggle.

Not for the love he bore the contented slaves and cowards who patiently submit to life-long servitude and remorseless tyranny, but because he hated, with a hate as cold as ice and then as hot as the fabled fires of hell, those institutions and conditions, with those who profit by them, that cause so much suffering and anguish, mental and physical, among the many millions of innocent, helpless men, women, and children, victims to the greed and lust of an idle, vicious, useless class, venomous and parasitical ; a class of mild and wild beasts that live only upon the blood, muscles, and sinews of our class ; who use as tools for their own selfish purposes our strength, our skill, our patience and ingenuity, and who, therefore, must as a class be destroyed or abolished.

Our comrade was not of an affectionate nature (I shall not ascribe to him virtues that he did not possess); but one virtue he excelled in, and that was tenacity of purpose; another was his intense heartfelt love for the movement. The movement, not that which comprises a few known men ; the movement, not of one party or one land, but a holy love for the world-wide movement of the workers towards emancipation, towards Freedom—social and economic; the movement of which we Anarchists are but as links in the chain encircling the known earth, only visible here and there wherever tyranny and oppression have forced it to the surface ; underneath, barely visible even to those who form connecting links, lies dormant yet powerful the natural, potential, forces of human solidarity that, in the course of time—that time which we Anarchists are bringing nearer, with an irresistible force will embrace and entwine the aspirations of a Universal Brotherhood of Labor, when a new era will have commenced and the peoples be on the high road to Peace and Harmony and Love.

It is owing to such comrades as Martial Bourdin, with their resolution and tenacity, that the social question has forced itself even so far upon the masters of the race. How droll, and yet how terrible !—a handful of creatures, fellow mortals, social atoms like ourselves, individually weak and helpless, yet masters of the race, with all-powerful influences, holding within their grasp the lives and liberties of millions—blind, stupid, and brutal. But only because of the mental blindness of the masses do the classes manage to retain their power ; the blindness that is fostered by all the cursed cliques of priests and politicians, who see in the people's intelligence their own destruction. Martial believed with us that no force outside individual physical force will ever suffice to show to our bloodsuckers and oppressors how really in earnest we are in our endeavours to win for the workers of the world real Freedom, in order that we should all have the fullest and freest opportunities for the cultivation and development of our highest and best faculties.

We had both read the great Wendell Phillips, where he wrote : "Every step of progress that the world has made has been from scaffold to scaffold, and from stake to stake. It is no exaggeration to say, that all the great truths relating to society and government have been first heard in the solemn protests of martyred patriotism or the loud cries of crushed and starving labor. The law has been always wrong. Government began in tyranny and force, began in the feudalism of the soldier and bigotry of the priest ; and the ideas of justice and humanity have been fighting their way like a thunderstorm, against the organized selfishness of human nature."

Martial was a relative of mine, but there was hardly any affection between us on that score. He had no affection, I believe, for anybody in the ordinary sense ; he was too much wrapped up with interest in the growth and development of the revolutionary movement to have time for any display of selfish personal affection or gratification, and although he was always to the fore in any frivolous yet necessary affair, it was for other reasons and with other motives that he seemingly threw off the serious and became the social. Just one or two instances of his dual nature will show what kind of comrade we have lost. Once he went with me to a lecture, and afterwards walked the whole distance back rather than change a sovereign, and then went to bed supperless for the same reason. Some time afterwards a comrade was obliged to leave London on important business, but he had no money for the expenses; he told our comrade so, and with an exhibition of impatience (he was always impatient) Martial took two sovereigns from his purse and gave them over, and the journey was made. I, naturally, was somewhat surprised, knowing his niggardly disposition generally ; and on asking for an explanation he said : "I don't require much for myself, but for the movement, and when something has to be done, everything I have would be too little ; I can make shift and manage easily for myself, but the work of the movement must be carried on."

On another occasion several comrades had been arrested and their wives and families rendered penniless; he came among the friends and, going to each one separately, soon collected enough for their immediate wants. When a comrade was in danger on the continent, and money had to be sent to pay the expenses here, Martial was always the most energetic in collecting and borrowing the needful ; when the funds of the club were run out, when money had to be raised by means of subscription lists, concerts, balls, excursions, and what not, Martial always brought in the most money ; when, a few weeks back, the *Commonweal* was without funds and we were obliged to attempt to print the paper by hand on our own antiquated press, Martial (although he did not stand any higher than the machine) was there offering Cantwell to do anything that might be useful in the work on hand ; when any suspicious characters entered the club, he was among the first to point them out and urge their expulsion, only on the Saturday before his unfortunate death he shouted the loudest and argued the most against the presence of persons he considered dangerous to the movement and the club. He was not always thanked, rather he was abused, but he was not moved from his uncompromising position or purpose which he carried with him to the end.

Such a comrade was he, and at the age of 26 he undertook the conveyance of dangerous explosive compounds to a secluded spot, where none could have been injured, in order to put to the test a new weapon of destruction that would have furnished the revolutionary armoury with another means of terrorizing those who consciously and unconsciously consign so many innocent lives to destitution and despair. In vain they tell us that force is no remedy; in vain they point out that these acts form the excuse for the most brutal repression ; in vain they hang, torture, and imprison : all this has no effect on those who know history, who know human nature, who know how in the past, in spite of persecution and oppression and torture and ostracism, the truth has still made itself heard and felt,—those who know how much the element of fear enters into the spirit that concedes anything whatever. Was it not an English statesman who, speaking at Carlisle, Jan. 13th, 1871, said that "Catholic Emancipation was passed through fear of revolution in Ireland ; the first Reform Bill was passed by the light of Nottingham and Bristol in flames ; Free Trade would not have been carried as it was, if there had not been a famine in Ireland that alarmed our statesmen ; the second Reform Bill was in danger of not being passed, until Hyde Park railings came down"? And again : "I am not sure whether the Irish Church would not have been standing still if the Fenians had not blown down Clerkenwell Prison ; and as to the Irish Land Bill, I doubt whether we would have got it if the Irishmen had not taken to the fatal practice of shooting their landlords." Believing this, we stand and look the whole world in the face, all those that hate us, misunderstand us, and who show no appreciation of our efforts on their behalf : to those workers who, like worms are content to squirm and grovel under the heel of injustice, those worms who are satisfied with getting enough dust to eat—even among those who knew Martial and who know us—to these and to the workers of the world generally we say, with our eyes fixed on the corpse of our comrade, that, come weal come woe, we pledge ourselves to the fallen dead and the living, we make this solemn vow : That we shall strive by every means in our power to destroy ignorance and oppression, prejudice and cruelty, fear and falsity, in order that it shall be impossible for some men to murder, rob, and dominate millions of their fellows for no other reason than their helplessness and simplicity.

Fig. 3. *The Commonweal*, 10 March 1894, p. 1. (British Library)

Whereas in December 1893, a placard posted in Paris stated, rather benignly, that England had been spared from terrorist outrages "on account of her hospitality to the anarchists,"[12] post-Bourdin, *The Times* presented a selection of the hostile "jibes of the Paris Press" towards "selfish England" (Ref. 7). Such righteous indignation continued, with the Paris correspondent of the *St James's Gazette* claiming that London "has become a standing menace on the Continent, because it is now the cave of Anarchism – the stronghold of the most dangerous men of all nations" (Ref. 9). The chorus of disapproval and accusation being levied at England supports Jacques Berthoud's observation that "the threat to state came not from anarchism but from its own permissiveness, which was provocative to those European powers that had reason to fear anarchism's campaigns of assassination and random terror" (1997: 109). It is precisely this perspective that Conrad chose for *The Secret Agent*, wherein Vladimir tells Verloc: "England lags. This country is absurd with its sentimental regard for individual liberty. … England must be brought into line" (28).

Despite Conrad's eventual disingenuousness regarding not only the Outrage but also David Nicoll's pamphlet, *The Greenwich Mystery*, it is none the less this account that he promotes in the novel. Nicoll contended that Samuels was an *agent provocateur* in the pay of Inspector Melville[13] and that he duped Bourdin into carrying the explosives that ultimately killed him. While conceding that the death was accidental and the presumed intention being for Bourdin to endure the "living death of penal servitude" once found in possession of the bomb by the police whom he suspects were waiting "in ambush not far from the Observatory" (Sherry 1971: 393), Nicoll proposes that the rationale for Samuels's action was to discredit the anarchists and give the middle classes, in Vladimir's prescription, "a jolly good scare" (28).

More recent opinion has found his claims to be exaggerated and informed by the enmity that clearly existed between the two men. Samuels, for example, usurped Nicoll as editor of *The Commonweal*.[14]

---

[12] HO 144 545 A55176/5 (File opened 2006).

[13] William Melville (1850-1918). His career and reputation began to flourish when he was appointed in 1893 to the Special Irish Branch, "a new covert branch of the CID based at Scotland Yard ... Established in response to the Fenian bombing campaign which had begun in 1881" (Cook 2004: 30). Later, this was known simply as the Special Branch.

[14] *The Commonweal* was first published in February 1885 as "The Official Journal of the Socialist League," with William Morris as editor, contributor, main

Various suppositions notwithstanding, Bourdin's real purpose for being at Greenwich with a bomb is unlikely ever to be known, but, contrary to the official line, it is equally unlikely that he was killed whilst attempting to commit a genuine Outrage in the one country that still provided asylum for political refugees, however loosely defined.[15] This was re-iterated in the aftermath of the explosion by one anarchist who stated "England is our refuge," whilst another blamed Bourdin for potentially "endangering the position of the Anarchists in the only country where they could move without obstruction" (Refs. 5 and 8).

Compared to the extensive and often sensationalist reporting of the incident in the popular press, the anarchist press coverage both in comment and column inches, was fairly muted. Not only were there considerably fewer anarchist publications in circulation at this time, but they also tended to appear on either a fortnightly or monthly basis, funds permitting, and so were never quite up to date on events as they occurred. Thus, *The Commonweal*'s first report on the affair was the Memorial Edition, published nearly a month after Bourdin's death (Fig. 3). The March edition of *Liberty* also comments on the event, and describes Colonel Majendie's testimony that the Observatory was Bourdin's target as being "utterly absurd" and designed to provoke "prejudice against Anarchism" (Ref. 19).

The January–February edition of *Freedom* had already been "put to bed" by the time of the explosion, but of interest is its account of "A Conference of Communist Anarchists" called by the Commonweal Group and held at the Autonomie Club on 26 December 1893. It reports that "Special emphasis was laid upon the fact that the work of Communist Anarchists is essentially one of *education* not of violence, but it was declared, as Anarchists, we acknowledge the right of individuals to act as they think best in furthering the spread of their ideas" (Ref. 14). It is doubtless at this conference that Nicoll recalled seeing "little Bourdin sitting at the feet of Samuels, and looking up into his eyes with loving trust. To the little man, he was evidently a hero to be loved and revered" (Sherry 1971: 388).[16] This places Bourdin at the conference, and as no

---

financial backer, and designer of the paper's masthead. By 1888, after dissension had developed in the Socialist League, more extreme anarchist members removed Morris, and he was replaced as editor by David Nicoll, under whom the paper became "A Revolutionary Journal of Anarchist-Communism."

[15] Samuels states his theory in the memorial to Bourdin in *The Commonweal* of 10 March 1894 (Ref. 17).

[16] Sherry also notes the similarity between this description and Winnie's observation to Verloc about Stevie: "That boy just worships you" (1971: 314).

dissent over the emphasis on *education* is recorded in *Freedom* 's report, it can be assumed that it met with general approval. Thus, it is "hardly credible" that within weeks of this consensus, Bourdin should conceive an attempt to blow up the Royal Observatory as a method of furthering the cause of anarchism.

Again, it is the March edition of the Supplement to *Freedom* that first mentions "The Bourdin Affair," and simply states that he "met his death by the explosion of a bomb, which for some purpose unknown he was carrying in Greenwich Park." It does, however, decry the "want of decency in the presence of death" displayed as the funeral cortège passed *en route* to the cemetery, yet it suspects this was the handiwork of "detectives scattered among the crowd." The final column relating to the incident, refers to the English "Third Section," an allusion to the Russian Secret Police, and states that a "political police force" is now in operation and paid for by English taxpayers "to be at the beck and call of foreign governments" (Refs. 10 and 15; see also Ref. 11). This is a reaction to Asquith's assertion in the Commons that to deal effectively with the anarchists, all that was required was a "more constant and concerted interchange of information ... between the Governments and police authorities of the different nations of the world."[17] However, all of the anarchist press reporting is distinguished by its lack of personal engagement with Bourdin and the presumed Outrage, nor was he claimed, Samuels's obituary apart, as a martyr for the cause.[18] This detached attitude is continued in *The Torch*'s retrospective of 1894.[19] Spanning almost three pages, the article is a veritable calendar of anarchist and labour activity throughout the world for 1894. That there is not one mention of Bourdin and his bomb is a damning indictment of the Greenwich Outrage. Perhaps the most fitting coda to the whole affair is

---

[17] Despite this response, Home Office files reveal a frustration with European authorities' continued practice of sending expelled anarchists to Britain, and ignoring repeated requests to only deport to this country British subjects. See HOB2840/3a and HOB8240/5a, "Memorandum of Laws relating to landing and residences of Aliens in Great Britain," which was revised by Secretary Asquith on 10 July 1894. For a detailed view of attempts to get an Aliens Act onto the statute books, see Collyer 2004.

[18] *The Commonweal* for 28 April 1894 dismissed the Outrage thus: "The Greenwich Park explosion proved how foolish and how dangerous it is to meddle with compounds one is not familiar with" (3).

[19] The journal was on hiatus from October 1893 until the following spring (Oliver 183: 122).

the depiction of the Outrage as yet another instalment in the capers of The Ball's Pond Banditti that appeared in the "funny paper" *Larks!* on 19 February 1894. It places the gang "At Greenwich Observatory," where the "pitiless horde" is thwarted in its attempt to capture "Britain's Home of Science" (see Fig. 4).

This Copy of "LARKS!" is a **Railway Accident Life Policy for £50.**

½D

Larks!

½D

FOUNDED AND CONDUCTED BY GILBERT DALZIEL.

Vol. 2.—No. 43.] MONDAY, FEBRUARY 19, 1894. [HALFPENNY

THE BALL'S POND BANDITTI AT GREENWICH OBSERVATORY

(1) MYSTERIOUS PASSENGERS

(2) THE ADVANCE.

(3) PREPARATIONS FOR THE ATTACK

(4) THE "CRIB-CRACKERS."

(5) A SORTIE.

(6) FLIGHT.

(1) Gallantly the good ship *Citizen X*, chartered specially for this occasion only, clove the six-inch billows of the Thames, as the dark and mysterious Bloodwing stood in the bow, surrounded by his ruthless and daring Band of Outlaws.

(2) Landed at Greenwich, the Bandits sought the Park, and lurked amid its woody recesses like fierce beasts of prey, until the darkening towers of the Observatory stood out bold and clear against the fading sunset.

(3) Stealing from their concealment, the Outlaws mounted the Hill with cat-like tread, halting for a moment upon the broad promenade before the stately edifice to assume their masks and prepare their lethal weapons, at the command of their reckless Chief.

(4) Nought stirred within, as the Robber Captain, mounting upon the herculean shoulders of Lurcher Geeson, flashed his bull'seye around the courtyard. A moment more and Britain's Home of Science must be in the hands of that pitiless horde. Will nought avert the calamity? The grim lieutenant, Gorger Pain, mounts guard, halbert in hand; but the sharp ears of Sweppy Titmarsh and Bocco have caught the click of a latch. Hark!

(5) A gate bursts open. The furious garrison dash out, scattering the startled Bandits before them like chaff before the gale.

(6) Amazement becomes panic. Greenwich Observatory is saved for this time, at any rate. Clearing the railings, the Ball's Pond Banditti are presently in headlong flight down the hill, escaping capture or destruction only by an accident, which delays the foremost of their pursuers, until the last Bandit has disappeared from sight.—(*See next week.*)

Fig. 4. *Larks!*, 19 February 1894 (British Library)

Acknowledgements

My sincere thanks are due to Allan H. Simmons not only for encouragement and tireless support but also, with J. H. Stape, for variously contributing to the information here and commenting on drafts of this essay. I should also like to express gratitude to: Mitch Abidor, historian of French anarchism and a member of the Steering Committee of the Marxist Internet Archive; Mme Agnès Renou, of "le SINDBAD," Département de Philosophie, histoire, sciences de l'homme, Bibliothèque Nationale de France; Dr Barry Pateman, Associate Editor of The Emma Goldman Papers, University of California, Berkeley; Linda Haas Davenport; and Evelyn Cornell, Special Collections Librarian, University of Leicester.

Works cited

"Anarchism: A Documentary History of Libertarian Ideas." <en.wikipedia.org>.

Anderson, Sir Robert. *Sidelights on the Home Rule Movement.* London: John Murray, 1906.

Berthoud, Jacques. "*The Secret Agent.*" In *The Cambridge Companion to Joseph Conrad*, edited by J. H. Stape. 100-21. Cambridge: Cambridge University Press, 1996.

Cook, Andrew. *M: MI5's First Spymaster.* London: Tempus, 2004.

Collyer, Michael. "Secret Agents: Anarchists, Islamists and Responses to Politically Active Refugees in London." *Ethnic and Racial Studies* 24.2 (2004): 278-302.

Ford, Ford Madox. *Joseph Conrad: A Personal Remembrance.* London: Duckworth, 1924.

Jean-Aubry, G. *Joseph Conrad: Life and Letters.* 2 vols. London: Heinemann, 1927.

Maitron, Jean, ed. *Dictionnaire biographique du mouvement ouvrier français.* 37 vols. Paris : Éditions ouvrières, 1964-90.

——. *Le Mouvement anarchiste en France.* Paris: F. Maspero, 1975.

"Meredith, Isabel." *A Girl Among the Anarchists* (1903). Lincoln: Nebraska University Press, 1993.

Oliver, Hermia. *The International Anarchist Movement in Late Victorian England.* London: Croom Helm/St. Martins, 1983.

Prieg, Benjamin. "1894: A Retrospect." *The Torch.* N.s. 8.18 January 1894 [= 1895]: 3-5.

Sherry, Norman. *Conrad's Western World.* London: Cambridge University Press, 1971.

Watt, Ian, ed. *Conrad: The Secret Agent.* Macmillan Casebook. London: Macmillan, 1973.

DOCUMENTS

1. *St James's Gazette*, 16 February 1894: 3

WORDS AND DEEDS

The explosion at Greenwich Park last night came as an unfortunate practical commentary on Mr. Asquith's apologetic reply to Mr. Knatchbull-Hugessen and Mr. W. F. Smith delivered in the House of Commons a couple of hours earlier. Mr. Asquith's position is that the London Anarchists are best treated by being left alone and allowed to blow off steam, and that for the press or for members of Parliament to take notice of "the mouthings of these obscure and contemptible ranters" is to create the very mischiefs and dangers which we all want to prevent. But if the "mischiefs and dangers" are going on all the same, if the "mouthers" are found marching step by step with the murderers, meeting at the same clubs and applauding the same speeches, what are we to do? Mr. Asquith says we are not to be guided by French precedents, and that, although the Republic by a recent law deals in a sharp and summary way with such incitements, "we must settle our own affairs according to our own ideas." That sounds well; it is thoroughly British and insular, and is the sort of thing that goes down with the House of Commons; but in view of the facts it is really a rather foolish remark. For, in the first place, the Anarchist business is in its essence not local but international; and, in the second, the distinction between those who talk about and advocate such crimes and those who commit them is such a thin and constantly shifting partition that it is exceedingly difficult at any moment to declare with any approach to certainty who is on this side and who is on that. Even assuming that the preaching of anarchy and the manufacture of bombs in our midst is a matter that does not concern us, since they are meant for foreign consumption, it must yet be admitted that these Anarchists are uncomfortable neighbours. The "respectably dressed" young man of thirty, who went down on the South-Eastern Railway yesterday afternoon from Charing-cross to Greenwich, doubtless jostled against many worthy citizens at the ticket office or on the platform and sat side by side with them in the railway carriage. He was, as we know, ready to "go off" at any moment, as he did a little later in the park. How many more respectable-looking foreigners are there in our streets and lodging-houses in the same uncomfortable position? The "right of asylum" may be a sacred thing, but we can have too much of it.

It becomes a very serious question, and Mr. Asquith would do well to consider it, whether our laws regarding free speech, personal liberty, and all the rest of it, excellent though they are under ordinary circumstances and in cases of ordinary crime, are at all fitted for dealing with international anarchy. Every Continental State now provides for this sort of thing by special laws. The natural result is that, as rats driven out of one corn-sack take refuge in the next, so these enemies of the human race come over quietly and settle down among us. Our legal theory, that every man is innocent until he is proved to be guilty, protects them admirably; for until the crime is committed we cannot deal with them effectively, and when it is committed it is too late to do so. The police in London know these men, and know their meeting places; but their hands are tied. In France or in Germany such clubs as exist in the slums of Tottenham-court-road and in the East End would be quietly surrounded and "raided," and every man present would have to give an account of himself; they would be rigorously examined, each apart from the other; and such of them as the law could not deal with directly would be shown across the frontier by a couple of gendarmes. A very harsh and arbitrary proceeding, our Radical friends would say; and some one of the type of Mr. Benn would get up and ask questions about it, and inquire whether somebody had not called the gentle dynamiter "idle" or "vicious," and if that wicked language was not the "cause" of his natural desire to commit wholesale murder. But if we are to have a scrupulous respect for personal liberty and personal safety in these matters, let the Anarchists begin.

But, says Mr. Asquith, you must not confound the real dynamiters with the "obscure and contemptible ranters" of Tower-hill. The distinction is one which, in practice, it is extremely difficult to draw. Take the case of Ireland at the time when the Invincibles and other murder clubs were active. Mr. James Carey was a prominent citizen and politician. In his trade society and in the Dublin Municipal Council he was noted for his "patriotic" speeches, and was in the running for the office of Lord Mayor. And yet all the while he was in touch with the "practical" criminals. It was the same with Daly and Egan, over whom Mr. Redmond and Mr. Dillon still shed rival tears. You cannot draw a hard-and-fast line and say, On this side are the talkers, on that side are the criminals. Your true criminal, Mr. Asquith will say, is silent and secret and does not come out to talk of his crimes. We are not so sure of that. A great deal of this crime is a matter of contagious excitement; and where one man will use explosive talk simply as a means of manœuvring himself into a safe seat in Parliament, another, with a weaker and more inflammable brain, will go out and do the act of which his leader merely prates. We do not profess for a moment that the question is free from serious difficulty. But if Mr. Asquith hopes to deal with it, he must try to get rid of his fine phrases and debating-society theories. Two things are clear. The first is, that wild talk, if it finds a suitable bed, quickly germinates into crime; and therefore, while so much crime is about the talk should be stopped, or should be kept within the bounds of decency. And the second and more important fact is, that London is being made the refuge and preparing-ground for the men who are spreading wounds and panic through the cities of the Continent. The alien pauper was bad enough; but we are told that in the sacred name of free trade we are bound to tolerate him. Are we also to have free trade in crime, which is the only stock-in-trade of the alien dynamiter?

2. *The Sheffield Daily Telegraph*, 17 February 1894: 3

THE BLOWN UP ANARCHIST

It was five o'clock yesterday afternoon when the Anarchist Bourdin was blown up in Greenwich Park. Yet not a word about it was known in London till the papers came out this morning. And even then we would probably have heard nothing of it but for the Central News which in this business enjoys the honour of been quoted in big type and the source of information of the great London dailies. Beyond this, the Central News also enjoyed the distinction of being the first to send the news round the world in its service of foreign telegrams. Mr. Secretary Asquith's extreme reticence in the House to-night continues a theory of mine that the police purposely withheld information of the tragedy from the Press inquirers in order that they might not alarm other Anarchists who were being watched.

[The Home Secretary's "extreme reticence" may well have been due to an extreme lack of knowledge. See Ref. 20.]

3. *The Evening News and Post*, 17 February 1894: 2

THE AUTONOMIE CLUB

The police have awakened at last. The raid upon the Autonomie Club, in Windmill-street, last night, appears to have been cleverly conceived and smartly carried out. The members of the Anarchist resort walked into the trap that had been set for them, without, apparently, the least suspicion that they would be detained and compelled to give an account of themselves. It is true that the whole proceeding is akin to the English official practice of locking the stable door after the steed has escaped; but it is better for the deed to be done late than never to be done at all. Why it was not done months ago is a question Mr. Asquith alone can answer. There is no reason why he should have waited until a Frenchman had accidentally relieved society of his presence by getting blown to pieces in front of a building which he may have intended to destroy. The raid ought at least to have been executed after the explosion in the French Chamber, if not soon after the outrage at Barcelona. Everyone knows that after these events there was a general stampede of Anarchists and that with one consent they made England their asylum. To every journalist it was notorious that the Autonomie Club was their recognised meeting place, and that under its roof might nightly be seen men who would not be allowed to set foot on their native soil. Yet not until last night, in spite of the protests that were raised in Spain and in France, did our police take the trouble to sift the club and give its members to understand that they were not free from surveillance. For this inaction Mr.

Asquith is responsible. He is a believer in the policy of what he is pleased to call "letting off steam." …

4. Home Office File A55176/12 | 17 February 1894

Question: Admission of dangerous characters into England

Colonel Howard Vincent – To ask the Secretary of State for the Home Department, whether he is aware that the executive authorities of nearly every Continental State have the power to expel and conduct to the frontier any person whose presence is considered dangerous to the commonwealth and that by these means considerable numbers of dangerous characters are reported to have been lately sent to England from France and elsewhere, every other State denying them admission:

And if, under the circumstances of the day, the Government propose to place any limit upon Foreign immigration or the reception in the overcrowded centres of the United Kingdom of the refuse population of Europe.

[Tabled on 17 February, the question was asked on Monday, 19 February 1894, and reported in *The Times* the next day.]

Included in this file is the following extract from *The Times*, 20 February 1894:

THE TREATMENT OF ANARCHISTS

COLONEL HOWARD VINCENT asked the Secretary of State for the Home Department whether he was aware that the executive authorities of nearly every Continental State had the power to expel and conduct to the frontier any persons whose presence was considered dangerous to the commonwealth, and that by these means considerable numbers of dangerous characters were reported to have been lately sent to England from France and elsewhere, every other State denying them admission; and whether, in the circumstances of the day, the Government proposed to place ant limit upon foreign immigration or the reception in the overcrowded centres of the United Kingdom of the refuse population of Europe.

Mr. ASQUITH.– It is the fact that in most of the Continental States the Executive possesses a power of expulsion which is not given to it by the Constitution of this country. There is no doubt also that, by reason of the exercise of this power, dangerous and objectionable characters from time to time find their way into England, not unfrequently, I regret to say, without any warning being given to us by the authorities of the country from which they are expelled. Her Majesty's Government are not of the opinion that , in this respect, any necessity has arisen for a change in the law which has for so long prevailed in Great Britain, and which they believe to be sufficient both for our own protection and for the due performance of our international duties. I should add that we are ready and anxious to co-operate with other countries in any practical measures that can be devised for dealing more effectually with Anarchists and similar enemies of society. (Cheers) But, in our opinion the direction which international efforts can most fruitfully take is to be found, not so much in an extension of the power of expulsion on suspicion, which is apt to confound the innocent with the guilty, and to shift the burden and the danger from one country to another, as a more constant and concerted interchange of information and combined action, both detective and punitive, between the Governments and police authorities of the different nations of the world. (Cheers.)

5. *The Daily Graphic* , 17 February 1894: 3

AN INTERVIEW WITH AN ANARCHIST

Only one Anarchist could be got to talk about Bourdin's death. He knew him, and expressed astonishment at his end, and he went on to explain: "None of us may have known what he intended to do. English people do not seem to understand that we have no plans in common; that each man can act on his own idea, and not mention it to any one."

"You mean that in the ordinary way an outrage could take place and only one man have schemed and carried it out? That there is no conspiracy because it takes more than one to conspire?"

"Yes, yes, that is it. In Anarchy every man or woman has no law except him or herself. Perhaps Bourdin had an idea to blow up Greenwich Observatory – I do not know. I don't think so. I think it was an accident – but if he had he could easily carry it out without telling anyone."

"But about the money he had on him. How could he, a working tailor out of employment, come by that?"

"How can I tell? I did not know he had money on him. Again I say I don't believe he intended anything. We Anarchists do not wish to do anything in England, because it is our refuge. It serves us by letting us alone, and the opinion is among our comrades not to do anything here so long as we are ourselves not attacked. If war was declared against us, then we, too, would have to make war against your English society."

"Did you know Emile Henri when he was here?"

"I would rather not say, and I do not wish to say anything more about Bourdin who has died."

6. *Weekly Times & Echo: A Liberal Newspaper of Political and Social Progress*, 18 February 1894: 1

FATAL BOMB EXPLOSION AT GREENWICH

SUPPOSED ANARCHIST PLOT

On Thursday evening an explosion was heard by a keeper at Greenwich-park on the hill close to the Royal Observatory. Proceeding thither he found a respectably-dressed foreign-looking man in a kneeling posture, terribly mutilated. His legs were shattered, one arm was blown away, and the stomach and abdomen were torn open. As the keeper came up to him the man faintly besought help and then fell forward on his face, unconscious, in a great pool of his own blood. He was taken to the Seamen's Hospital on an ambulance, and died in less than half an hour. A bottle, in many pieces, which had apparently contained an explosive substance, was found near the spot where the explosion took place, and it is conjectured that the deceased man fell and caused its contents to explode. A card inscribed Mr. H. Bourbon [*sic*], 18, Great Titchfield-street, and several letters and papers were found on the body by the police. There were also several small packages containing a suspicious-looking powder.

THE PARK-KEEPER'S STATEMENT

The park-keeper Sullivan, who was the first to reach the dying man, made the following statement: "Yesterday afternoon at 4.50, I was on duty at St. Mary's-gate, which is nearest to the hospital, and I heard a sharp, loud report. I spoke to another keeper, who believed it was the report of a cannon. I thought there had been an explosion at the Observatory, and to satisfy myself ran immediately towards it. There were only a few boys in the park and they called to me. As I approached the zigzag path I saw a man who seemed to have been hurt. . . . Hurrying forward I saw the man in a kneeling posture, holding himself together, with his head bent towards the ground, and covered with blood. His left hand and forearm had been blown off, and he was groaning and moaning. I asked him what had happened and he cried 'Take me home, take me home.' 'Where do you live?' I said, and he made no reply, but after a pause, said again, 'Take me home.' He spoke in good English, but his accent was foreign. His face was towards the Observatory. I held the weight of his body until Dr. Willes arrived. There was a strong odour of acid. In examining his clothing and the contents of his pockets my hands were covered with a sticky, black stuff which I had some difficulty in washing off."

Alleged Discovery of a Conspiracy

The London police have, according to the Central News, discovered an Anarchist conspiracy. These facts, among others, are beyond dispute – that the inquiries of the detectives, although cautiously made, frightened the plotters, that the gang hurriedly scattered, and that its chief met with his death on Thursday evening when endeavouring to carry away to some place the explosives which were to have been used against society either in this country or in France.

The Police Theory

The police authorities think there is practically no room for doubt that the victim was fleeing from the police, and that his immediate desire was to rid himself safely of the explosives which he had taken away with him. He reached Greenwich about half an hour before dusk, and turning to the left on leaving the station, he walked to the park by way of London-street and Stockwell-street. Walking along the main avenue lined with great trees on both sides, he reached the top of the hill, near the Observatory. Across the pathway the roots of the older trees protrude through the gravel, and it may be assumed that, it now being dusk, the man stumbled and fell, with the result that the infernal machine or machines which he was carrying exploded on his own person. It is possible at the last moment, remembering that the Observatory was a Government building, he decided to expend his explosives against it.

Identification of the Deceased

The deceased has been identified as a young Frenchman, named Martial Bourdin. A card in his pocket showed him to have been a member of the Autonomie Club, in Windmill-street, Tottenham-court-road, a well-known resort of Anarchists of all nations. A sum of £13 in gold was found on his body.

A member of the Autonomie Club, interviewed on Friday, said "We are all intensely grieved that this affair should have occurred. We are sorry that he should have been so ill advised as to attempt anything of the kind here, as we fully recognise the opportunity it gives the Government for taking some repressive action."

Interview with his Brother

On Friday morning, at 18, Great Titchfield-street, W. C., a reporter interviewed the victim's brother, M. Henri Bourdin. He is a tailor by occupation, and rents a small workshop which forms a portion of the back premises of the address above given. "My brother was," he said "a quiet and reserved man, and never conversed with me on aught except the most trifling things. His private affairs he always kept to himself. He had numerous references from his employers describing him as a good honest workman. He has been in this country on and off for about six years." "Had you," asked the interviewer, "any idea that he was in any way, either here or abroad, associated with societies holding extreme views?" "I had not, and I may say my residence here has extended over ten years. My brother was twenty-six years of age, and was born in Tours. My own birthplace was Sanserre [sic]. He was a tailor, but had been unfortunately out of work. Occasionally he visited me for the purpose of obtaining work, but latterly business has been very slack. I last saw him about twelve o'clock (noon) yesterday, when he entered my workshop here and told me he had no work to do. He asked if I could help him, and I said, "I cannot, for at present I have nothing to do myself. He was a batchelor, and whenever he had work he could earn very good wages."

BOURDIN'S ANTECEDENTS

A representative of the Press Association learned on Friday morning, in the course of an interview with one who was intimately acquainted with Bourdin, that the latter first came from Paris – where his parents live – to London about six years ago. He was then a raw lad of sixteen years of age, and any ideas of political intrigue did not appear to enter his mind. Like the majority of French youths he was lively and excitable, but nothing beyond. On reaching London he worked for his brother in Great Titchfield-street, and gradually began to visit the clubs in the vicinity, until falling in with the Anarchist ring, he became imbued with their opinions and at last did not withhold from his companions that he was of one their number [*sic*] and believed in their methods of operation. Three years ago Bourdin went to America, but whether he journeyed thither on an Anarchist mission is not at present quite plain. While in America he found employment as a lady's tailor with a Jew named Wingard or Weingard, and was never short of money. The suggestion is that he received funds from head-quarters, but of this there is at present no actual proof, as Bourdin, after entering the inner ring of the movement, was extremely reticent as to his friends and actions. On leaving America he returned to Paris, and thence proceeded to London, where he resumed his employment as a lady's [sic] tailor at the establishment of his brother, who, like his parents, had no connection whatever with the Anarchist movement. The brother does not live at his business premises, but at a private house, and Bourdin himself lodged at a house in Cleveland-street. Once in London again Bourdin returned to his old haunts and habits. Implicit confidence was placed in him by his associates, and it is not denied that they themselves regret the loss of one of their most zealous organisers.

HIS LIFE IN PARIS

PARIS, Saturday. – The Anarchist Bourdin, who was killed at Greenwich on Thursday evening, was when in Paris connected with an association of Anarchists known as the "Needles," because all the members were tailors. In 1884 he was sentenced to two months' imprisonment for having attempted, by means of placards and other appeals, to organize a meeting in a public thoroughfare. After his release from prison he went abroad, but has since made several visits to Paris. He is a married man, and his wife is of English ancestry. – *Dalziel.*

QUESTION IN PARLIAMENT

In the House of Commons, on Friday, Mr. Darling said that in the absence of the hon. member for Greenwich, and as his constituency was contiguous to it, he would ask whether the Home Secretary could give the House any information as to the explosion reported to have taken place on Thursday. Particularly he would ask whether it was a fact, as stated in several of the newspapers, that it was known to the police that the Anarchists in a particular club were in the habit of meeting at the club, and had in their possession explosives, and if this was so, why these persons had not been arrested before they had an opportunity of doing any damage to themselves or to anybody else. Mr. Asquith replied that he was not in a position at this moment to give the House any information on the subject except that the whole matter was being carefully investigated. (Hear, hear).

ALLEGED INTERNATIONAL PLOT

The Exchange Telegraph Company states that the London police authorities are satisfied Bourdin was one of the travelling conspirators attached to the chief Anarchist group connected with an international dynamite plot, and this view is strengthened by several corroborative circumstances. In the first place, it has just transpired that bombs of a similar character, viz., fluid in a glass receptacle, were discovered in the city of Brussels a few days ago, and from the hotel bills found on Bourdin it is argued he could quite possibly have been concerned in the deposit of those bombs, as he is now proved to have been away from England on and off for two months past.

REPRESSIVE MEASURES CONTEMPLATED

The Exchange Telegraph Company has official authority for stating that the authorities take the gravest possible view of the circumstances connected with Bourdin's death. The strictest secrecy has been enjoined on all officials connected with the case, and the Home Secretary is understood to regard the foreign Anarchist gatherings as fraught with grave danger to the public safety.

Either legislation or drastically repressive police measures in connection with Anarchist conspirators resident in England are certain to follow the disclosures which will be made at the inquest.

Police Raid on the Autonomie Club

At nine o'clock on Friday evening the police made a raid on the Autonomie Club, Windmill-street, Tottenham-court-road, which was believed to be the resort of Anarchists. Having installed themselves in the building, the detectives detained the callers as they arrived, and each one was questioned as to his address and other matters. By eleven o'clock no fewer than eighty persons were thus detained, and were grouped together in the hall in the basement. A little later a Frenchman presented himself, and finding the place in possession of the police tried to escape, but after a struggle he was overpowered. About midnight the police were withdrawn from the Club, none of those present being taken into custody. It is stated that the police made an important seizure of documents at the club, one being the copy of a placard recently circulated in France and headed "Death to Carnot." The house where Bourdin lodged was also searched, and some explosives were found.

Latest Details. – Expect Arrest

A representative of the Press Association says: "As a result of exhaustive investigation, it will be no surprise to the leaders of the London Anarchist Group if the arrest of at least one of the prominent members of the party is effected shortly, as a result of recent developments in London. It is not regarded as possible that any immediate action will be taken against the members of the Autonomie, for although the police seized the members' book, it was found to contain only the bare names of the members of the club, and not their addresses. Neither did the membership cards found on those present bear any addresses. Private letters were, however, taken from persons present, and conveyed to Scotland Yard. Last night the club was crowded, though the premises were known to be "under observation."

The Inquest

Mr. Carttar, the coroner, has decided that the inquest shall take place at eleven o'clock on Monday, at the Lecture Hall, Royal-hill, Greenwich.

7. *The Times*, 19 February 1894: 5

LATEST INTELLIGENCE
THE ANARCHIST CONSPIRACY

PARIS, FEB. 18.

Mr. Asquith's placid inactivity up to the time of the Greenwich explosion brings down, not only on him, but on "selfish England," the jibes of the Paris Press.

The *République Française* says: "The English have two pairs of spectacles, one for looking at their own affairs, the other at those of their neighbours. So long as the Anarchists were content with operating in France, Spain, and Belgium, they were free to 'demonstrate' on Tower-hill, and to form their abominable plots at the Autonomie Club, but it was seen in London that people there ran the risk of having their own fingers burnt at the game, and that bombs exploded at Greenwich, as well as at the Café Terminus and the Licéo, a different tone is taken . . . Everybody will benefit by this tardy awakening of conscience, and we cannot but congratulate ourselves on it. M. Bourdin was therefore well inspired, if not for himself, at least for others, in stumbling with his bottle."

The *Liberté,* in like manner remarks: "The British mind requires the paramount motive of self-interest. The trials of others do not affect it, but it is extremely sensible to its own. . . . Among us, as in England and everywhere else, there exists an infernal band of conspirators who have sworn to compass the extermination of society, and who carry on their abominable designs by blood, fire, and iron. Our neighbours are beginning to understand this, and their direct interest in preserving themselves from the attacks of all these bandits will, perhaps, at last induce them to take precautions, guaranteeing also the safety of other States. . . . Whenever England is closed to Continental Anarchists, so that they have to flee beyond the ocean, there will then be substantial guarantees for the general security. It seems to us that our neighbours ought to make it a point of honour to give this pledge to European order."

The *Paix* likewise holds that the danger will disappear when the Anarchists are driven beyond the sea to countries which will give them the reception they deserve and it adds: "After long hesitation England seems to have understood this duty. To congratulate her on it would be insulting."

8. *The Times*, 20 February 1894: 5

LATEST INTELLIGENCE
THE ANARCHIST CONSPIRACY

PARIS, FEB. 19.

... A French Anarchist in London named Milcent a tailor, is reported by the *Soir* to have blamed Bourdin for endangering the position of the Anarchists in the only country where they could meet without obstruction. He added however, that, London being so large, they could baffle the police, and could hold private meetings. They were to have met last night in the Strand, but this was given up, because the police would have arrested the speaker and there would have been scuffles. – *Our Own Correspondent.*

9. *St James's Gazette*, 21 February 1894: 4

THE CAVE OF ANARCHISM

LENTEN PREACHNG IN PARIS – THE OLD AND NEW JOURNALISM

(*From Our Paris Correspondent.*)

"C'est la faute aux Anglais." Everything bad that now happens to the French is, in their opinion, to be laid to the account of the English. Although Anarchism may almost be catalogued with *articles de Paris* – foreign imitations being for the most part rather weak – the French press for some days past has been very near the point of casting upon England the responsibility of Vaillant's exploit at the Chamber of Deputies and Henry's at the Hôtel du Terminus. We are told that England, in accordance with her habitual and traditional selfishness, has entered into a sort of informal pact with the Anarchists, by which on one side is granted the right of asylum and on the other immunity from the dynamite campaign. By virtue of this tacit and immoral understanding, London, it is said, has become a standing menace on the Continent, because it is now the cave of Anarchism – the stronghold of the most dangerous men of all nations, men inflamed by the worst kind of fanaticism that the world has yet known. Although in other Continental countries opinion may not be quite so outspoken on this subject as it is in France, its tendency is the same. The effect of the recent explosions has been to put back the clock of what is called "progress" several hours and to bring into very general contempt those principles and laws touching individual liberty, under the shelter of which it becomes possible for systematic and indiscriminate murder to be carried on, in the name of the "Propaganda of Deeds," by men who make no secret of their intentions. In the old days, when England was overrun with genuine political refugees, she earned the admiration of the Continent for her hospitality to foreigners. Hers was the "land of liberty," and the idea, together with the phrase, became fixed in the minds of millions who could not speak the English language. But the conditions have changed. The old-fashioned political conspirators were not necessarily assassins and scoundrels; indeed, they frequently possessed the qualities which cause men to be respected. The same cannot be said of the conspirators of the new school, who do not plot against any particular dynasty or form of government, but against society. They should either be treated as criminals or as dangerous lunatics. England, with her love of liberty, has naturally a righteous horror of all arbitrary measures founded on the *raison d'état.* But the world, having yielded too much to the seductive reasons of democratic philosophers, is being forced by the sinister brood of reformers that other reformers have hatched to take up the old weapons again. It is hard to see how England will be able to resist much longer the strong current of opinion that is now setting in favour of a common action on the part of civilized nations in grappling with the new danger by which they are threatened. If all the sinister individuals whom the London police lately had in their power were shipped off to some cannibal island and there left to convert the anthropophagi, there would be great thanksgiving in Europe. Perhaps it is not too late for Mr. Gladstone's Government to act upon the suggestion.

10. HO144/257/A55660/5 | Letter from Home Secretary H. H. Asquith to Commissioner of Police Sir Edward Bradford

Sir E. Bradford,

With reference to the proposed demonstration at the funeral of Bourdin tomorrow, I desire you to carry out the following instructions.

The funeral is to proceed by the shortest and most direct route. No procession of any kind is to be allowed to follow the hearse.

If any attempt is made, either at the starting place, or en route, to form a procession it must be at once prevented and broken up by the police. Only the mourning coach and officials of the undertakers shall be allowed to follow. At the cemetery no one is to be permitted to make a speech of any kind.

If any one attempts to do so, he shall be stopped and if necessary remanded.

(sd) HHA.
22 Feb.94

11. *St James's Gazette*, 24 February 1894: 9

BOURDIN'S FUNERAL

HOSTILE DEMONSTRATIONS

The incidents which marked the progress of the procession which yesterday accompanied the body of the Anarchist Bourdin from the undertaker's premises in Chapel-street, Edgeware-road, to the grave in Finchley Cemetery must have had a very wholesome corrective effect upon any foreign Anarchists, if such there were among the crowd who witnessed them, who may have entertained the notion that their special methods were likely to find sympathy in England. From first to last the attitude of the crowd was distinctly hostile.

RED FLAGS TORN UP

Shortly before the hour appointed for the departure of the procession a number of men, said to have come from Fitzroy-square, appeared at the Lisson-grove end of Chapel-street, carrying two red banners edged with black. They were jeered and hustled by the crowd as they endeavoured to force their way through. Having arrived where the police were stationed, they were at once ordered to withdraw, and being somewhat slow in obeying, they were collared unceremoniously by a number of stalwart constables, and were soon flying from the scene, having left behind them, only to be torn up by the crowd, the shabby old flags which they were not even allowed time to unfurl. This incident was a significant test as to the temper of the crowd, and the officials in charge of the arrangements began to realize that so far from any trouble arising in connection with the Anarchists their efforts must be directed towards protecting the funeral party.

THE MOURNERS THREATENED

The appearance of the coffin as it was borne forth to be placed in the hearse, was greeted with a storm of hissing and hooting, which became even more general and pronounced after the mourners had entered the carriage and the journey to the cemetery began. So threatening, indeed, was the attitude of those who thronged round the hearse and mourning coach that the mounted police had to be summoned from Lisson-grove, where they had been kept in reserve. The mounted men having formed an escort, the constables on foot employed themselves in keeping the crowds from closing in upon the funeral car and its occupants, who were more than once threatened with violence and presented quite a scared appearance. The excitement increased as the cortège proceeded along Lisson-grove, the hearse and carriage being surrounded with a howling mob, many of whom, amidst cries of "Down with the Anarchists," "Go back to your own country," "No bombs here," and other hostile exclamations forcing their way past the police, rushed wildly after the vehicles. The tumult had reached its highest pitch when, at the entrance to Grove-road, the mounted police galloped on in front and formed into line across the thoroughfare. They were supported by fifty constables armed with truncheons. When the procession reached this point only the hearse and funeral car were allowed to pass, the entire force of police being brought into requisition to prevent the passage of the mob. No doubt this movement on the part of the police prevented what threatened to be an attack on the funeral party.

EXCITING SCENE AT THE CEMETERY

The cemetery was reached about half-past three. There was a good deal of hissing on the arrival of the hearse; but the crowds were kept at a safe distance by the constables who escorted the party. A grave had been prepared on the chapel side of the cemetery in the unconsecrated ground, and here there was an assemblage of about one thousand persons awaiting the arrival of the funeral. The number was considerably increased by a mob which followed the hearse from the entrance to the cemetery. The funeral was allowed to proceed in complete peace. While the coffin was being lowered into the grave a lady, clad in black, was seen to place a wreath of white flowers on the lid. It bore the inscription, "With deepest sympathy, from Fanny." The moment the coffin had disappeared a remarkable episode occurred. A short, fair man, dressed I dark clothes, who had previously been unobserved, suddenly sprang upon the narrow wooden platform which led up to the grave, and gesticulating wildly, exclaimed in stentorian tones, "Friends and Anarchists." No sooner were the words out of his mouth than the cry went up "No speeches here," followed by a shout, "Throw him out." Instantaneously the would-be orator, without ceremony, was seized by two or three stalwart constables and forcibly removed. Thereupon the assembled crowds sent up a wild cheer, mingled with cries of "Hang him," "Lynch him," and similar exclamations, and the individual who turned out to be a Charles Thomas Quinn, a member of the Commonweal Club, was hurried bareheaded from the grave across the grass, to the gates of the cemetery, followed by a noisy throng of persons. The mob, which had rapidly attained considerable proportions, was diverted by constables into the high road, and there was immediately dispersed. Quinn was detained at the gate until the mourning coach approached. It stopped for barely a second and into it Quinn jumped with as much alacrity probably as he had ever exhibited in his life. For a considerable time the crowds remained in the vicinity of the grave but eventually the police dispersed them. Several women who attended the funeral were, it is stated, recognized by officers from Scotland yard as "lady Anarchists," who are frequently employed in secret missions between the fraternity in this country and the Continent.

The Attack on the Autonomie Club

There was, as we reported last evening, a hostile demonstration yesterday afternoon outside the Autonomie Club in Windmill-street. Two young men, in their endeavours to enter the club, were very roughly handled by the mob. The felt hat of one was seized and torn to pieces. A tall young fellow shortly after left the club, and was immediately set upon. He sought shelter in the dairy next door, but the door was bolted against him, and he was hustled out of the street. Just then a missile was thrown through the fanlight over the door of the club, and it was followed by others in quick succession, and soon the words "Club Autonomie" had almost disappeared. Two missiles next went through a window on the first floor, and, amidst cries of Down with 'em, burn it down," a rush was made for the door and shutters. One pair of shutters had just given way, when three hackney cabs came by, each containing two students and two policemen, followed by several constables. The mob at once left the club and followed the cabs, hooting the police and shouting words of cheer to the students.

12. *The Morning Leader*, 26 February 1894: 5

THE AUTONOMIE THREATENED

A batch of threatening letters has been received at the Club Autonomie. Perhaps the most striking was the subjoined, written in a bold round hand, with apparently no attempt at disguise. It bore neither name nor address, and was directed simply to "The Members of the Autonomie Club, Windmill-st., Tottenham-court-rd." An extract from the letter, which bore the West Central postmark, dated 23 Feb., is as follows:

> Now, you may take this as written by a man who can probably make a better bomb than the best of you, and who, not being suspected, would not need to make it in secret, and I give you full notice that on the first explosion caused by any of your dirty crew in England it shall soon be followed by a second, and the second will be by the firing of a bomb in your club, and I shall take care that there is a full household of you, and that your carcasses shall be blown sky high.

Amongst other missives received at the Autonomie Club was a post-card, couched in very violent forms and unfit for publication. The windows of the club which were smashed last week have not been replaced and are at present boarded up.

13. *The Daily Graphic*, 27 February 1894: 3

NOT HIS BROTHERS KEEPER

Henri Bourdin was re-called at this point, and had his evidence read over to him. He added that his brother could both speak, read and write English. He and his brother came to England seven years ago, but his brother had been on the Continent several times since. …

EVIDENCE OF THE LANDLORD

Ernest Delebscque, a cabinet maker, living at 30, Fitzroy Street, a Frenchman, said he knew the dead man as his lodger. He last saw him alive at ten o'clock on the Wednesday night. He was in the house and there was nothing unusual about him. He could not account for Bourdin being found at Greenwich. He had known him for about four years. He did not believe Bourdin could read or write English. …

14. *Freedom: A Journal of Anarchist Communism*, January–February 1894: 7

THE PROPAGANDA
REPORTS

London – A Conference of Communist Anarchists, called by the Commonweal Group, was held at the Autonomie Club, on Dec. 26th. Delegates from Norwich, Manchester, Portsmouth, Brighton, Sheffield and other places attended, as well as representatives of all the London groups. Letters were read from provincial and Scotch groups unable to send delegates. The Conference was very successful, and the agenda as well adhered to. A statement of aims and policy was agreed upon. Special emphasis was laid upon the fact that the work of the Communist Anarchists is essentially one of *education*, not of violence, but it was declared, as Anarchists, we acknowledge the right of individuals to act as they think best in furthering the spread of their ideas. It was agreed that, realising the immensity of the task that we and all revolutionary propagandists have undertaken, the abolition of classes, privileges and distinctions, and the emancipation of labor throughout the world, we hold that, in a struggle like this, all means, however desperate, are justifiable. The second part of the Conference was devoted to a consideration of the policy of the *Commonweal*. It was decided to adopt a sympathetic attitude towards Trade Unions and to devote a column regularly to Trade Union matter. Comrade Samuels was asked to remain editor, and literary and financial support was invited from comrades throughout the country. All matter (with the exception of short notes) to be revised by the *Commonweal*-Group. Information concerning local affairs of general interest was specifically requested.

[The report goes on to identify various anarchist meetings, including those in Regents Park "every Sunday morning," where Cantwell and Nicoll are listed as speakers, and Trafalgar Square, where "The meeting at which H. Samuels proposed to explain the 'Aims and Principles of Anarchism' was prohibited Sunday, Dec. 3rd, by Mr. Asquith."]

15. Supplement to *"Freedom,"* March 1894: 12

NOTES
THE BOURDIN AFFAIR.

On Thursday, Feb. 15, a French Anarchist, named Martial Bourdin, met his death by the explosion of a bomb, which for some unknown he was carrying in Greenwich Park. His funeral, on Feb. 25, was the occasion of a disgraceful exhibition of rowdyism on the part of certain medical students, who smashed the windows of the Autonomie Club, and created a disturbance in the street, whilst the crowd from Lisson Grove and the neighbourhood hissed and showed some inclination to attack the hearse and mourners. A Fabian Anarchist comments on the scene as follows:

> The aristocracy of Lisson Grove don't like Anarchism. Indeed why should they? Take away their policeman, and life will be robbed of well-nigh its only gleam of interest. Without intermittent visits to Marylebone police court existence in the Grove would be duller even that the dismal houses which line that detestable thoroughfare. No! the patience of Lisson Grove has its limitations, and when a dead Anarchist hads the effrontery to rest his unhallowed body – though but temporarily – in a district sacred to second-hand furniture and yellow-haired ladies, it is high time for Lisson Grove to assert itself. And what more tasteful occasion could there possibly arise for a display of virtuous indignation than that afforded by the passage to its last resting-place of the poor, mangled, weary body wherein had lately burned a maddened hate of capitalist oppression! So Lisson Grove has turned out in its thousands to "boo" at the coffin and the handful of mourners accompanying it.
>
> It was immense fun. The mourners looked quite scared when we rushed at them – or at least we imagined they did, which came to much the same thing. Certainly the police were rather stupid. They spoiled one bit of harmless frolic completely; for we meant to take the coffin out of the hearse, and dance on it. This would have made a capital diversion, and would have eased our pent-up feelings greatly, especially if we could have obtained the services of a piano-organ to give a suitable accompaniment, say "The Rowdy Dowdy Boys." The police, however, partly compensated for this loss by providing an excellent game of hide and seek after the cortège. But we *should* have enjoyed being let into the cemetery. Great opportunities for rollicking were missed there. And, to take a more serious view of it, the graveside would have been such an appropriate place for Lisson Grove to make its dignified protest against Anarchism. There we could really have warmed to the subject and denounced with proper energy the infamous monsters who would, if they had their wicked way, abolish our great commercial system. The prospect of what would ensue, were these wretches to triumph, hardly bears thinking of. What would become of the profits of the worthy tradesman who sells rickety chairs to poor married people? And how would the lady lodgers on the first and second floors be able to continue their patronage of the "Pig and Whistle" if they no longer had the opportunity of selling their bodies, like honest commercial people, in the open market? Savagery would come again, and Lisson Grove be a wilderness! Well, we did succeed in

> making some kind of protest. And, take it all in all, we don't remember such a jolly demonstration since we cheered H. M. Stanley on his safe return from slaughtering niggers. This time we were able to vary our vocal exercises. Altogether, a pleasant and profitable day.

If indeed the hisses of the crowd were directed against Anarchism, Anarchists are not the first social reformers by many thousands whose earnest efforts to come to the aid of their fellow men have been met by shouts of "Crucify them, Crucify them"; but we are inclined to believe that the bulk of the Lisson Grove people knew and cared nothing about Anarchist principles, and were simply giving vent to the national dislike of "furriners" and "dynamiters." Also, we should not be surprised to find that the presence of a large number of detectives scattered amongst the crowd, and the fact that a street row would not ill serve the purposes of the agitators for a continental police system had something to do with a want of decency in the presence of death rarely shown by the English public.

THE AUTONOMIE CLUB

The English "Third Section" – for we free-born English now pay out of the taxes for the maintenance of a force of secret political police, who are in future to be at the beck and call of foreign governments as well as our own (see the Home Secretary's reply to Colonel Howard Vincent, Feb. 19) – the English "Third Section" profited by the excitement resulting from the Greenwich explosion to raid the Autonomie Club with impunity. As all London comrades know, the Autonomie was a foreign (principally German and French) Anarchist Club, which in the days of the German Anti-Socialist laws published a German paper and did much propaganda in that country. Its members have always been very generous in lending their hall for English lectures and giving any help they could to the English movement. On Feb. 16th, Inspector Melville and his gang took possession of the Club premises, where they violently wrenched open doors, overturned furniture, and seized papers of every description, including the private letters of the family living in the house and their Christmas cards. All persons who turned up were kept under arrest until the close of the search. A frequent attendant at the lectures in the Club Hall recently, Mr. Passmore Edwards, proprietor of the *Echo*, says that had he had been summarily deprived of liberty for no offence he would have had the law of the men who acted in so high-handed a fashion. (*Echo*, Feb. 17.) The Club has now been closed, not on account of the open violence of the police, but of their secret spy system, which has rendered the place useless and dangerous. The last public meeting was held in the Hall on Feb. 18, when Gittens, of the Social Democratic Federation addressed a handful of foreign comrades and some Scotland Yarders in an impromptu speech which is said, by those who heard it, to have been shamefully misquoted in the capitalist press.

16. *The Standard*, 9 March 1894: 3

(THROUGH REUTERS AGENCY)

PARIS, March 8.

Seven Anarchists were arrested to-day, among them being the father of the Anarchist Bourdin, who was killed by the explosion of the bomb in Greenwich Park.

Domiciliary visits were made yesterday at the residences of the Anarchist arrested on Thursday night at the shop of the man Duprat, and resulted in the discovery of important documents.

17. *The Commonweal: A Revolutionary Journal of Anarchist-Communism* (2.23) 10 March 1894: 1-2 (see Fig. 3)

IN MEMORIAM

MARTIAL BOURDIN. DIED FEB. 15, 1894.

AGED 26 YEARS.

Spurning the name of a slave,
Fearless of gaol or grave,
Fighting for Freedom he gave
His life in the Revolution.

Time shall not rob him of fame;
Hating the Tyrant, and game
In the spirit that rings in his name
He died for the Revolution.

Our noble comrade lies now beneath the sod. At an early age he risked his future chances of comfort, pleasure, and life itself, for the benefit of suffering humanity, – ignorant brutish, suffering humanity, – that greeted his funeral cortege with derision, contempt, and hatred, bred from their brutalizing surroundings and prejudices which enable the classes, who "toil not, neither do they spin," to live in splendour and voluptuousness upon the degradations and miseries to which the workers are condemned by the present capitalist system, which Martial Bourdin labored to destroy and for which he sacrificed his life. He was not one of the poorest, the most wretched, the most exploited or oppressed; he earned a tolerably comfortable livelihood, but he had seen enough of the cruelties and injustices inflicted upon the class to which he belonged – the workers – in France, in America, and in London, to make him determined to throw himself entirely into the struggle of the workers against the shirkers.

He was no writer, he had not any oratorical ability; so he contented himself with working in a quieter and more effective way as he considered, rather than do nothing except criticize and waste his time in bickerings and unmanly actions, as some do. His old father and mother, nearly ninety years of age, still obliged to work and still in poverty after working their whole lives and rearing a family of eight to be useful workers in this rotten society: seeing that this is the end that we must, nearly all of us, reach if we are fortunate enough to escape disease, starvation, or the workhouse, he threw himself into the struggle.

Not for the love he bore the contented slaves and cowards who patiently submit to life-long servitude and remorseless tyranny, but because he hated, with a hate as cold as ice and then as hot as the fabled fires of hell, those institutions and conditions, with those who profit by them, that cause so much suffering and anguish, mental and physical, among the many millions of innocent, helpless men, women, and children, victims of the greed and lust of an idle, vicious, useless class, venomous and parasitical; a class of mild and wild beasts that live only upon the blood, muscles, and sinews of our class; who use as tools for their own selfish purposes our strength, our skill, our patience and ingenuity, and who, therefore, must as a class be destroyed or abolished.

Our comrade was not of an affectionate nature (I shall not ascribe to him virtues that he did not possess); but one virtue he excelled in, and that was tenacity of purpose; another was his heartfelt love for the movement. The movement, not that which comprises a few well known men; the movement, not of one party or one land, but a holy love for the world-wide movement of the workers towards emancipation, towards Freedom – social and economic; the movement of which we Anarchists are but as links in the chain encircling the known earth, only visible here and there wherever tyranny and oppression have forced it to the surface; underneath, barely visible even to those who form connecting links, lies dormant yet powerful the natural, potential forces of human solidarity that, in the course of time – that time which we Anarchists are bringing nearer, with an irresistible force will embrace and entwine the aspirations of a Universal Brotherhood of Labor, when a new era will have commenced and the peoples be on the high road to Peace and Harmony and Love.

It is owing to such comrades as Martial Bourdin, with their resolution and tenacity, that the social question has forced itself even so far upon the masters of the race. How droll, and yet how terrible! – a handful of creatures, fellow mortals, social atoms like ourselves, individually weak and helpless, yet masters of the race, with all-powerful influences, holding within their grasp the lives and liberties of millions – blind, stupid, and brutal. But only because of the mental blindness of the masses do the classes manage to retain their power; the blindness that is fostered by all the cursed cliques of priests and politicians, who see in the people's intelligence their own destruction. Martial believed with us that no force outside individual physical force will ever suffice to show to our bloodsuckers and oppressors how really in earnest we are in our endeavours to win for the workers of the world real Freedom, in order that we should all have the fullest and freest opportunities for the cultivation and development of our highest and best faculties.

We had both read the great Wendell Phillips, where he wrote: "Every step of progress that the world has made has been from scaffold to scaffold, and from stake to stake. It is no exaggeration to say, that all the great truths relating to society and government have been first heard in the solemn protests of martyred patriotism or the loud cries of crushed and starving labor. The law has been always wrong. Government began in tyranny and force, began in the feudalism of the soldier and bigotry of the priest; and the ideas of justice and humanity have been fighting their way like a thunderstorm, against the organized selfishness of human nature."

Martial was a relative of mine, but there was hardly any affection between us on that score. He had no affection, I believe, for anybody in the ordinary sense; he was too much wrapped up with interest in the growth and development of the revolutionary movement to have time for any display of selfish personal affection or gratification, and although he was always to the fore in any frivolous yet necessary affair, it was for other reasons and with other motives that he seemingly threw off the serious and became the social. Just one or two instances of his dual nature will show what kind of comrade we have lost. Once he went with me to a lecture, and afterwards walked the whole distance back rather than change a sovereign, and then went to bed supperless for the same reason. Some time afterwards a comrade was obliged to leave London on important business, but he had no money for the expenses; he told our comrade so, and with an exhibition of impatience (he was always impatient) Martial took two sovereigns from his purse and gave them over, and the journey was made. I, naturally, was somewhat surprised, knowing his niggardly disposition generally; and on asking for an explanation he said: "I don't require much for myself, but for the movement, and when something has to be done, everything I have would be too little; I can make shift and manage easily for myself, but the work of the movement must be carried on."

On another occasion several comrades had been arrested and their wives and families rendered penniless; he came among the friends and, going to each one separately, soon collected enough for their individual wants. When a comrade was in danger on the continent, and money had to be sent to pay the expenses here, Martial was always the most energetic in collecting and borrowing the needful; when the funds of the club were run out, when money had to be raised by means of subscription lists, concerts, balls, excursions, and what not, Martial always brought in the most money; when, a few weeks back, the *Commonweal* was without funds and we were obliged to attempt to print the paper by hand on our own antiquated press, Martial (although he did not stand any higher than the machine) was there offering Cantwell to do anything that might be useful in the work on hand; when any suspicious characters entered the club, he was among the first to point them out and urge their expulsion, only on the Saturday before his unfortunate death he shouted the loudest and argued the most against the presence of persons he considered dangerous to the movement and the club. He was not always thanked, rather he was abused, but he was not moved from his uncompromising position or purpose which he carried with him to the end.

Such a comrade was he, and at the age of 26 he undertook the conveyance of dangerous explosive compounds to a secluded spot, where none could have been injured, in order to put to the test a new weapon of destruction that would have furnished the revolutionary armoury with another means of terrorizing those who consciously and unconsciously consign so many innocent lives to destitution and despair. In vain they tell us that force is no remedy; in vain they point out that these acts form the excuse for the most brutal repression; in vain they hang, torture, and imprison; all this has no effect on those who know history, who know human nature, who know how in the past, in spite of persecution and oppression and torture and ostracism, the truth has still made itself heard and felt, – those who know how much the element of fear enters into the spirit that concedes anything whatever. Was it not an English statesman who, speaking at Carlisle, Jan. 13th, 1871, said that "Catholic Emancipation was passed through fear of revolution in Ireland; the first Reform Bill was passed by the light of Nottingham and Bristol in flames; Free Trade would not have been carried as it was, if there had not been a famine in Ireland that alarmed our statesmen; the second Reform Bill was in danger of not being passed, until Hyde Park railings came down"? And again: "I am not sure whether the Irish Church would not have been standing still if the Fenians had not blown down Clerkenwell Prison; and as to the Irish Land Bill, I doubt whether we would have got it if the Irishmen had not taken to the fatal practice of shooting the landlords." Believing this, we stand and look the whole in the face, all those that hate us, misunderstand us, and who show no appreciation of our efforts on their behalf: to those workers who, like worms are content to squirm and grovel under the heel of injustice, those worms who are satisfied with getting enough dust to eat – even among those who knew Martial and who know us – to these and to the workers of the world generally we say, with our eyes fixed on the corpse of our comrade, that, come weal come woe, we pledge ourselves to the fallen dead and the living, we make this solemn vow: That we shall strive by every means in our power to destroy ignorance and oppression, prejudice and cruelty, fear and falsity, in order that it shall be impossible for some men to murder, rob, and dominate millions of their fellows for no other reason than their helplessness and simplicity.

Were the authorities afraid that these words spoken at the graveside on the platform of death, carried over the whole world through the telegraph and telephone by the representatives of a world's press, who had assembled by the graveside to do that work; their very presence being a proof of the fact that the peoples are interested in our principles and practices: were they afraid of the effect our words would have on the minds and hearts of the workers, that they ruthlessly prevented any speaking? Well, our speeches they may prevent, but the very system that they maintain is breeding, in ever increasing numbers, such men as Pallas, Berkman, Ravachol, Vaillant, and Bourdin, who will rather face sudden and violent death than endure the sight of the intense suffering that is the lot of the majority of the workers of the world.

Comrades, be of good courage! We have a world to win, and nothing to lose but our chains. Prepare for the Social Revolution.

Martial, in spirit I clasp your hand and vow at all costs to continue the work for Liberty, Equality, and Fraternity. *Vive l'Anarchie.*

H. B. SAMUELS.

The undertaker, Mr Enefer, 6 Chapel Street, Marylebone Road, W., has cabinet photos of Martial Bourdin on sale at a shilling each, taken in two positions. Memorial cards will be sent to all the groups to whom we send *Commonweal.* A few large ones for framing may be had on application to me. All these cards contain the two verses that are at the top of the page.

18. From *Liberty*, March 1894: 20

BETWEEN OURSELVES

Colonel Majendie's assumption that Martial Bourdin's intention was the immediate use of the explosive – probably against the Observatory, its contents, or inmates," is utterly absurd; but it is what we would naturally expect from Colonel Majendie, intent, no doubt, on creating a prejudice against Anarchism. It is impossible to say more, the whole affair being involved in mystery.

… Scarcely had Society avenged itself on Valliant, than it was again thrown into a state of consternation by the explosion at the Café du Terminus. So the war goes on. Not long ago it was Ravachol; almosy yesterday, Vaillant; to-day Henry. Our views on the explosion at Café du Terminus are well expressed by our comrade in his Paris letter.

The police make raids, seize literature and arrest well known Anarchists, still the blows fall. The press cries out for the arrest of Anarchist speakers who incite these deeds; they are arrested, but still the outrages do not cease. Oh no, messieurs! it is not the agitator who is creating the mischief, but your rotten corrupt society. Go on guillotining, but you will find it useless, sooner or later you must try something else.

Correspondence

Paris, February 27th.

Dear Comrades,

I have but just received "Liberty," and I hasten to scribble a few words on the present state of affairs in Paris. Let me speak first of the all absorbing event, the bomb thrown into the Café Terminus. Far from delighting in or approving of the act of Henry, I must tell you that a great number of devoted Anarchists are entirely opposed to it. We find it not only ill timed, but wholly wrong. The Anarchist's idea is to bring happiness into the world, to create liberty and develop man's nature by giving full play in all directions. Have we a right to attempt to take our fellow-citizens' lives? We must respect the feelings of others, all the more so their lives. Of course in a moment of struggle, when there is a fight between the army of reaction and that of progress, between armed bourgeoisie and armed people we shall do our duty, and use the same means as our enemies to defend ourselves and attain our ends. But this is not the case, we are at a moment of propaganda and not of actual struggle. Shall we, besides, imitate the abominable actions we blame in the government. Shall we murder women and children, like the English at Alexandria and in Matabeleland etc., like the French in Tonquin, in Senegal, and after the Commune, like the Prussians at Strassburg, Belfort and Paris! We are not murderers like them. If Henry's act were useful to the propaganda it might be endorsed, but far from being useful it has done a lot of harm, hundreds of friends have been estranged from us. The people for whom we wish to work would be the first to fall upon us and tear us in pieces. Throughout Europe the propaganda has stopped and the cause has suffered greatly by the indiscriminate use of dynamite.

The program of Anarchy has been changed; the defenders of the late explosions have left off talking of the happiness of the people, of communism, they have become a political party, they want their party to get to power! What a jumble of words, Anarchy in power! That fact alone would suffice to show the harm done to the cause. These men return to the Anarchy of Proudhon – or that of Lord Wemyss in England. Moreover, is it not a pity to lose so many devoted, intrepid comrades as those who sacrifice their lives for their ideas. We can ill spare men who may be useful in so many ways. All our best friends are driven abroad by the terrible wave of reaction. France will feel the loss of some of her most intelligent and active children who can do nothing in a foreign land.

The domiciliary visits and arrests continue everywhere. They have searched the houses of every known comrade, and have found nothing except the addresses of sympathizers who have been thus exposed to petty persecutions.

Paris Comrade.

19. *Liberty: A Journal of Anarchist-Communism*, March 1894: n.p.

BETWEEN OURSELVES

Colonel Majendie's assumption that Martial Bourdin's "intention was the immediate use of the explosive-probably against the Observatory, its contents, or inmates," is utterly absurd; but it is what we would naturally expect from Colonel Majendie, intent, no doubt, on creating a prejudice against Anarchism. It is impossible to say more, the whole affair being involved in mystery.

20. HO144545 / A55176/26 | 25 April 1894

Mr. Murdoch,

In the newspapers of Monday last there appeared an account of the capture of an Anarchist, and it was not until the following Wednesday morning that the S of S received any official communication on the subject, and then only after a request to the Commissioner of Police by desire of the S of S.

Would you inform whoever is responsible for this oversight, that in future the S of S desires that he may have immediate official information in all matters relating to the Anarchists, and not be left to obtain this news from the papers.

H. W.[20]
19.4.94

[noted below:] So inform Mr. Anderson from whom reports as to Anarchists come. Sir E. Bradford has already been informed of S.S wishes on 20 Ap[ril] 94.

---

[20] Presumably H. W. Primrose, Undersecretary of State, Home Office.